This book presents Southeast Asian scholars writing full throttle about Southeast Asian literature and cinema–crossing languages, crossing borders, crossing the boundaries of conventional sexualities and racial politics. Hold on tight. The future of Southeast Asian literary studies has arrived.
— *Harry Aveling, Professor of Translation Studies,*
Monash University

This important collection builds upon the discipline of comparative cultural studies in Southeast Asia by exploring contestations of race, gender and sexuality through the lens of "translational politics." The objects under view are the region's nationally based or globally shared filmic and literary texts. This lens also reveals the imbrication of both the contradictions and homogeneity, which late neoliberal globalization has fostered throughout the region, with its seductive mediascapes and commodity culture often disruptive of pre-existing norms. This disruption includes the private and public contestations over definitions and shifting values associated with legalized entitlements attributed to race, gender, and sexuality. It is this disrupted positionality, an experience shared by many South East Asians, that is explored in this noteworthy collection of essays through the lens of translational politics.
— *Teri Shaffer Yamada, Professor Emerita of*
Asian and Asian American Studies,
California State University

Translational Politics in Southeast Asian Literatures

Highlighting the interconnections between Southeast Asia and the world through literature, this book calls for a different reading approach to the literatures of Southeast Asia by using translation as the main conceptual framework in the analyses and interpretation of the texts, languages, and cultures of the following countries: Cambodia, Malaysia, Singapore, Indonesia, Brunei Darussalam, and the Philippines.

Through the theme of "translational politics," the contributors critically examine not only the linguistic properties but also the metaphoric, symbolic, and semiotic meanings, images, and representations that have been translated across societies and cultures through local and global consumption and circulation of literature, (new) media, and other cultural forms. Using translation to unlock and decode multiple, different languages, narratives, histories, and worldviews emerging from Southeast Asian geo-literary contexts, this book builds on current scholarship and offers new approaches to the contestations of race, gender, and sexuality in literature, which often involve the politically charged discourses of identity, language, and representation. At the same time, this book provides new perspectives and future directions in the study of Southeast Asian literatures.

Exploring a range of literary and cultural products, including written texts, performance, and cinema, this volume will be a key resource for students and researchers interested in translation and cultural studies, comparative and world literature, and Southeast Asian studies.

Grace V.S. Chin is Senior Lecturer in English Language Studies at Universiti Sains Malaysia. She specialises in postcolonial Southeast Asian literatures in English and has published journal articles and essays on writers and literary works from Malaysia, Singapore, Brunei Darussalam, Indonesia, and the Philippines. Her publications include two co-edited volumes: *The Southeast Asian Woman Writes Back: Gender, Identity and Nation in the Literatures of Brunei Darussalam, Malaysia, Singapore, Indonesia and the Philippines* (2018) and *Appropriating Kartini: Colonial, National and Transnational Memories of an Indonesian Icon* (2020).

Routledge Contemporary Southeast Asia Series

The aim of this series is to publish original, high-quality work by both new and established scholars on all aspects of Southeast Asia.

The Army and Ideology in Indonesia
From *Dwifungsi* to *Bela Negara*
Muhamad Haripin, Adhi Priamarizki and Keoni Indrabayu Marzuki

The 2018 and 2019 Indonesian Elections
Identity Politics and Regional Perspectives
Edited by Leonard C. Sebastian and Alexander R. Arifianto

Embodied Performativity in Southeast Asia
Multidisciplinary Corporealities
Edited by Stephanie Burridge

The History of South Vietnam
The Quest for Legitimacy and Stability, 1963–1967
Vinh-The Lam

Singapore after Lee Kuan Yew
S.C.Y. Luk and P.W. Preston

Affect, Narratives and Politics of Southeast Asian Migration
Carlos M. Piocos III

Translational Politics in Southeast Asian Literatures
Contesting Race, Gender, and Sexuality
Edited by Grace V.S. Chin

For more information about this series, please visit: www.routledge.com/Routledge-Contemporary-Southeast-Asia-Series/book-series/RCSEA

Translational Politics in Southeast Asian Literatures
Contesting Race, Gender, and Sexuality

**Edited by
Grace V.S. Chin**

Taylor & Francis Group

LONDON AND NEW YORK

First published 2021
by Routledge
2 Park Square, Milton Park, Abingdon, Oxon OX14 4RN

and by Routledge
52 Vanderbilt Avenue, New York, NY 10017

Routledge is an imprint of the Taylor & Francis Group, an informa business

© 2021 selection and editorial matter, Grace V.S. Chin; individual chapters, the contributors

The right of Grace V.S. Chin to be identified as the author of the editorial material, and of the authors for their individual chapters, has been asserted in accordance with sections 77 and 78 of the Copyright, Designs and Patents Act 1988.

All rights reserved. No part of this book may be reprinted or reproduced or utilised in any form or by any electronic, mechanical, or other means, now known or hereafter invented, including photocopying and recording, or in any information storage or retrieval system, without permission in writing from the publishers.

Trademark notice: Product or corporate names may be trademarks or registered trademarks, and are used only for identification and explanation without intent to infringe.

British Library Cataloguing-in-Publication Data
A catalogue record for this book is available from the British Library

Library of Congress Cataloging-in-Publication Data
Names: Chin, Grace V.S., editor.
Title: Translational politics in Southeast Asian literatures : contesting race, gender, and sexuality / edited by Grace V.S. Chin.
Description: London ; New York : Routledge, 2021. | Series: Routledge contemporary Southeast Asia series | Includes bibliographical references and index.
Identifiers: LCCN 2020046329 (print) | LCCN 2020046330 (ebook) | ISBN 9780367470234 (hardback) | ISBN 9781000363180 (adobe pdf) | ISBN 9781000363326 (epub) | ISBN 9781000363258 (mobi)
Subjects: LCSH: Translating and interpreting—Political aspects—South Asia—History. | South Asia—Languages—Translating. | South Asian literature—Translations—History and criticism. | Language and culture—South Asia.
Classification: LCC P306.8.S68 T73 2021 (print) | LCC P306.8.S68 (ebook) | DDC 418/.020959—dc23
LC record available at https://lccn.loc.gov/2020046329
LC ebook record available at https://lccn.loc.gov/2020046330

ISBN: 978-0-367-47023-4 (hbk)
ISBN: 978-1-003-03612-8 (ebk)
ISBN: 978-0-367-74109-9 (pbk)

Typeset in Times New Roman
by codeMantra

Contents

Acknowledgements		ix
Notes on contributors		xi

1 **Introduction** 1
GRACE V.S. CHIN

2 **Self-conscious and queer: translating the pasts of Singapore and Malaysia in Lydia Kwa's *This Place Called Absence* and Tan Twan Eng's *The Gift of Rain*** 22
ANGELIA POON

3 **Performance and translation: Hang Li Po and the politics of history** 42
GRACE V.S. CHIN

4 **Were-tigers in were-texts: cultural translation and indigeneity in the Malay Archipelago** 66
NAZRY BAHRAWI

5 **Translating the ideal girl: female images in Khmer literature and cinema** 82
DARIA OKHVAT

6 **Gained in translation: the politics of localising Western stories in late-colonial Indonesia** 100
TOM G. HOOGERVORST

7 **Translating Islam: conversion and love in Bruneian fiction** 132
KATHRINA MOHD DAUD

8	**Cinematic erasure: translating Southeast/Asia in *Crazy Rich Asians***	151
	KELLY YIN NGA TSE	
9	**Translation and LGBT Studies in the Philippines**	171
	J. NEIL C. GARCIA	

Index 193

Acknowledgements

My deepest gratitude goes to Henk Schulte Nordholt, who first invited me to organise and run a trial laboratory at the 2017 European Association for Southeast Asian Studies (EuroSEAS) Conference at Oxford, UK—an event that led to the inception of this edited volume. I am also indebted to the Royal Netherlands Institute of Southeast Asian and Caribbean Studies (KITLV) for sponsoring my trip to Oxford and for ensuring that I had the support I needed to set up the laboratory. To this end, I am grateful to Yayah Siegers and Tom G. Hoogervorst, especially the latter, who provided sound advice and assistance. Where the volume is concerned, I thank Tom again as well as Angelia Poon for their perceptive insights and suggestions for improvement. I am also deeply appreciative of Universiti Sains Malaysia for supporting my work and of my research assistant, Viniy Vimalar, whose help with the edits and formatting has been invaluable. Above all, I thank my spouse, Francisco Roldan, for being as supportive and patient as he has been throughout this entire project.

Notes on contributors

Grace V.S. Chin is Senior Lecturer in English Language Studies at Universiti Sains Malaysia. She specialises in postcolonial Southeast Asian literatures in English and has published journal articles and essays on writers and literary works from Malaysia, Singapore, Brunei Darussalam, Indonesia, and the Philippines. Her publications also include two co-edited volumes, *The Southeast Asian Woman Writes Back: Gender, Identity and Nation in the Literatures of Brunei Darussalam, Malaysia, Singapore, Indonesia and the Philippines* (2018) and *Appropriating Kartini: Colonial, National and Transnational Memories of an Indonesian Icon* (2020).

J. Neil C. Garcia teaches creative writing and comparative literature at the University of the Philippines, Diliman, where he serves as Director of the university press and a Fellow for Poetry in the Institute of Creative Writing. He is the author of numerous poetry collections and works in literary and cultural criticism. Between 1994 and 2014, he co-edited the famous *Ladlad* series of Philippine gay writing. He is the director for the Philippines of Project GlobalGRACE: Global Gender and Cultures of Equality, a world-wide research and arts consortium sponsored by the Research Councils of the United Kingdom and Goldsmiths, University of London. He is currently at work on "Likha," his seventh poetry book.

Tom G. Hoogervorst is a historical linguist based at the Royal Netherlands Institute of Southeast Asian and Caribbean Studies (KITLV) in Leiden. He has worked on Malay- and Javanese-language history, using textual sources and loanwords as prisms to reconstruct cultural contact in Southeast Asia. His forthcoming book is a language history of Indonesia's Chinese minority, which focusses on the linguistic characteristics of the "Sino-Malay" literature and its lessons for a more intimate understanding of colonial hierarchies from a non-European perspective. He is also interested in Indian Ocean Studies, youth language, and food history.

Kathrina Mohd Daud is an Assistant Professor specialising in Creative Writing and Literature at Universiti Brunei Darussalam. She has previously held research fellowships at the Oxford Centre for Islamic Studies (2013) and the Centre for Southeast Asian Studies at Kyoto University (2017), and her work has been published in volumes on Southeast Asian Islam, popular romance studies, and Bruneian studies. She co-edited *The Southeast Asian Women Writes Back: Gender, Nation and Identity in the Literatures of Brunei Darussalam, Malaysia, Singapore, Indonesia and the Philippines* (2018), and her debut novel, *The Fisherman King,* was shortlisted for the Epigram Books Fiction Prize 2020 and published in 2020.

Nazry Bahrawi is Senior Lecturer at Singapore University of Technology and Design. Trained in comparative literature, he specialises in the study of Indian Ocean cultures and texts between the Malay Archipelago and the Arab world. His essays in these areas have been published in *Journal of World Literature, Counter Text, Literature and Theology, Journal of Intercultural Studies, Moving Worlds,* and *Green Letters.* He has also translated literary works by Singapore's Cultural Medallion winners from Bahasa to English.

Daria Okhvat is a lecturer at the Department of Philology of South-East Asia, Faculty of Asian and African studies, St. Petersburg University, and has been teaching there since 2013. She received her BA and MA specialising in Cambodian drama at St. Petersburg University. Her primary research interests are in the field of modern Khmer literature. She has developed new teaching courses on Cambodian literature and is now on track to complete her PhD on "Modern Khmer prose" at St. Petersburg University.

Angelia Poon is Associate Professor of Literature at the National Institute of Education, Nanyang Technological University. Her research interests include postcolonial studies and contemporary Anglophone writing, with a focus on racial and gender politics, globalisation, and transnationalism. She is a co-editor of *Singapore Literature and Culture: Current Directions in Local and Global Contexts* (Routledge, 2017) and *Writing Singapore: An Historical Anthology of Singapore Literature* (2009). She is also the author of *Enacting Englishness in the Victorian Period: Colonialism and the Politics of Performance* (2008) and numerous journal articles on postcolonial writing, including Singaporean and Malaysian literatures in English.

Kelly Yin Nga Tse is Assistant Professor of English at the Education University of Hong Kong. Prior to this, she was Visiting Lecturer at the University of Cambridge. She received her DPhil in English from the University of Oxford. Her research and teaching interests lie in postcolonial and world literatures with a focus on Asia Pacific, law and literature, and environmental humanities. Her publications have appeared in *The Journal of Commonwealth Literature, Interventions: International Journal of Postcolonial Studies,* and *The Oxford History of the Novel in English: Volume 10: The Novel in South and South East Asia since 1945,* among others.

1 Introduction

Grace V.S. Chin

The identity politics of race, gender, and sexuality in the study of Southeast Asian literatures is by no means a new subject in the field. In the past few decades, there has been a steady stream of scholarship on this subject, with the majority dominated by concerns about race, ethnicity, and language, followed by gender and sexuality as subjects of inquiry.[1] Influenced by the postcolonial turn in the 1980s (Bachmann-Medick 2016), these studies have contributed much to our understanding and exploration of the literatures of Southeast Asia as a fertile field of inquiry and theorising, especially in terms of the representational politics of identity and their relation to power, hegemony, resistance, diaspora, transnationalism, cross-culturalism, the nation-state, hybridity, and globalisation, among others.

Despite the inroads made, there are, nonetheless, limits to these studies as many tend to revolve around the literary productions of individual countries.[2] When a comparative lens is employed, the analysis is often motivated by language, which can be coupled with race and ethnicity; examples include the Malay-language and Chinese-language (sinophone) literary and cultural productions in the region.[3] Another area of comparison is the literary form and canon.[4] The drawing of ideological lines based on country/nation and language in fact highlights the "bounded" nature of literary activity and production in the postcolonial contexts of Southeast Asia, where much of the creative output takes place in the native/mother tongue or national language—a phenomenon that has largely been shaped by the decolonising ideologies and strategies of the region's post-independent nation-states, and also by the nationalising (and often homogenising) prerogatives and impetuses of the ruling governments in the developmental nation-building years.[5]

While the resulting language barrier is an obstacle for international researchers who have to learn the language or else rely on works produced in English (or other global languages) and/or translations for their material, it is also worthwhile noting that national policies on language and culture—instrumental to the construction and regulation of "national literature," "national writer," and, ultimately, "national identity" as demarcating categories of independence, sovereignty, and difference—have also resulted in the segregated manner with which the literatures of Southeast Asia have traditionally been constructed and perpetuated as a field of research and knowledge production. Consequently, much of the current scholarship is based on country-specific and, more often than not, language-specific canons and productions.[6] Another complication is the divided scholarly attention between the "mainland" states (Myanmar, Thailand, Cambodia, Laos, and Vietnam) and the "island" states (Malaysia, Singapore, Brunei Darussalam, Indonesia, and the Philippines) in the region, with the international scholarship on literary studies centred mostly on the anglophone productions emerging from ex-British and ex-American colonies among the "island" states: Malaysia, Singapore, and the Philippines (Chin and Rajandran 2020). These developments have disadvantaged the research on Southeast Asia, affecting those of us working in our respective locations and language-bound fields as we find ourselves mostly ignorant of the works produced in other languages, whether in our own or neighbouring countries.

According to Chua Beng Huat, the production of Southeast Asian texts in non-European languages may be one of the central reasons why the region "does not figure significantly, if at all" (2008, 231) in the field of postcolonial studies, adding that the exclusion indicates "a very colonial practice at work in the production of knowledge of postcoloniality" (2008, 232).[7] The same exclusionary practice can be seen in the study of Southeast Asian literatures, which have still not been given the kind of attention that has been showered on the literatures of their bigger, and more popular, Asian neighbours, notably India, a veritable "giant" in the construction and production of postcolonial studies, not to mention China and Japan, both of which are favourite locations for the study of world literature. As for comparative literature programmes, the majority are found in the US, where much of the focus is on European texts, or Asian texts from South Asia and East Asia. Sandwiched between East Asia and South Asia, Southeast Asia—being neither one nor the other but a liminal space in-between—has remained relatively obscure (despite its wealth of literary offerings) as an area of study in the fields of postcolonial literature, comparative literature, and world literature. As an academic subject, "Southeast Asian Literature" is offered mainly by Southeast Asian/Asian studies programmes and institutes or is found in local academic programmes, albeit in association with the country; for instance, the subject of "Malaysian Literature in English" is offered by a few university-affiliated English language and literature programmes in Malaysia.

Eurocentric practices and biases are also reflected in the epistemological hierarchies derived from the unequal positioning of literatures on a global scale, which are mirrored to an extent within the region itself. As noted earlier, anglophone productions from former British and American colonies—in particular Malaysia, Singapore, and the Philippines—have traditionally received higher recognition compared to other regional productions by virtue of the language medium used: English (see also

Chin and Rajandran 2020). In recent years, the visibility of these places as favoured reading destinations has been heightened by the emergence of international award-winning authors such as Malaysia's Tan Twan Eng and Tash Aw, or bestselling authors turned Hollywood darlings like Singapore's Kevin Kwan, all of whom are now feted as global or postcolonial anglophone luminaries. This development has been reinforced by literary market trends, seen in the growing corpus and increased visibility of diasporic and transnational literatures produced by Southeast Asian writers who have made their homes in Australia, the UK, and the US. As a result, "transnationalism," "diaspora," "hybridity," and hyphenated identity categories have emerged as key terms and domains of research in the study of Southeast Asian literatures, with scores of studies and research publications attesting to the popularity of these subjects. However, the downside to this development is that literary works written in national or native languages have continued to be excluded from the global limelight, until and unless they are translated into English or other global languages.

Language lies at the very heart of the investigations found in this volume. An ideological minefield in the geopolitics of the postcolonial and modern Southeast Asian nation-state, language is inextricable from the politics of identity and representation. Historically linked to the movements of anti-colonialism, decolonisation, independence, and nation-building, language has—especially for the bilingual or multilingual Southeast Asian writer—emerged as a negotiated ideological choice, whereby the decision to write in one's national language/mother tongue, or not, invariably taps into the discourse of nationalism and its attendant articulations of loyalty, homeland, and belonging.[8] Although this situation has been mitigated by the region's increasingly internationalised outlook—with English acknowledged as the premier language of global trade, commerce, technology, diplomacy, and travel, the multiple challenges arising from language and literary barriers and hierarchies as well as the prevailing Eurocentric views and practices in the region and the world have, as noted earlier, remained; they include the lack of trans-Southeast Asian connections, the relative obscurity of Southeast Asian literatures, and the imbalances in regional and global literary productions and readership. These challenges not only influence literary and academic trends, readership, and the publishing market, but also directly impact the way we "read" and perceive Southeast Asia as a geo-literary phenomenon.

Tackling these key concerns and challenges, this volume calls for a different approach to the reading of Southeast Asian literatures through the theme of "translational politics," with translation deployed as the main conceptual framework in the analyses and interpretation of texts, languages, and cultures of the following countries: Cambodia, Malaysia, Singapore, Indonesia, Brunei Darussalam, and the Philippines. Derived from the Latin *translatio*, which means to "carry across" or "bring across," translation has been inextricably linked to literary research in the fields of postcolonial literature, comparative literature, world literature, and cultural studies—a development also known as "literary translation" in translation studies, which involves the study of translated literature and texts within social, cultural, and political contexts and systems, and approaches to the text as process and product, among others (Albaladejo and Chico-Rico 2018; Jones 2009; Wright 2016). In Southeast Asia, the scholarship on translated literature is fairly substantial, based on either country-specific or regional and cross-country comparative research.[9] However, the approaches used are still quite conventional as they typically focus on the literary or linguistic analysis of local texts translated into English (or other global languages) by the researcher, who may also undertake the task of translating the materials or texts. While this volume continues to work within this tradition, the contributors and I nonetheless hope to expand the boundaries of literary scholarship and conventions by using translation concepts, theories, and approaches to inform our research. Specifically, we aim to fill a significant gap in the field by examining the politics of translation in relation to race, gender, and sexuality in Southeast Asian texts and contexts, with emphasis on local perspectives and practices.

Since the 1990s, scholars working in translation studies have emerged with bold and exciting theories, paradigms, perspectives, and approaches that challenge the limits of translation traditions. Calling this phenomenon the "translational turn," Doris Bachmann-Medick (2009, 2016) observes the transformative force and influence of translation on other disciplinary fields across the humanities and the ways in which interdisciplinary scholarship has led to the development of new domains of inquiry and theorising; they include translation and postcoloniality (Bassnett and Trivedi 1999; Bhabha 1994; Niranjana 1992; Simon and St-Pierre 2000; Spivak 1993), translation and culture (Harding and Cortés 2018; Maitland 2017; Muñoz-Calvo et al. 2008), translation and feminism (Simon 1996; Spivak 1993), and translation and power (Tymoczko and Gentzler 2002). The millennium has since witnessed the explosion of translation research in new fields that include the mass media, performance, art, music, film-making, comics, animation, video games, the Internet, and new media forms (YouTube, social networking sites like Twitter, Instagram, and Facebook, and chat apps like WhatsApp, etc.), to the point where "*nearly* every discipline derives from and depends upon translation" (Gentzler 2017, 5). These studies are, in fact, testament to the crucial role played by translation in a plurivocal world, where cross-cultural, multilingual, transnational, and diasporic contact and communication have engendered heterogeneity and hybridity as well as new and emerging terrains of thought, perception, feeling, experience, and expression in globalised cultures and societies around the world.

These latest developments in translation studies can also be seen in Southeast Asian scholarship, although such research remains limited. Research monographs and edited volumes that employ translation as the main conceptual framework and approach include Jennifer Lindsay's edited volume *Between*

Tongues: Translation and/of/in Performance in Asia (2006), Henri Chambert-Loir's *Sadur: Sejarah Terjemahan di Indonesia dan Malaysia* (Adapting: A History of Translation in Indonesia and Malaysia, 2009), Ronit Ricci's *Islam Translated: Literature, Conversion, and the Arabic Cosmopolis of South and Southeast Asia* (2011), E.K. Tan's *Rethinking Chineseness: Translational Sinophone Identities in the Nanyang Literary World* (2013), and Harry Aveling's *Perceptions: Essays on Translation and Literature of the Malay World* (2019). Then there are the edited volumes on translation studies in Asia, which include chapters on Southeast Asia: Eva Hung and Judy Wakabayashi's *Asian Translation Traditions* (2005), Ronit Ricci and Jan van der Putten's *Translation in Asia: Theories, Practices, Histories* (2011), and *Asia through Art and Anthropology: Cultural Translation across Borders* by Fuyubi Nakamura et al. (2013), among others. By and large, however, chapters and articles focussed on translation in Southeast Asia are still on the meagre side, with the odd chapter found in collections here and there; the same holds true for journals in translation studies.[10] Furthermore, translation studies in the region are still driven by Eurocentric approaches and traditions that have also displaced and marginalised the Southeast Asian perspective (see Nazry Bahrawi's Chapter 4).

Taking our cue from the ground-breaking scholarship in translation studies, the contributors of this volume aim to go beyond the traditional function and terminology of translation[11] to critically examine not only the linguistic properties but also the metaphoric, symbolic, and semiotic meanings as well as images and representations that have been translated across societies and cultures through local and global consumption and circulation of literature, (new) media, and other cultural forms. Using translation to unlock and decode the multiple, different languages, narratives, histories, and worldviews emerging from Southeast Asian geo-literary contexts, this volume builds on current scholarship by inviting us to rethink the ways we can approach the contestations of race, gender, and sexuality in literature, which often involve the politically charged discourses of identity, language, and representation. Focussing on the interconnections and dialogic relationships enables us to go beyond the conventional interpretative strategies that are often text-centred. As the chapters here demonstrate, the analyses take into account the relations not only between texts, forms, words, representations, and perspectives but also between cultures, histories, and spaces (temporal, geographical, and ideological). In the course of doing so, they provide a much more informed, and an infinitely richer, understanding of the significant role played by literature in narrating Southeast Asia.

Acting as a symbolic bridge, translation can be harnessed to build trans-Southeast Asian connections among scholars and within the field itself; it can potentially breach, subvert, or dismantle binarisms—what Homi K. Bhabha describes as the "politics of polarity" (1995, 209)—and "[confound] tendencies towards homogenization" (Bachmann-Medick 2009, 6). Translation can thus be employed to bridge, cross, vex, or even transgress borders and boundaries, the process of which also enables us to address the intertextual, intercultural, transnational, trans-spatial, and trans-temporal continuities, contestations, interactions, mediations, and engagements as well as the inherent complexities, contradictions, and tensions that underline these relationships. In this way, we bring new perspectives and directions to the study of Southeast Asian literatures.

It is also important to reflect on why this volume has retained its focus on the identity politics of race, gender, and sexuality—an already well-established ground in the field. These identity categories are heavily politicised domains of meaning making and knowledge/power production in Southeast Asian geopolitics. Characterised by ethnic, cultural, religious, and linguistic heterogeneity, the region has been wrestling with ways of managing diversity and difference, with race and ethnicity—usually yoked to religion, culture, and language—placed at the forefront of political contestations and debates, followed by gender and sexuality. Known also as the region where some of the world's best-known authoritarian regimes have emerged (Day 2002) and continued to endure till today (Einzenberger and Schaffar 2018), Southeast Asia has historically witnessed how race, gender, and sexuality have been subjected to the regulatory and disciplinary forces of *both* the colonial and the postcolonial state, whose repressive and ideological apparatuses have been harnessed in the name of the Empire or the Nation. Then there are the entrenched social and cultural discourses of honour and shame, which have continued to exert a strong influence on identities on the ground, notably where gender and sexuality are concerned. Although gender and sexuality have a less visible or prominent presence compared to race and ethnicity in the study of Southeast Asian literatures (see Chin and Kathrina 2018), they nonetheless form important sites for our investigation, especially given the paternalistic-patriarchal systems of governance in Southeast Asian societies and cultures, both in the past and in the present.

Paternalistic-patriarchal rule and authority are dominant facets of Southeast Asian histories and politics. While colonial paternalism develops the "familial" bonds of dependency between the colonial master and the colonised subject through the Orientalist discourse of the Empire's "benevolent and paternal supervision and of the 'child' or 'childlike' qualities of the 'primitive' peoples" (Ashcroft 2001, 42), postcolonial state "fatherhood" is based on the appropriated local cultural forms of paternalistic leadership (Chin and Kathrina 2018; Pye 1985). It is not surprising to find that, very often, the postcolonial Southeast Asian nation-state spotlights the centrality of the heteronormative, patriarchal family and the vital role it plays in upholding social order and cohesion in the national imaginary.

Operating as a powerful symbol of the nation itself, the heteronormative, patriarchal family that is led by the father figure espouses traditional (and desirable) values that are in alignment with religious, social, and national principles. However, it is also against the masculine, heterosexual father figure that the gendered and sexed other—represented by woman, and LGBTQ (lesbian, gay, bisexual, transgender, queer) identities—is constructed as "feminine," "effeminate," "subordinate," "different," and therefore marginal, even deviant, in the phallo- and hetero-centric politics of the nation-state. To date, homosexuality is illegal in Malaysia, Singapore, Myanmar, Brunei,[12] and Aceh, a province of Indonesia.[13] Recent reports, however, have also revealed positive changes towards LGBTQ identities and rights, with the most progress seen in Thailand and the Philippines, both of which have made legal inroads in protecting LGBTQ rights (APCom Foundation 2020; Ariffin 2018; Wilkins 2019; Yulius 2018). As the identity politics of race, gender, and sexuality continue to shape ideologies and discourses as well as influence perspectives, attitudes, and material practices on a daily basis, they remain as relevant as ever to the study of Southeast Asian cultures and literatures.

Covering a wide spectrum of texts and genres, the chapters in this volume engage with not just linguistically translated works but also adaptations, performance, and rewriting projects—involving acts of revision, appropriation, deconstruction, and intertextuality—across a wide temporal spectrum, ranging from precolonial to colonial and postcolonial periods. The volume as a whole thus addresses cross-cultural, transnational, or global connections between texts written in different countries, periods, genres, languages, and traditions. At the same time, it interrogates the tensions, contradictions, ambivalences, violence, ruptures, or gaps involved in the process of translation—what gets "lost" (see Chin, Chapter 3), "gained" (see Hoogervorst, Chapter 6), "erased" (see Tse, Chapter 8), or even "rendered opaque" (see Garcia, Chapter 9). Throughout the volume too, there is a shared concern in the politicisation of meaning that keeps recurring through the process of translation. This process, defined here as a shift or transition in meaning, is invariably transformative, constituted as it is by the acts of (re)interpretation, (re)writing, (re)mediation, and (re)appropriation, all of which involve a certain amount of agency.

In short, the process of translating ideas, language, and imagery, or contexts (time and space), emotions, and perspectives, is one that goes beyond the conventional understanding of "carrying over," as it brings forth "new" articulations of identity as a discourse, a point significant to the invention and shaping of the Southeast Asian identity, particularly during the decolonising years. The act of translation is thus a political one that also reveals the embedded structures of racial, gender, and sexual inequalities and biases within discourse. Through the theme of translational politics, the volume explores ideas important to the changing historical and social contexts of Southeast Asia, including the ways in which knowledge and power intersect with local and global discourses of race, gender, and sexuality through writing, performance, and representation. At the forefront of our inquiry is the critical question of identity: the manner in which it has been translated time and again, and how it has been contested with each and every shift, and in ways that expose the nexus of power relations underlying the discursive productions of race, gender, and sexuality.

8 *Grace V.S. Chin*

Conception and the contributors

The idea for this volume emerged from the laboratory[14] session—titled "Contesting race, gender and sexuality in Southeast Asian literature: From colonial past to postcolonial present"—that I had convened at the 2017 European Association for Southeast Asian Studies (EuroSEAS) conference in Oxford. I'd invited a group of scholars from different parts of the world (with the majority from Southeast Asia) to discuss and exchange ideas on how the literatures of this part of the world constituted the symbolic space through which the historically contested identity discourses of race, gender, and sexuality could be fruitfully engaged as political and cultural domains of expression and representation. As the scholars specialised in different areas and fields, their distinct work and expertise would be—in my mind—an excellent foundation to kick-start the discussion on various aspects, issues, and ideas related to literature and culture, one that encompassed indigenous (precolonial), colonial, and postcolonial productions. Another objective was to form a network through which we could share and exchange ideas and information about Southeast Asian literary formations and productions, with a book publication as a possible outcome.

The laboratory session, lasting a whole afternoon, was not without its challenges. As the dialogue commenced, it very quickly became clear that we espoused different perspectives, voices, and directions in our research goals and interests, which were reflected in the broad range of topics presented at the laboratory: "Violent heterosexualities and mapping Muslim gender relations in popular romance"; "Masculinity in Dutch Indies late-colonial press and literature"; "Historical aspects of gender and sexuality in Southeast Asian literature and culture"; "Singaporean women writers"; "Cross-cultural romance in Bruneian, Singaporean, Malaysian and Indonesian fiction"; "Female stereotypes in Khmer literature"; "The overseas Filipina worker (OFW) in literature and film"; "Arabisation and Nusantara literature"; "Translation and LGBT studies in the Philippines"; and "The Chinese female body and sexuality in Malaysian and Singaporean fiction." I realised later that, to some extent, the diverse voices and viewpoints raised during the laboratory had also mirrored the discursive and distinct ways in which the literatures of Southeast Asia have been approached and shaped as an academic field of study.

The seed for translation as a possible common theme and framework was implanted when J. Neil C. Garcia from the University of the Philippines employed "translationality" in his presentation to critique the Western discourses and theories of sexuality that currently dominate LGBT studies in the Philippines, arguing that they failed to capture indigenous vocabulary and notions of "gay" identity that carried different meanings and inflections. Garcia's presentation and the ensuing group discussions helped to further germinate the idea for using translation as the starting-point of an inclusive dialogue through which our differences could be bridged. And so, this volume was conceived. Given our shared interest in the politics of race, gender, and sexuality, I naturally decided to retain this focus in the present volume, seen in the inherited subtitle—*Contesting Race, Gender, and Sexuality*—from the laboratory. I'm pleased to say that many of the scholars who had participated in the laboratory have also joined me in the making of this volume, including Garcia, whose presentation has been turned into Chapter 9 here.

It is also fitting that translation is used to approach the Southeast Asian literary text, since all of us involved in the volume are bilingual or multilingual speakers and translators who straddle two or more language cultures and histories. Tapping into our own multicultural heritage also means we need not rely solely on anglophone or translated works—as has been the norm—from the region; instead, we work with the full range of our own polyglossic and translational capabilities. As a result, several chapters here present original translated material in English by the contributors themselves, a number of whom are already involved in translational research. I should also point out that the contributors here work primarily in literary, cultural, language, and comparative studies rather than translation studies. Hence the analyses in this volume are focussed on the literary, artistic, or creative text, which includes film and performance, as the reference point.

As can be seen from the chapter descriptions further below, the ways in which translation is employed are varied and diverse, depending on individual perspective, interpretation, and approach. Broadly speaking, the use of translation in the volume can be divided into three categories: (1) language and linguistic properties (also the most commonly understood category in translation studies); (2) translational elements, such as creative rewriting or revision, appropriation, adaptation, and intertextuality, among others; and (3) metaphorical translation, based on the attributes, process, and effect of translation, such as movement, shift, and transformation through creative representations or (re)mediations of the past, for instance. While language is pivotal to our investigations, what matters just as much, if not more, is the question of representation itself, and the imaginary, ideological, discursive, and psychological implications and forces that underpin or are evoked by its articulation. For this reason, the analyses undertaken here also involve a close scrutiny of the literary strategies or rhetorical devices used to construct and convey translational ideas, meanings, and viewpoints.

For all the positive associations with translation—building connections, crossing, or transgressing binaries and boundaries, there are also limits to the investigations in this volume. As a testament to the "bounded" nature of the field, the contributors here have remained very much within their own geo-literary and language domains, the result of which is that the academic divisions observed earlier are still very much in evidence in this volume. The majority of the chapters draw on the literatures of the "island" states of Malaysia, Singapore, Brunei Darussalam, Indonesia, and the Philippines. With the exception of Cambodia, the rest of the "mainland" states are not represented here, though not for want of trying.[15] While this lopsided representation is unfortunate, it does reflect the fragmented and uneven field of study that is Southeast Asian literatures, and the challenges it poses due to existing academic and language barriers.

Another issue too is the continued reliance on Eurocentric concepts and theories of translation that can be found in this volume. Nevertheless, these limitations should not detract from the very important work being done here for, by engaging with the translational dimensions of Southeast Asian literatures, some of the contributors have emerged with new ideas and approaches to the study of translation and literature in the region. At the same time, we also pave the way for an inclusive pan-regional approach that is both contemporary and relevant. This approach can be seen at work in the chapters, which examine literary texts and genres as well as terms and concepts produced in a multitude of languages, including English, Malay, Chinese, Dutch, Tagalog, and Khmer; these texts and languages provide a small glimpse into the wonderfully complex Babel-like terrain that is postcolonial Southeast Asia. At the same time, local and indigenous history and perspective, or worldview,[16] are emphasised across the volume.

The chapters

In putting this volume together, I've grouped the chapters into two thematic sections: "Time" and "Culture." Reflecting key preoccupations in the field of postcolonial Southeast Asian literatures, the themes of "Time" and "Culture" capture a pan-regional concern with history and the past as well as with culture as symbolic sites of negotiating identity. Indeed, one of the major themes that kept cropping up during the EuroSEAS laboratory was the way the past had been revisited across Southeast Asian literary imaginaries. The concern with the precolonial and/or colonial past has been instrumental to the anti-colonial and decolonising projects of reclaiming identity, whether in the name of "indigenous," "native," or "local" culture, or of the independent and sovereign nation. Central to postcolonial studies, the project of reclaiming identity and the past is one that both fascinates and troubles the scholars working in the field, since we are cognisant of the psychological and emotional ways in which we have been interpellated as racialised, gendered, and sexed subjects by the state and society, even as we interrogate, resist, and dismantle the very system that constructs history and the past, and our very place in it. Almost all the chapters here tap into history and the past in some form or another (even when the objectives of doing so differ) in order to examine the hidden matrices of power and entrenched inequalities and biases that underline the act and process of translation itself, especially when it involves the contested categories of race, gender, and sexuality. In doing so, they also question and critique the concept of "time," including the way it is translated through the construction and production of history and the past, whether as official, indigenous, subaltern, or interventionist discourses.

The volume thus begins with the very important theme of "Translating across Time," which explores how the indigenous, precolonial, or colonial past continues to reside in, vex, or influence present imaginaries through the appropriation, revision, or (re)articulation of history, myth, legend, and archetype. Featuring four chapters, the section examines the different ways in which the past is translated into the present, revealing in the process the pull of larger forces—whether of the global market, the nation-state, or cultural traditions—that continues to affect and shape how race, gender, and sexuality are perceived and represented.

The first of the chapters to be presented here is Angelia Poon's "Self-Conscious and Queer: Translating the Pasts of Singapore and Malaysia in Lydia Kwa's *This Place Called Absence* and Tan Twan Eng's *The Gift of Rain*" in Chapter 2, which reflects on the critical function of historical fiction in interrogating the past through "informed creative and interpretive acts of translation" (22). In her analysis of Lydia Kwa's and Tan Twan Eng's historical novels, respectively titled *This Place Called Absence* and *The Gift of Rain*, Poon argues that they use metatextual or metafictional strategies—which involve self-conscious writing in exploring the relationship between literature and reality—to disrupt official history's linearity and articulate the contentious issues of queer desire and sexuality, which have conventionally been silenced in the "politics of historiography, dominant histories, and hegemonic cultural imaginaries" (38). Drawing on translation as a metaphoric act of creative revision, Poon frames her arguments by employing concepts of queer time and space to translate queer desire and sexuality in the novels; in doing so, she shows how they reimagine a past that both accommodates and gives expression to queer sexuality and desire. Significantly, the novels' acts of articulating queerness can be considered subversive and transgressive, even "anti-national," within the contentious contexts of "straight" Singapore and Malaysia where LGBTQ identities and acts are illegal. Hence the act of translating the past is also one that probes the ideological and formal impetuses that construct official history and the identity categories of race, gender, and sexuality. Poon also argues that this process is made possible by the novels' positioning as transnational or "global" Malaysian and Singaporean literary products that traverse Anglo-American and Southeast Asian/Asian literary traditions as well as national culture.

Chapter 3, also to do with the constructed nature of "history" and the past, features Grace V.S. Chin's "Performance and Translation: Hang Li Po and the Politics of History." This chapter provides a critical perspective into the politics of history by analysing two contemporary plays on Hang Li Po, a legendary Chinese princess who was once inscribed as a historical figure in Malaysian history textbooks. According to Chin, the historicised figure of Hang Li Po as a silent and powerless object of the Malay male gaze not only establishes patriarchal Malay authority and dominance as a historical and legitimate right in the nation space, but also perpetuates the subordination of the Malaysian Chinese as racialised and gendered other through the hegemonic tropes of difference and exclusion. The state's appropriation of Hang Li Po in the formation of official history in national discourse thus bears significant ramifications for Chinese-Malay relations and for Malaysian Chinese identity and position, which are reflected in the treatment of race, gender, and language in the two plays. Using performance translation as her approach, Chin examines the dialogic relations between language and performance in the two plays to reveal ironies, inconsistencies, or "schisms" (51) which, she argues, underline the "textuality of history" and the way it "is subjected to the politics of appropriation, manipulation, and revision" (61). Her reading also shows that, although both plays perform and translate the legend very differently, they nevertheless engage with the local and global discourses of their time to represent and articulate very specific viewpoints about race and gender identities and relations. In the course of doing so, they reflect "a preoccupation with the idea of Malaysia as a nation, and what it means to be Malaysian" (43).

Next is Nazry Bahrawi's "Were-Tigers in Were-Texts: Cultural Translation and Indigeneity in the Malay Archipelago" in Chapter 4, which maps the cultural translation and transformation of the "were-tiger," an oral folktale or mythology from the Malay Archipelago that dates back to a precolonial era, in two respective modern texts from Malaysia and Indonesia. While this chapter shares common ground with Chapter 3 in revisiting "old" literary narratives to show how they are pertinent to present concerns, its motivation stems not from the problematic of the nation-state, but rather from "the dominance of Euro-American epistemology" (67) across academic disciplines, including translation studies. Indigenous Malay narratives of the region can be deployed, he contends, as a vital interventionist strategy to decolonise the Eurocentric epistemological system, which involves challenging hegemonic concepts like the self/other dichotomy and the Cartesian mind/body dualism. To demonstrate how this interventionist strategy works, Nazry looks to cultural translation to shed light on the "transformations that transpire within a single culture across time and context" (68), that is, by analysing how indigenous cultural or literary legacies of the past—in this case, the Malay mythology of the "were-tiger"—help deconstruct and decolonise contemporary Eurocentric epistemology in the field of translation studies. At the same time, Nazry ponders on the transformations effected within the cultural trope of the "were-tiger," and how its re-appearance in the modern narrative forms of film and novel has engendered "were-texts" that are "not quite original, but not quite archetypal either" (78). In short, these contemporary "were-texts" are a hybrid product of old (tradition and beliefs) and new (ways of thinking)—the primordial past made relevant in present, modern form.

In Chapter 5, titled "Translating the Ideal Girl: Female Images in Khmer Literature and Cinema," Daria Okhvat reveals how the traditional figure of the "ideal" Khmer girl has persisted as a germane cultural symbol, even in the postcolonial present. Using intralingual translation, she traces the cultural archetypes of Khmer women in literary and cinematic representation across the temporal arc of colonial and postcolonial contexts, only to find that they are still subjected to strict literary and patriarchal conventions established by religious literature (*Chbap*) several centuries ago. Like Nazry, Okhvat is interested in exploring the shifts in meaning and ideas within the same language discourse and culture (Khmer in this case), and she similarly does so by tracing cultural tropes and archetypes in twentieth-century narratives; however, her focus and findings are very different. By comparing two classic Khmer novels of the colonial period and two postcolonial film texts, all of which have been framed by a decidedly masculine perspective, Okhvat discovers that time has made little impact on the gender identities, roles, and expectations in Khmer culture and society, even with the changes wrought by independence, revolution, and civil war as well as modernisation and globalisation. Modern Khmer literature, it seems, has remained as "one of the main broadcasters of cultural tradition through which the ideal Khmer girl is upheld" (98). However, this is not to say that there is no change at all, only that it is limited, and slow in coming. This can be seen in contemporary Cambodian cinema, which is at the forefront of exploring modern images of Khmer femininity by representing women in ways that depart from the prescribed literary trope and figure of the ideal Khmer girl.

The second thematic section, titled "Translating across Cultures," is informed by the chapters' shared emphasis on culture as the defining focus— an aspect also discernible in Chapters 4 and 5; both these chapters thus form a "natural" bridge between the two thematic sections. Culture is another highly contested ideological site in postcolonial Southeast Asian studies. In the early years of independence and decolonisation, culture—often interpreted as "indigenous" or "native"—was held as the symbolic repository of cherished traditional values, customs, and practices. Partha Chatterjee[17] ([1991]2010) in fact argues that the space of culture, defined as the "spiritual" or "inner" domain that "[bears] the 'essential' marks of cultural identity" (27), is what drives Asian anti-colonial nationalism. As the spiritual domain is the source of cultural identity and therefore the basis of national culture, it must be protected from the corroding influence of Western liberalism and modernity. This defensive posturing can be seen in the nationalistic rhetoric and attacks on the loss of tradition and cultural values, not to mention the erosion of the mother tongue and national language (and correspondingly, national literature). This tune is still being sung today by nationalists and conservatives in globalising Southeast Asian societies. Within the contemporary contexts of late capitalism and globalisation, identities, subjectivities, and practices on the ground have been influenced, even transformed, by economic development, modernisation projects, social changes, and technological innovation, all of which have occurred at an accelerated pace since the 1990s. These changes have affected the Southeast Asian nation-state whose participation in the global marketplace and technologies has to be mediated by concerns related to national identity and culture. The negotiation between local and global, Asian and Western, cultures and ideas powerfully links the next few chapters, which address the politics of race, gender, and sexuality that undergird and shape cross-cultural, transnational, or glocalised identities and experiences, and how they inform translational practices on the ground, including intercultural, cross-cultural, or transcultural relations and dialogue.

We start with Tom G. Hoogervorst's "Gained in Translation: The Politics of Localising Western Stories in Late-Colonial Indonesia" in Chapter 6, which draws on postcolonial translation studies to examine how translation can serve as a politicised act of anti-colonial resistance. Analysing writings and translations across three language cultures—English, Dutch, and (hybrid) Malay, Hoogervorst shows how Indonesian author-translators of Eurasian and localised Chinese (*Peranakan*) background in the Dutch colony "write back" to the imperial centre through strategic translations that articulate and affirm their local viewpoints and sensibilities, notably by removing or excising racist elements from Western narratives, a technique Hoogervorst calls "deracialising" (117). Deploying creative linguistic strategies like "strategic omission and semantic broadening" (123), the author-translators "assert agency over the literature of their colonisers" (111) by producing popular translations that tapped into the psychology of the local reading market, made up of colonised and racialised subjects. Since they resist colonial racism and epistemology, these localised translations should be seen as insurrectionary texts whose popularity and widespread circulation among the masses also perpetuate anti-colonialism in the "local" imaginary. The use of early twentieth-century Malay as the master code in translation is another empowering act, for it provides the author-translators with the linguistic means of localising and deracialising the narratives, while enabling their anti-colonial resistance in the same breath. Defiant and transgressive, these Malay translations vex the Empire's epistemological boundaries and hierarchies by undermining established European ideas of race and language through bold assertions of the local voice, viewpoint, and agency in late-colonial Indonesia.

Chapter 7 looks at how racial/ethnic and gender identities and expectations are negotiated through religious conversion and cross-cultural romance in two Bruneian novels in Kathrina Mohd Daud's "Translating Islam: Conversion and Love in Bruneian Fiction." Especially relevant in the current context of Islamophobia and Brunei's controversial implementation of the Syariah Penal Code Order, this chapter constitutes an interventionist reading into the ways Islam is perceived and articulated in literature by examining how the cross-cultural conversion romance in the Bruneian novel intersects with the larger global narrative of Islam and conversion. As a genre, conversion romances are by nature of its thematic subject necessarily cross-cultural. Here, however, Kathrina invites us to reflect on how local Bruneian conversion romance and its global counterpart, particularly American conversion romance, are actually in dialogue with each other, even when they diverge where the converts' identity and positionality are concerned. In so doing, she deepens the discussion on the cross-cultural experience of conversion, an already complex subject-matter, by analysing the trope in multifaceted ways: locally, glocally, and globally. Although translation here is used in its metaphoric sense, its role in facilitating our understanding of the cross-cultural connections between local and global narratives of Islam should not be underestimated. Indeed, translation is deployed in three crucial ways. First, it is used to initiate the conversation between local and global discourses on Islam through conversion romance; second, it highlights the underlying power dynamics that shape the ways in which the convert figure is defined, perceived, and positioned in both local and global Islamic frameworks; and, finally, it "throws into relief the fault-lines and clash-points of identity" (134) in the negotiation of racial and gender expectations in these different spaces. What Kathrina finds out in the process is also revealing of the ways in which race/ethnicity and gender as well as national and cultural identities are managed and regulated through conversion in Brunei and globally.

The following Chapter 8 by Kelly Yin Nga Tse, titled "Cinematic Erasure: Translating Southeast/Asia in *Crazy Rich Asians*," also engages the local-global trajectory in the reading of Jon M. Chu's 2018 cinematic adaptation of Kevin Kwan's best-selling 2013 novel *Crazy Rich Asians* Instead of looking at dialogic connections and intersections, however, Tse interrogates the *lack* of critical conversation between local and global discourses of identity, the result of which is the insidious mistranslation and erasure of Southeast Asia. Using related concepts of cultural and interlingual translation as well as cinematic excess, Tse carefully unpacks the film's embedded "layers of unspoken cultural biases and representational violence" (159) as she examines the complex politics of race and class and how they are translated at different levels and registers—cultural, national, regional, and global—in varying contexts across the trans-Pacific: Singapore, Southeast Asia, Asia, and (Asian) America. As empowering as the film is in redressing the historicised racist discourses of white America and Hollywood through the recuperative narrative of Asia's ascendance in the world, Tse argues that it still problematically hinges on Chinese hegemony and capitalistic wealth. By supporting a Chinese-centric Asia through the depictions of crazy rich Chinese in Singapore, and by conflating Southeast Asia with (East) Asia, the film's cultural (mis)translation ignores, and even elides, the racial, cultural, and linguistic diversity of Singapore and the region. Singapore, too, is guilty for playing a complicit role in promoting the Chinese capitalistic narrative, which reinforces its own self-image as Southeast Asia's most prosperous country as well as the only one with a Chinese-majority population. Although the film reproduces "the same logic of violence" (160) inherent in ideologies and discourses of race and class, Tse nonetheless points out the "parodic potential" (161) of the film's visual excess, which allows for the possibility of self-critique, if only to highlight the exclusion and erasure of the Southeast Asian other whose voice and agency have been denied.

We come full circle by ending the volume with J. Neil C. Garcia's "Translation and LGBT Studies in the Philippines," the chapter that first raised the idea of translation as a possible common theme and framework at the EuroSEAS laboratory. The idea of translation, or interlinguality, is particularly relevant to the polyglossic and hybridised spaces of postcolonial Philippines. Although Garcia, like Nazry, is also critical of Western epistemological hegemony in global LGBT discourse, which he argues is being "conducted in the anglophonic register" (171), he reserves his biggest criticism for the lack of self-reflexivity of local scholars who merely replicate Western ideas and theories of gender and sexuality without considering local conditions in the development of the Filipino LGBT field, known also as "Bakla and Tomboy (or Lesbyana) Studies." This lack of mediation between local and global cultural discourses furthermore undermines the tradition of Filipino writing in English, which has employed cultural translation as a postcolonial interventionist technique to "nativise" or "localise" narratives. Reading two of the earliest "gay" texts—a novel and a poem—in English by Philippine writers, Garcia considers how their cultural translations of homosexuality as a theme can be troubling, painful, ambivalent, and paradoxical, all because of the language used. English has been appropriated by the writer to create a symbolic space through which homosexual desire can be expressed and articulated; but on the other hand, there is no equivalence in English to translate "native" vocabulary sources or words that are rooted in localised gender and sexual experiences. One such word is *bakla*, which embraces a fluid range of meanings such as "intramale sexual attraction, male femininity, and male-to-female gender-crossing" (174).[18] Although terms like *bakla* challenge Western binaries of sex and gender, they have in the course of translation been remoulded and essentialised to fit Western, and global, views. Unless it is recuperated, the *bakla* will "ever 'haunt'" (188) the Filipino gay culture.

I would like to end by expressing the hope that the future scholarship on Southeast Asian literatures will involve more translational research, and that this volume is a positive contribution in that direction. As evinced by the chapters here, translational research can be very exciting and enriching. By crossing imaginary and ideological borders, and making connections where none seemingly exist, the contributors here bring in fresh insights and innovative ideas that break the conventional patterns of reading and writing about Southeast Asian literatures, which have stayed well within the confines of language, academic, and market trends as well as geopolitics. Although tensions and challenges will still exist as such work troubles and resists the established boundaries and nationalising impulses of the nation-state, there is also much to be gained. It is this thought that should be kept in mind as we explore the frontiers of translational Southeast Asia and push the existing scholarship out of internalised comfort zones (remember: artists, writers, readers, and researchers are equally the subjects of specific times and spaces/places, even as they work to express, resist, trouble, or

Introduction 17

conform to the contexts, exigencies, and imperatives of their cultures and societies). Only then can we do justice to the region's rich literary, linguistic, and cultural heritage.

Notes

1 Read Chin and Kathrina (2018) for a fuller discussion of this topic and for examples of scholarly publications.
2 For examples of country-specific research in Southeast Asian literatures, read Chin and Rajandran (2020), which provides a comprehensive overview of the trends and directions in the study of language, literature, and culture in Southeast Asia, including publication samples. However, it should be noted that these samples refer mainly to English-language scholarship. Many more studies are written in the national or native languages, and are not readily accessible due to the language barrier.
3 See Chin and Rajandran (2020) for more details about and examples of literatures written and produced in different languages within the region, notably English (anglophone), Malay, and Chinese (sinophone).
4 Examples include Smyth (2000) and Yamada (2009).
5 There are, of course, exceptions. In postcolonial Singapore and Philippines, the ex-colonial tongue of English is recognised as one of the official languages; as such, literary productions in English receive national recognition.
6 This observation is also based on my own teaching experiences in Malaysia, Brunei, and Hong Kong. For instance, the undergraduate course "Malaysian Literature in English" falls under the English Language and Literature Studies programme at Universiti Sains Malaysia, and is promoted as an anglophone field of study (which is reinforced by the academic research market). At Universiti Brunei Darussalam, an attempt was made in 2011 to merge both Malay and English language drama under the Drama and Theatre Studies minor programme, but the move proved so unpopular with students that the proposal was scrapped, and drama was again taught according to the language medium under the respective programmes of Malay Studies and English Studies.
7 See also Heryanto (2002), who criticises the ethnocentric and Western-dominated practices in Southeast Asian studies, which have led to the subordination and marginalisation of Southeast Asian academics and scholars in the field.
8 In Malaysia and Singapore, for example, the decision to write in English, a language burdened by British colonialism, has resulted in the "negative psychological condition" described as "*alienation, anomie, anxiety, detachment, dislocation, displacement, rootlessness,* or in terms of being *deculturalized, deracinated, detribalized, homeless* or *marginalized*" (original emphasis, Ismail S. Talib 1994, 206). See also Chin (2006) for an interesting analysis of the anxieties of authorship faced by English-language writers in Malaysia and Singapore.
9 Examples of scholarly works based on specific countries include Arimbi (2009), Chigas (2005), Echols ([1956] 2009), Galam (2009), Groppe (2013), Platt (2013), and Salmon (1981), while regional or cross-country comparative literatures in translation include Aveling (2019), Braginsky (2004), Ding and van der Molen (2018), Jenner (1973), Mohamad Rashidi Pakri and Graf (2013), Smyth (2000), and Yamada (2009). For more examples of such studies, see Chin and Rajandran (2020), who also discuss the significance of translation studies (and literary translation) in the research of Southeast Asian literatures and cultures.
10 A brief survey of journals that include *Translation Studies* and *Asia Pacific Translation and Intercultural Studies*, for instance, reveals fewer articles on translation in Southeast Asia compared to those written about East Asia and South Asia.

11 Translation traditions usually focus on the textual and linguistic dimensions involved in the translation process between the source text and target text (with the writer as originator of the source and the translation as the target), and the issues that arise, including the role of the translator, and topics related to fidelity, transfer, and equivalence as well as the linguistic mediations and choices of taxonomy, lexical, and other linguistic features. Much of this work still remains at the heart of translation studies even as the discipline is being reshaped.
12 In 2019, Brunei's move to enforce the death penalty for adultery and same-sex sexual relations under the 2013 Syariah Penal Code Order resulted in a celebrity-led global backlash against the kingdom. Consequently, the Sultan of Brunei announced a moratorium on the death penalty, which is extended to cover the Syariah law.
13 While Indonesia has not criminalised LGBTQ activities, homosexuality is widely considered taboo. Rising homophobia has been reported in Indonesia, with the LGBTQ community attacked by hate rhetoric and subjected to acts of harassment and shaming due to increasingly conservative religious views and attitudes on the ground (see Yulius 2018).
14 The laboratory was then a novel concept, designed to help incubate new and innovative ideas as well as generate dialogue and exchange among a group of scholars behind closed doors. It is now one of the distinct features of the EuroSEAS Conference (https://www.euroseas.org/content/euroseas-conference).
15 The researchers I'd approached were unable to join us mainly because of existing commitments. Others either did not meet the aims or scope of this volume, or were unable to meet the deadlines.
16 The terms "local" and "indigenous" should not be conflated with "national," which derives its meaning and imperative from the state itself.
17 Chatterjee's powerful essay "Whose Imagined Community?" categorically rejects Benedict Anderson's premise that anti-colonial nationalism in Asia is influenced by Western models of nationalism, arguing instead that Asian nationalism is defined by the spiritual domain (represented by culture, community, and family) rather than the material, an area dominated by Western legacies of colonialism, economy, technology, and political system. In short, anti-colonial nationalism in Asia is characterised by *"difference"* ([1991] 2010, 26; original emphasis) from Western models.
18 This linguistic phenomenon is by no means exclusive to the Philippines within the region. Parallels can also be found in Thailand. See Sinnott (2004) and Jackson (2016).

References

Albaladejo, Tomás, and Francisco Chico-Rico. 2018. "Translation, Style and Poetics." In *The Routledge Handbook of Translation and Culture*, edited by Sue-Ann Harding and Ovidi Carbonell Cortés, 115–33. London and New York: Routledge.

APCom Foundation. 2020. "Building Space for Lasting Change—LGBTI in Southeast Asia." *Heinrich Böll Stiftung: South East Asia*, January 30. https://th.boell.org/en/2020/01/30/building-space-lasting-change-lgbti-southeast-asia.

Ariffin, Eijas. 2018. "ASEAN's Shifting Attitudes towards LGBT Rights." *The ASEAN Post*, November 8. https://theaseanpost.com/article/aseans-shifting-attitudes-towards-lgbt-rights.

Arimbi, Diah Ariani. 2009. *Reading Contemporary Indonesian Muslim Women Writers: Representation, Identity and Religion of Muslim Women in Indonesian Fiction*. Amsterdam: Amsterdam University Press.

Ashcroft, Bill. 2001. *On Post-Colonial Futures: Transformations of Colonial Culture*. London: Continuum.

Aveling, Harry. 2019. *Perceptions: Essays on Translation and Literature of the Malay World*. Bangi: UKM Press.

Bachmann-Medick, Doris. 2009. "Introduction: The Translational Turn." *Translation Studies* 2, no. 1: 2–16.

———. 2016. *Cultural Turns: New Orientations in the Study of Culture*. Translated by Adam Blauhut. Berlin: Walter De Gruyter.

Bassnett, Susan, and Harish Trivedi, eds. 1999. *Post-Colonial Translation: Theory and Practice*. London and New York: Routledge.

Bhabha, Homi K. 1994. "How Newness Enters the World: Postmodern Space, Postcolonial Times and the Trials of Cultural Translation." In *The Location of Culture*, edited by Homi K. Bhabha, 303–37. London and New York: Routledge.

———.1995. "Cultural Diversity and Cultural Differences." In *The Post-Colonial Studies Reader*, edited by Bill Ashcroft, Gareth Griffiths, and Helen Tiffin, 206–10. London and New York: Routledge.

Braginsky, V. I. 2004. *The Heritage of Traditional Malay Literature: A Historical Survey of Genres, Writings and Literary Views*. Leiden: KITLV Press.

Chambert-Loir, Henri. 2009. *Sadur: Sejarah Terjemahan di Indonesia dan Malaysia*. Jakarta: Kepustakaan Populer Gramedia.

Chatterjee, Partha. (1991) 2010. "Whose Imagined Community?" In *Empire and Nation: Selected Essays*, by Partha Chatterjee, 23–36. New York: Columbia University Press.

Chigas, George. 2005. *Tum Teav: A Translation and Analysis of a Cambodian Literary Classic*. Cambodia: Documentation Center of Cambodia.

Chin, Grace V.S. 2006. "The Anxieties of Authorship in Malaysian and Singaporean Writings in English: Locating the English Language Writer and the Question of Freedom in the Postcolonial Era." *Postcolonial Text* 2, no. 4: 1–24.

Chin, Grace V.S., and Kathrina Mohd Daud. 2018. "Introduction." In *The Southeast Asian Woman Writes Back: Gender, Identity and Nation in the Literatures of Brunei Darussalam, Malaysia, Singapore, Indonesia and the Philippines*, edited by Grace V.S. Chin and Kathrina Mohd Daud, 1–17. Singapore: Springer.

Chin, Grace V.S., and Kumaran Rajandran. 2020. "Change and Preservation in Language, Literature and Culture in Southeast / Asia: Trends and Directions." *KEMANUSIAAN: The Asian Journal of Humanities* 27, no. 2: 79–101. https://doi.org/10.21315/kajh2020.27.2.5

Chua, Beng Huat. 2008. "Southeast Asia in Postcolonial Studies: An Introduction." *Postcolonial Studies* 11, no. 3: 231–40.

Day, Tony. 2002. *Fluid Iron: State Formation in Southeast Asia*. Honolulu: University of Hawai'i Press.

Ding, Choo Ming, and Willem van der Molen, eds. 2018. *Traces of the Ramayana and Mahabharata in Javanese and Malay Literature*. Singapore: ISEAS Publishing.

Echols, John M. (1956) 2009. *Indonesian Writing in Translation*. Jakarta and Kuala Lumpur: Equinox Publishing.

Einzenberger, Rainer, and Wolfram Schaffar. 2018. "The Political Economy of New Authoritarianism in Southeast Asia." *Austrian Journal of South-East Asian Studies* 11, no. 1: 1–12.

Galam, Roderick G. 2009. *The Promise of the Nation: Gender, History, and Nationalism in Contemporary Ilokano Literature*. Quezon City: Ateneo de Manila University Press.

Gentzler, Edwin. 2017. *Translation and Rewriting in the Age of Post-Translation Studies*. London and New York: Routledge.

Groppe, Alison M. 2013. *Sinophone Malaysian Literature: Not Made in China*. Amherst, NY: Cambria Press.

Harding, Sue-Ann, and Ovidi Carbonell Cortés, eds. 2018. *The Routledge Handbook of Translation and Culture*. London and New York: Routledge.

Heryanto, Ariel. 2002. "Can There Be Southeast Asians in Southeast Asian Studies?" *Moussons* 5: 3–30.

Hung, Eva, and Judy Wakabayashi, eds. 2005. *Asian Translation Traditions*. London and New York: Routledge.

Ismail S. Talib. 1994. "Responses to the Language of Singaporean Literature in English." In *Language, Society and Education in Singapore: Issues and Trends*, edited by S. Gopinathan, Anne Pakir, Ho Wah Kam, and Vanithamani Saravanan, 203–18. Singapore: Times Academic Press.

Jackson, Peter A. 2016. *First Queer Voices from Thailand: Uncle Go's Advice Columns for Gays, Lesbians and Kathoeys*. Hong Kong: Hong Kong University Press.

Jenner, Philip N. 1973. *Southeast Asian Literatures in Translation: A Preliminary Bibliography*. Honolulu: University Press of Hawaii.

Jones, Francis R. 2009. "Literary Translation." In *Routledge Encyclopedia of Translation Studies*, 2nd ed., edited by Mona Baker and Gabriela Saldanha, 152–57. London: Routledge.

Lindsay, Jennifer, ed. 2006. *In between Tongues: Translation and/of/in Performance in Asia*. Singapore: NUS Press.

Maitland, Sarah. 2017. *What Is Cultural Translation?* London: Bloomsbury Academic.

Mohamad Rashidi Pakri, and Arndt Graf, eds. 2013. *Fiction and Faction in the Malay World*. Newcastle upon Tyne: Cambridge Scholars Publishing.

Muñoz-Calvo, Micaela, Carmen Buesa-Gómez, and M. Ángeles Ruiz-Moneva, eds. 2008. *New Trends in Translation and Cultural Identity*. Cambridge: Cambridge Scholars Publishing.

Nakamura, Fuyubi, Morgan Perkins, and Olivier Krischer, eds. 2013. *Asia through Art and Anthropology: Cultural Translation across Borders*. London: Bloomsbury.

Niranjana, Tejaswini. 1992. *Siting Translation: History, Post-Structuralism, and the Colonial Context*. Berkeley: University of California Press.

Platt, Martin B. 2013. *Isan Writers, Thai Literature: Writing and Regionalism in Modern Thailand*. Singapore: NUS Press; Denmark: NIAS Press.

Pye, Lucian W. 1985. *Asian Power and Politics: The Cultural Dimensions of Authority*. Cambridge, MA: Belknap Press.

Ricci, Ronit. 2011. *Islam Translated: Literature, Conversion, and the Arabic Cosmopolis of South and Southeast Asia*. Chicago, IL and London: The University of Chicago Press.

Ricci, Ronit, and Jan van der Putten, eds. 2011. *Translation in Asia: Theories, Practices, Histories*. London and New York: Routledge.

Salmon, Claudine. 1981. *Literature in Malay by the Chinese of Indonesia: A Provisional Annotated Bibliography.* Paris: Editions de la Maison des Sciences de l'Homme.

Simon, Sherry. 1996. *Gender in Translation: Cultural Identity and the Politics of Transmission.* London and New York: Routledge.

Simon, Sherry, and Paul St-Pierre, eds. 2000. *Changing the Terms: Translation in the Postcolonial Era.* Ottawa: University of Ottawa Press.

Sinnott, Megan J. 2004. *Toms and Dees: Transgender Identity and Female Same-Sex Relationships in Thailand.* Honolulu: University of Hawai'i Press.

Smyth, David, ed. 2000. *The Canon in Southeast Asian Literature: Literatures of Burma, Cambodia, Indonesia, Laos, Malaysia, Philippines, Thailand and Vietnam.* Richmond, Surrey: Curzon Press.

Spivak, Gayatri Chakravorty. 1993. "The Politics of Translation." In *Outside in the Teaching Machine*, by Gayatri Chakravorty Spivak, 179–200. London and New York: Routledge.

Tan, E.K. 2013. *Rethinking Chineseness: Translational Sinophone Identities in the Nanyang Literary World.* Amherst, NY: Cambria Press.

Tymoczko, Maria, and Edwin Gentzler. 2002. *Translation and Power.* Amherst/Boston: University of Massachusetts Press.

Wilkins, Albert. 2019. "The Battle for LGBT Rights Is Far from Over." *Asia Times*, June 24. https://asiatimes.com/2019/06/the-fight-for-lgbt-rights-is-far-from-over/.

Wright, Chantal. 2016. *Literary Translation.* London and New York: Routledge.

Yamada, Teri Shaffer, ed. 2009. *Modern Short Fiction of Southeast Asia: A Literary History.* Ann Arbor, MI: Association for Asian Studies, Inc.

Yulius, Hendri. 2018. "Rethinking the Mobility (and Immobility) of Queer Rights in Southeast Asia: A Provocation." *Heinrich Böll Stiftung: South East Asia*, December 26. https://th.boell.org/en/2018/12/26/rethinking-mobility-and-immobility-queer-rights-southeast-asia-provocation.

2 Self-conscious and queer

Translating the pasts of Singapore and Malaysia in Lydia Kwa's *This Place Called Absence* and Tan Twan Eng's *The Gift of Rain*

Angelia Poon

Introduction

In a lecture delivered as part of the BBC's annual Reith lectures in 2017, novelist Dame Hilary Mantel posed a rhetorical question to her audience, "And without art, what have you, to inform you about the past?" (2017, 6). Her observation is a profound one simply put. The past comes to us in the present always already with commentary, through a creative act and artifice. Writers who write about the past—whether the historian or the novelist of historical fiction—invariably engage in acts of translation, rather than simply acts of recovery, in order to make the past meaningful to their contemporary readers. In her chapter for an edited collection of essays entitled *Reading the Past*, cultural historian and literary scholar Catherine Belsey explains her discomfort with "living history"—places which attempt to recreate the past and transport the visitor back in time—by noting how the experience leaves her disoriented because it entails the removal of the purchase on familiar knowledge provided by the present. In contrast, conventional historiography "translates the past into the present [...] the idea is to make the past present to our *understanding*. An earlier epoch exists as a document written in an unfamiliar language for the linguistically competent historian to render in a language we know" (italics in original) (Belsey 2000, 105). Both Belsey and Mantel make the case for understanding writing about the past as informed creative and interpretive acts of translation, a critical point to bear in mind when considering contemporary Malaysian and Singaporean anglophone novels set in prior historical moments in these two places, often with the politics of memory and historiography as key thematic asseverations.

The new millennium has witnessed an increase in anglophone literature about Malaysia and Singapore, especially in the number of so-called "global" Malaysian and Singaporean novels. These novels are the ostensible products of globalisation and the large-scale transnational flows of people, capital, and commodities commonly associated with it. Many of these novels are written by writers who either have left or are not permanently based in their countries of birth. They are works published by UK and US publishers and sold and distributed beyond local markets. Addressing diverse readers situated in multiple locations, these texts typically reflect an amalgamation of multicultural influences in creative tension with each other, including not just the Anglo-American literary tradition but Southeast Asian and Asian cultural traditions as well as specific national cultures. As "transnational commodities," these novels, as Philip Holden argues, have a "different purchase" on the local and the national from the previous generation of postcolonial novels (2012, 57).[1] A noticeable though hardly unique feature of many global Malaysian and Singaporean novels is a preoccupation with the history and past of these two separate and sovereign nations that were once part of British colonial Malaya more than half a century ago.[2] Writers originally from Malaysia like Tash Aw, Tan Twan Eng, Vyvyane Loh, and Rani Manicka, for example, have all chosen the Second World War and the Japanese occupation of Malaya as the setting for their novels.[3] Singapore-born writers like Lydia Kwa in Canada, Fiona Cheong in the US, and Balli Kaur Jaswal have drawn on particular and specific moments of the island-nation's past as inspiration for their fiction.[4] Shaped inevitably by their individual experiences—including, for many, new lives in their adopted countries—these writers often seek to dramatise daily living in the past, exploring the personal, affective, and cultural dimensions of life in specific historical periods, even if they do not all ultimately present an alternative history to the orthodoxies about British colonialism, the Second World War, and the postcolonial independence period familiar to those who know Malaysia and Singapore well. Such fictive (re)writing of the past in the contemporary moment effectively represents an act of translation that opens up numerous possibilities. For one, it serves to invite comparison with the present, not so much in order to pronounce historical advancement or progress over time as to reveal—by holding up a broken mirror—the contingent nature of the past in order to refute the teleological inevitability of the present. It also provides an opportunity for re-examining official narratives as well as received knowledge and long-held assumptions about sedimented identity categories, like those of race, gender, sexuality, and nationality, thus effectively historicising the present.

In this chapter, I focus on two novels about Singapore and Malaysia set at the dawn of and in the first half of the twentieth century, respectively—Lydia Kwa's *This Place Called Absence* (2000) and Tan Twan Eng's *The Gift of Rain* (2008). Kwa's novel depicts the lives of two Chinese prostitutes in turn-of-the-century colonial Singapore while Tan's novel traces the relationship between Philip Hutton, a young British-Chinese man, and a mysterious Japanese spy during the Second World War in Penang, Malaya. Both novels are not, however, solely stories *about* the past set *in* the past but narrative texts which frequently remind us of their constructed nature. Both writers use metafictional elements to dislodge and disrupt traditional narrative realism. According to Patricia Waugh, "metafiction" is a term given to "fictional writing which self-consciously and systematically draws attention to its status as an artefact in order to pose questions about the relationship between fiction and reality" (1984, 2). Primarily through a split narrative frame which juxtaposes the historical period in focus with the immediate present of the main protagonists in the 1990s, the novels by Kwa and Tan foreground reflexively their own textuality and mode of translating the past. The emphasis on the power of words, language, and the creative imagination in *This Place Called Absence* and the importance of story and storytelling in *The Gift of Rain* are the other specific ways in which each text casts light on its own construction. Both novels attempt to disrupt strict linearity in their narrative structure to convey a sense of the past subjectively experienced. As characters in the two novels seek to remember and memorialise aspects of the past, they foreground competing ideological tensions at work in the texts' representation of Singaporean and Malaysian histories. Both novels critique and implicitly contest the historical hierarchies and arrangements of sexuality, race, class, and gender, which continue into the present in significant ways, while also compelling the reader to confront the limits of historical knowledge and knowability.

In fact, the two novels are particularly significant for their depiction of queer desire and sexuality in their translations of the past. By representing same-sex attraction and far from straight male and female subjects in historical periods of Singapore and Malaysia typically silent about such matters, the texts perform a queering of time and space that has implications for present perspectives on the identity logics and politics of the nation in these two places. The queering of time and space, self-consciously effected, further reinforces the overall metafictional orientation of both novels. Queer studies scholarship—with its self-reflexive processes of critique that have moved beyond a "fixed political referent" (Eng et al. 2005, 3) to stress the need to interrogate normalisation and intersectionality more expansively—provides a useful analytical lens for understanding this.[5] According to queer studies scholar Carla Freccero, "queer" is "the name of a certain unsettling in relation to heteronormativity" (2007, 485). To Judith Halberstam, the term "queer" refers to "nonnormative logics and organisations of community, sexual identity, embodiment, and activity in space and time" (2005, 6). These logics and organisations counter the heteronormative institutions of family and reproduction, for example, operating according to alternative spatio-temporal rhythms of movement, location, and daily living. As Halberstam explains,

> "Queer time" is a term for those specific models of temporality that emerge within postmodernism once one leaves the temporal frames of bourgeois reproduction and family, longevity, risk/safety, and inheritance. "Queer space" refers to the place-making practices within postmodernism in which queer people engage and it also describes the new understandings of space enabled by the production of queer counterpublics.
>
> (2005, 6)

Although Halberstam deals with queering as a postmodern practice in contemporary society in the late twentieth and early twenty-first centuries by queer groups resisting mainstream straight society in the Anglo-American West, her work is useful for helping us understand how heteronormativity governs the most fundamental aspects of daily routines, ordinary time, and everyday spaces. In so doing, it also sustains conventional modes of association, identification, and understanding pertaining to national belonging and citizenship. Thus, for example, the notion of inheritance is based on an understanding of "generational time" where "values, wealth, goods, and morals are passed through family ties from one generation to the next" (Halberstam 2005, 5). Generational time enables the private family to be co-articulated with the larger nation in terms of a shared past as well as a common investment in a future of stability and progress.

As a corollary, it follows then that any attempt to resist the totalising logic of heteronormativity must involve challenging discursive and conceptual foundations in time and space. By interrogating normalised notions of inheritance, child rearing and family time, the biological clock for women, and bourgeois rules of respectability, Halberstam strives to open up alternative narratives and re-envision futures and lives according to different relations to time and space. She writes, "I try to use the concept of queer time to make clear how respectability, and notions of the normal on which it depends, may be upheld by a middle-class logic of reproductive temporality" (2005, 4). Queer subjects may use time and space to challenge and imaginatively dislodge conventional logics of development, maturity, adulthood, and responsibility, where queerness always suggests a stance of opposition, anti-essentialism, destabilisation, and a refusal to assimilate. In her book, *Time Binds*, Elizabeth Freeman similarly locates queerness in "ways of living aslant to dominant forms of object-choice, coupledom, family, marriage, sociability, and self-presentation [which are] thus out of synch with state-sponsored narratives of belonging and becoming" (2010, xv). She focusses on nonsequential experiences of time, including textual moments of asynchronicity, anachronism, repetition, and reversal: for example, to disrupt what Walter Benjamin has called "homogeneous empty time" (2010, xxii). In confronting the temporal and spatial basis of heteronormativity, queer studies has sought to account for its hegemonic force beyond sexuality and sexual orientation. Natalie Oswin makes a similar argument but with specific relation to Singapore when she argues that one needs to analyse and critique heteronormativity as it "works through teleological narratives of progress and social reproduction," rather than apprehend its hegemonic force solely in terms of a single issue like the struggle for LGBTQ rights (2014, 414). The Singapore state, as Oswin makes clear, enshrines a particular ideal of family that it considers proper for its generation of a core population of citizens according to its narrative of national progress and development. This "straight time" can also create "multiple queer asynchronies" inhabited by queered others like single women and migrant workers who fall outside the norm (Oswin 2014, 417).

One needs, of course, to also view contemporary anglophone writers queering the pasts of Singapore and Malaysia in fiction marketed globally alongside the specific political and socio-cultural contexts of these two neighbouring countries where homosexuality remains a crime and different racially and religiously charged heteronormative narratives underpin their post-independence histories and trajectories.[6] Since the 1980s, although to varying degrees of iteration, a consistent strand of the Asian Values debate in both Singapore and Malaysia has depended on a "traditional" notion of the heterosexual family to the marginalisation or exclusion of LGBTQ claims (Offord 2013, 341). In Singapore, with a population of 5.6 million, the state's approach towards homosexuality has been described as one of "illiberal pragmatism," significantly different from the rights-based discourse of liberal Western democracies (Yue 2012, 5). It is a political stance which helps explain how the criminalisation of homosexual acts can yet co-exist with a relatively vibrant LGBTQ scene and significant cultural production of gay and queer-themed work in the small nation-state and global city. In contrast to multiracial but majority-Chinese Singapore, Malaysia is the much larger neighbour with a population of thirty-two million and considerable material and ideological differences between its urban centres and rural areas. More than 60 percent of the population are Muslims and Islam plays a large determining role in the way Malaysian society has traditionally been, and continues to be, organised, especially with regard to sexuality and gender. Discrimination and repressive acts against sexual minorities, including homosexuals in Malaysia, are often the intertwined result of religious beliefs, deliberate government policies, and politicking among the different political parties (Williams 2010, 1–22).[7] Through their depiction of the moral and emotional predicaments of their queer protagonists in their translations of the past, Kwa and Tan throw into greater relief the way in which national histories in postcolonial Singapore and Malaysia are invariably presented as "straight" narratives with queer desire and queerness completely absent from the historical script. That Kwa and Tan wrote and published their books outside the countries of their birth is a point worth remembering. Read alongside the official narratives and informed by current political struggles over LGBTQ issues in the two nations, these texts implicitly raise questions about the kinds of national futures being imagined.

Having mapped out the main coordinates of the context within which to situate the queered translations of the past by *This Place Called Absence* and *The Gift of Rain*, I turn now to examine each novel more closely. My analysis is guided by these key questions: What is the view of the past and history that each text presents? How does each text foreground its investment in translating the past in narrative and metatextual terms? How and in what ways is this metatextual self-consciousness intertwined with the queering of the past in each text, and what kinds of ideological and formal tensions arise as a result?

This Place Called Absence: queering the past

Split between Canada in the narrative present of the 1990s and Singapore in 1900, *This Place Called Absence* imagines a queer colonial past for the latter through its depiction of lesbian sexuality in two Chinese prostitutes.[8] Comprising what is at first glance four first-person accounts interwoven and braided together, the novel begins in Vancouver on Remembrance Day in 1994 as we are introduced to the protagonist, Wu Lan, whose father has committed suicide in Singapore. Besides Wu Lan, a psychologist originally from Singapore and now a Canadian, the other three narrative voices in the novel are those of her mother, known as Mahmee, and two Ah Kus or prostitutes from China living in turn-of-the-century Singapore. Of the two Ah Kus, Lee Ah Choi was sold into prostitution by her peasant father while Chow Chat Mui escaped from her life in China with her cousin, Ah Loong, to seek better economic opportunities in Singapore. In a tone that is for the most part introspective and confessional, each female narrator shares her story about her past and her thoughts and troubles in her respective immediate present.

Her father's death precipitates Wu Lan's identity crisis as she takes a year of absence from work, struggling to come to terms with her past and family while also seeking sexual and emotional intimacy with various women she meets in Vancouver. She remembers her father as a distant and moody man, exclaiming—while examining a picture of him—how ironic it was that "[h]e was already a ghost so early on!" (Kwa 2000, 174); Wu Lan is haunted by her father's suicide just as her mother is haunted by her husband's ghost. Looking back on her life, Wu Lan reflects upon the fact that the act of fleeing Singapore for a faraway country had not meant complete freedom after all:

> Proud of my escape from Singapore, I convinced myself that leaving the country was the solution—a flight into exile which resulted in internal fissures in the psyche, the cleaving of memory from memory. Here I've been in this country two decades, with the unsaid and the unsayable still swirling inside of me.
>
> (123)

The past exists for Wu Lan as "the unsaid and the unsayable" (123) but its mute presence is registered in palpable and visceral terms. Frequently musing over her absent daughter's life, Mahmee in Singapore laments the visits she receives from the ghost of her late husband, Yen. With her voice conveyed in fractured English, to register her age and the fact that she is a non-native speaker of English, Mahmee wonders and worries about her daughter who came out as a lesbian in a letter she wrote to the family from Canada—an event Mahmee refers to as the "Big Shock" (20).

In what initially appears to be their respective first-person narratives in the novel, Lee Ah Choi and Chow Chat Mui recall their previous lives in

China and relate their current hardships as prostitutes and virtual sex slaves at the hands of their pimps and madams. Both women are in debt to their brothels and, like the other prostitutes there, have no means of escaping their circumstances except perhaps through the rare possibility of becoming a concubine to a wealthy client. They smoke opium to ease their daily misery while accepting the fact that their fate in the end would likely be death through disease or suicide. Kwa gives a sense of colonial Singapore through the walks her prostitute characters take during the day. Through their gaze and observations of street life, we are presented with the familiar, standard features of colonial society as described in historical accounts of Singapore as a plural society with multiracial and ethnic groups divided according to economic function and organised into discrete geographic areas for living. As she acknowledges at the end of the novel, Kwa drew inspiration for her work from the subaltern histories of Singapore by James Francis Warren, *Rickshaw Coolie: A People's History of Singapore, 1880–1940* (1986) and *Ah Ku and Karayuki-San: Prostitution in Singapore, 1870–1940* (1993). In focussing on the everyday lives of marginalised groups in colonial Singapore, Warren (1986, 1993) casts a spotlight on the underbelly of colonial society where prostitution in a colonial port city with an overwhelmingly male immigrant population is recognised as a necessity that must yet be strictly managed (Levine 2002, 64). Kwa's reliance on Warren's work is significant as it marks a political commitment to the importance of history about ordinary people rather than the so-called great men of history. The quotation from the poet Adrienne Rich that Kwa places at the start of the novel as an epigraph—"freedom is daily, prose-bound, routine/remembering"—also suggests her endorsement of the political strategy of focussing on the everyday, of indeed the moral imperative of seeing and locating liberatory possibilities in the mundane.

Kwa extends and deepens this political strategy by queering the past through her lowly historical characters as she writes her Ah Ku characters as sexualised and erotic agents with private desires of their own and a hunger for intimacy. In love with each other, Lee and Chow rely on their physical relationship to sustain themselves even as they struggle to find the language with which to explain the nature of their feelings for each other. Thus Lee wonders:

> Who fooled whom first? How did we come to our first kiss?
> I have never seen other women kiss each other. I dare not ask. For isn't it a strange thing? No one pays us for this pleasure.
> (Kwa 2000, 48)

For Lee, the value of what she shares with Chow is something she struggles to understand as she can only express it as an exchange measured against the economic nexus of paying for sexual pleasure that forms the core of their livelihoods. Nevertheless, these lines also reflect Lee's growing sense of empowerment and consciousness of possible resistance to the status quo. The private spatio-temporal experience shared by Lee and Chow is asynchronous not only to their material socio-economic conditions as sex workers constrained by an exploitative and patriarchal system but also to dominant historical accounts that marginalise prostitutes, discounting their labour from the immigrant narrative of hard work, suffering, and sacrifice accorded to other groups like coolies, domestic servants, and *samsui* women (female Chinese migrants from the *sanshui* area in southern China who worked in construction), for example, who are more often regarded as pioneers laying the foundation for future nation-building.

Yet Kwa's queering of Singapore's past in the novel is not simply a matter of giving voice to forgotten or marginal actors in the nation's history. She complicates that gesture of recuperation by making the lives of the Ah Kus the product of Wu Lan's imagination. Initially, there is no clear connection between the accounts by the Ah Kus of their exploited lives as prostitutes in 1900 Singapore, and the modern-day narratives of Wu Lan and her mother. There are echoes though of Chow Chat Mui in Wu Lan, the former seeming like the nineteenth-century doppelganger of the latter. Both are feisty characters and physically tall for a woman; both have difficult relationships with their fathers. The reader learns only about thirty pages into the novel that the two Ah Kus are not "real" historical personages but imagined characters whom Wu Lan has conjured up while reading about nineteenth-century prostitution in the public library as a way of immersing herself in something that might distract her from the emotional turbulence caused by her father's suicide. This is the first explicit connection made between nineteenth-century Singapore and modern-day Canada, between the Ah Kus and Wu Lan, and the moment we learn that Wu Lan has in effect created a queer ancestor for herself.

By presenting the Ah Kus's narratives as a product of Wu Lan's imagination rather than as retrieved or recovered pieces of the past which Kwa the writer lays before the reader, Kwa engages in a metafictional strategy that mirrors her own creative act as a writer. In this way, Kwa's message is arguably more radical and complex for suggesting the democratising power of empathetic imagination which is potentially within everyone's reach. In a similar way to how the queering of the past is a creative and empowering act, private imaginative freedom also allows taboos about race to be voiced. Chow relates the incident of a Malay man applying to marry an Ah Ku and freeing her from the brothel. She notes the rarity of Malay men as customers, "The lines are drawn, the invisible lines that separate our allegiances. We serve our own, while the British and the Japanese and some Malays go to the *karayuki-san* [term for Japanese prostitutes]" (43). Sex and prostitution are organised along racial lines as per the colonial system of differentiation according to the racial and colour bar but in her musings, she dares to defy official strictures to imagine interracial coupling and sex. Thus, she wonders sensually what Malay men must be like with "[t]heir dark skin, their different smells" (43).

In keeping with the liberatory possibilities of the imagination, we see a related and metatextual importance placed on words, language, representing, and giving meaning throughout the text. At the same time, this also serves as a reminder to the reader of the politics of language in the translation of the past. In one incident, Chow remembers how her pimp, Ah Sek, had once inscribed some romantic words of poetry about her onto the window frame in the brothel. In those early years, she had still been an object of desire for Ah Sek, although the lines he had carved for her were quite conceivably done upon the direction of the fortune-teller to ensure more business for the brothel. Wracked now by years of sexual slavery and opium addiction, Chow finds the lines singing her praises as a "willow of supple limbs bending to the wind" (55) doubly derisible. Using the symbolism afforded by the window and the willow, Chow characterises her love for Lee as liberating and free precisely because it is unnamed. Ah Sek's gesture—less a sentimental lapse than a continuation of the patriarchal domination, forced heterosexuality, and brutish exploitation that constitute his trade—is marked by carved words and actions that affix and imprison. Chow thinks:

> How to speak the unspeakable? This desire for her. Without language to name it, it is not fixed like the window frame. Free like the wind, not a willow rooted to the ground, dependent on earth for its fate.
> This is my secret and my power.
>
> (55–56)

The queer space she has carved out for herself is one that falls through the cracks of named categories. Yet even as she relishes the freedom from language when it comes to expressing her sexual desire, Chow also understands the power of words and her strategic need for them. Words can stabilise and provide certainty. Thus she describes stories as "[r]eliable companions. Keep telling them, and they live on, changeless" (55). Indeed, the importance of language is symbolised in the novel by Chow's treasuring of what she calls a "word-gift" (210) bestowed on her by the scholar who eventually helps her to leave Singapore. This takes the form of the Chinese ideograph "si," meaning "thought," written on a piece of paper. The word-gift is a powerful talisman, and an injunction to think and imagine in language. The novel ends with Wu Lan going to meet Tze Cheng, the one who told her about the possible meanings of her name, just as Chow too is on the threshold of another life, leaving for a new world outside of Singapore with her word-gift. Self-reflexively, the novel relishes the idea of the materiality of language, paying tribute to the power of words thematically and symbolically within its main narrative.

Within the narrative present of the novel, Wu Lan struggles to come to terms with her identity, her personal history, and the meaning of her name. "Once I had been Lan-Lan, my mother's precious child. Lan-Lan stayed close to home, homing in on her parents' needs. But who is Wu Lan?" (123). She ponders over the multiple meanings of the Chinese word "wu" depending on the tone with which it is pronounced—the word could mean "a medium, shaman";

"without"; "dancing"; or "a mistake." The multiple possibilities of her name is metonymically linked to the possibility that there are also always other histories not yet revealed or articulated. Wu Lan reveals to her female lover, Francis, later in the novel, her attraction towards the hidden lives of the Ah Kus and their untold stories: "They weren't rich or politically powerful so most history books tend to ignore them" (163). Confessing that she "[did] not even know for sure if lesbianism existed among the ah ku of that time," she, however, felt "compelled" (163) to imagine their relationship. Any need for certitude offered by knowledge yields instead to the power of the imagination as Wu Lan notes, "I don't pretend to know. It's more that I've needed to imagine them so that I won't. . . can't be. . . defeated by their anonymity" (163). Later in the novel, as Wu Lan gazes at her reflection in the mirror, she observes,

> Wu Lan, the sum of which is greater than its parts. She is neither Ah Choi nor Chat Mui, although they are parts of her. An image seeks itself, the particular truths. Today I notice more details that distinguish me from my parents: the three small moles along the left side of my face, the faint scars from catching chicken pox as an adult.
>
> (207)

In these lines, Wu Lan shows how one can exceed the past and not be wholly determined by it. One can compensate for the accident of birth by dissociating from, if not completely disowning, one's biological parents. Indeed, the fact that the text begins with the death of Wu Lan's father is significant for signalling the symbolic erasure of the patriarch as well as patriarchal and homophobic Singapore society. The continued exorcism of the patriarchal as the novel progresses operates in tandem with the delineation of a queer genealogy and an all-female history.

Thus, once the reader learns the "truth" about the Ah Kus's narratives and how they were borne out of Wu Lan's need for a queer ancestor, the fact that Chow escapes her life of prostitution and has the chance for a new life in the end is consequently framed as part of Wu's wish-fulfilment fantasy and desire for a history of survival. In the novel, when Lee eventually commits suicide as the money she had stashed away is discovered by those who run the brothel, Chow is grief-stricken and accidentally kills her pimp. In her desperation, she runs to a temple and seeks out the scholar she had met there before. The scholar, Koh Tian Chin, offers to marry her and give her an opportunity to escape to Indonesia. It is a marriage of convenience as Koh reveals he is not attracted to women, explaining instead that his "deepest love is reserved for men" (205). Chat Mui thinks that she has noticed "this tender love between men," adding,

> Of course it was not meant for my eyes, but how can I not see? In the small distances between their bodies, there was a subtle language. The way their hands gently touched each other's shoulder or arm in greeting or parting.
>
> (205)

Koh's offer of help marks an alliance between sexual minorities which is of course wholly imagined by Wu Lan. In Wu Lan's fantasy, Chow has a future: she will escape to Indonesia and live with Koh's mother and pregnant sister. With no mention of any man in this future temporality, the image of the three women forming a supportive and nurturing family unit is an idealised queer fantasy which rewrites the patriarchal, heteronormative family. The idea of a self-contained and self-sustaining female community finds an echo in the narrative present at the novel's conclusion when Wu Lan watches a mother at a park playing with her three-year-old daughter on a swing. In this life-affirming scene that appears at the same time suggestively queer in its openness to parallel temporalities, the child's "vibrant energy" is infectious as Wu Lan hears "[her] own heart beating loudly" (212).

Christopher Patterson offers a satirical interpretation of *This Place Called Absence*, arguing that Wu Lan "reimagines the trauma and violence of the past to reaffirm her own development from such origins, thereby establishing Vancouver as a utopic space of arrival" (2018, 107). Her act of translating the past, according to this argument, is revealed as a self-serving one since the imagined history of the two sex workers helps underwrite Wu Lan's position as the successful migrant—an economically independent professional woman who is openly gay—while also enabling Vancouver to be seen as a tolerant, liberal space. Yet Wu Lan's journey of self-discovery and redemption which involves the imagining of a queer past and queer foremothers resists, however, the strict linearity of teleological and developmental logic. Hers is a journey that is crucially both a linear progression and a doubling back. The lines Kwa uses from T.S. Eliot's "Little Gidding" which preface the novel exemplify this movement in time and space as, for "all our exploring," we always end up where we started and only then would we come to "know the place for the first time" (Kwa 2000, n.p.). These words embody a recursive gesture which incorporates the past rather than sees the past and present in strictly dichotomous and sequential terms. In the context of the novel, the "place" that we will come to know could be any point of origin—a physical geographical space like Singapore or a private psychological space. The referential ambiguity of the word "place" in the last line also recalls the novel's evocative and multivalent title. The related suggestion here perhaps is that this place called absence from which Wu Lan began her journey of self-discovery will ultimately be known, not as a void, but as a creative starting-point for imagining and writing.

The Gift of Rain: telling stories and queering time

Like *This Place Called Absence*, *The Gift of Rain* by Malaysian-born writer Tan Twan Eng is a text that draws specific attention to its task of translating the past while also seeking to imaginatively present a defamiliarising view of an important period of Malayan history to contemporary readers.[9] Traditionally, representations of the Japanese occupation in Malaya—whether in literary writing, film, or more conventional historical narratives in the form of memoirs, oral histories, textbooks, and public exhibitions—have typically and not unexpectedly focussed on the brutality of the Japanese occupying force. While not avoiding the depiction of scenes of hardship and torture like the *sook ching* or murderous cleansing of Chinese civilians, Tan also makes a concerted attempt to humanise the Japanese enemy in *The Gift of Rain*. Tan's novel is set largely on the island of Penang in the northwestern part of Peninsular Malaysia. Penang was ruled by the British as part of the Straits Settlements together with Malacca and Singapore from 1826 until 1946 (disrupted only by the Japanese Occupation) before it became part of the Federation of Malaya in 1948.

The novel is split into the narrative present of the septuagenarian protagonist, Philip Hutton, and the period 1939 to 1945, just before and during the Japanese occupation of British Malaya in the Second World War. Half a century after the end of the war, Philip recounts the experiences that left him the last surviving member of the storied Hutton family; his great-grandfather had been among the earliest British men to arrive in Penang after Francis Light established a free port there in 1786, eventually founding a lucrative trading house. The product of a biracial union between an Englishman and a Chinese woman from a prominent family in Penang, Philip grew up alongside two half-brothers and a half-sister from his father's first marriage, never quite fitting into his family or Penang society. Always more comfortable describing his outsider rather than privileged status in a plural, multicultural colonial society, he says,

> That was my burden—I looked too foreign for the Chinese, and too Oriental for the Europeans. I was not the only one—there was a whole society of so-called Eurasians in Malaya—but even then I felt I would not belong among them.
>
> (Tan 2008, 96)

Philip's life is transformed when, as a teenager, he meets a Japanese consulate official and spy named Hayato Endo. Intelligent, cosmopolitan, and well-read, Endo becomes Philip's *aikijutsu* sensei. The two share a queer attraction and homoerotic relationship. In his naïveté, Philip cannot think ill of the seemingly pacifist Endo who is making use of him to learn more about Penang in order to exploit its strategic location. Once Penang falls to the invading Japanese army, Philip decides to work for the Japanese government to protect his family and safeguard the family business. But realising soon the futility of his efforts to save those around him through such collusion, he becomes a double agent, passing key information to the Chinese triads and to anti-Japanese resistance forces. His actions during this time earn him a mixed reputation in the post-war period; some fête him as a war hero who saved their families while others revile him as a traitor and a collaborator.

The Gift of Rain may be read as a metatextual meditation on the importance of storytelling. Structurally, the novel is full of embedded stories which various characters tell one another. These include the personal and family histories of Endo's father and Philip's mother which, since they allude to various periods and places like the pre-war years in Japan and Qing-dynasty China, widen the novel's historical focus to far beyond the Malayan war-time years to take in a broader swath of Asian history and territorial space as part of the text's cosmopolitan aesthetic.[10] The novel's main narrative frame is built around Philip recounting his war-time past to Michiko Murakami, an elderly woman from Japan who had been in love with Endo before the war. Now a widow, Michiko seeks Philip out, arriving in Penang with a fifty-year-old letter written by Endo, together with the latter's sword. Michiko's arrival precipitates the action in the novel and her presence is the catalyst for the elderly Philip to confront his past and to narrate his story about the war and his relationship with Endo. As Philip observes,

> Fifty years I had waited to tell my tale, as long as the time Endo-san's letter took to reach Michiko. Still I hesitated—like a penitent sinner facing my confessor, unsure if I wanted another person to know my many shames, my failures, my unforgiveable sins.
>
> (23)

But the crucial act of relating the past heals both teller and listener emotionally. Before Michiko's arrival, Philip had kept the past to himself and led a solitary existence, content to live in a kind of stasis with his memories and removed from, if not outside of, calendrical time. Within this context then, storytelling emerges as a carefully crafted gesture of conviviality and hospitality. It is a profound act of socialisation which ushers Philip back into society and the narrative present moment, and prompts reciprocity as Michiko too shares her history and knowledge of the past with him.

The importance of stories and storytelling in the novel is also apparent in Tan's depiction of the relationship between Philip and his maternal grandfather Khoo, a man the youth initially resents for having opposed his parents' marriage. Both establish a bond once Philip hears the tale his estranged maternal grandfather shares about how he had once been a tutor to the forgotten heir-apparent to the Chinese imperial throne in the waning years of the Qing dynasty before the last Emperor Pu Yi. Philip muses over how this "strange tale. . . had made him human, a man with a history, not the caricature of a controlling, narrow-minded man" (124). In this way, the act of storytelling is rendered thematically and symbolically significant in the novel as a humanising and fundamentally human endeavour. The incident, however, gives one pause because the story of Wen Zu, the "Forgotten Emperor," is entirely fabricated as Tan admits in an author's note at the end of his novel (433). Unintentionally perhaps, this piece of paratextual detail raises an uncomfortable question about the ethics of storytelling, for the power of stories to humanise is also of a piece with narrative's susceptibility to possible manipulation to effect a falsification of the past, an exculpation of wrongs, and a justification of injustice.

In *The Gift of Rain*, the employment of a bifurcated temporal structure, similar to *This Place Called Absence*, foregrounds the processes of historiography and shows how the past is rendered present or absent in the here and now. In the novel, the past resurfaces in the present in an unexplained random fashion as when Michiko receives Endo's letter, fifty years late. The letter is likened to "a ghost" (6) sent to haunt the living. But if the letter is like a ghost, it is also the case that it serves as a trope for Philip's existence after the war when he actively sought to suppress his memories. Thus he compares himself to Endo's folded letter: "The life I had lived was folded, only a blank page exposed to the world, emptiness wrapped around the days of my life; faint traces of it could be discerned, but only if one looked closely, very closely" (23). The shifting, multivalent relationship between the past and the present is kept thematically visible in the novel through key acts of memorialisation. As Philip's retrospective narrative draws to a close, he bequeaths his father's *keris* (Malay dagger) collection and the twin *katana* or samurai swords by Nagamitsu that had belonged to Endo and him to the Penang Historical Society. In relinquishing these personal objects, he allows them to become museum-ised artefacts, part of an official public history that is stripped of the emotive and the private. Thus, as Philip himself notes, displayed before the public gaze, the swords now "appeared almost unremarkable" (430). The transformation of the objects is symbolically significant for reminding the reader of the pending erasure of Philip—a queer and elderly figure without any heirs to carry on the Hutton name—from the official and always heteronormative historical narrative. Just as the meaning of historical objects may change, so, too, may differences in historical perspective qualify judgement. While not downplaying the brutality of the Japanese army, for example, the novel also makes clear the hypocrisy of the British colonisers as it inveighs against them for their refusal to acknowledge in Japanese imperialism a mirror of their own territorial, economic, and cultural aggression in Asia for nearly two centuries. As Endo reminds Philip, the British had "turn[ed] a nation of healthy Chinese into opium addicts just so it could force the Chinese government to trade with it" (41). Bringing into view a longer history through bifocal lenses raises the question of the possibly self-interested and expedient nature of narratives we tell ourselves in the more immediate present.

In his representation of the past, Tan also makes a self-conscious attempt to disrupt linearity and sequential time. To do this, he draws upon a range of strategies from various textual and visual genres like manga, anime, Japanese drama, and Chinese martial arts written and filmic texts. These trans-genre allusions underline the text's status as a contemporary cultural artefact; they also constitute an important aspect of Tan's exploration of the politics and aesthetics of representation in literary historical fiction. Thus he seeks, for example, to capture in words the cinematic ripple of time effect when Philip's grandfather and Endo meet for the first time: "At the instant that they shook hands, I sensed something shift, something move out of focus, and then sharpen again" (208). The suggestion here is that these two significant men in Philip's life have met each other before, in previous moments and iterations of time as part of their past lives and the looping process of reincarnation. The use of flashback, the overlaying of character voices, the presence of objects and their replicas, and the strategic deployment of ritual and symbolic objects like the jade pin Philip receives from his grandfather are other trans-genre strategies employed to convey both a "telescoping of time" (217) and the cyclical sense of time that Tan places in tension with linear temporality.

In the novel, the self-conscious disruption of linear time is brought together with queer sexuality in the relationship between Philip and Endo which is figured as a fantasy of everlasting romance. Tan employs the Buddhist belief in reincarnation to inform his portrayal of the sensei-student pair as romantic actors doomed always to be on opposing sides in history. This accounts for the sense of déjà vu in the novel, and the feeling of uncanny familiarity which inflects the straightforward historical realism of the novel. Thus, just as Philip was killed by Endo in a past life, so Endo must be executed by Philip to complete the cycle and achieve cosmic balance. As Endo explains to Philip, they have "known each other for many lifetimes" and their paths have criss-crossed just like footprints in the sand. They are "forced to live again and again, to meet, and to resolve [their] lives" (217). In this way, past, present, and future are explained in terms of cycles of reincarnation which suggest a higher force or pre-destined fate at work. Cyclical time is thus an example of queer time in the novel that serves as an alternative, if not direct counterpoint, to heteronormative generational time, producing for the reader a sense of time thrown out of joint. Despite Tan's disavowal of the centrality of the "queer dimension" to understanding Philip and Endo's relationship (Lim 2017, 16), it is clear, nevertheless, that this represents a critical aspect of the novel.[11] David C.L. Lim suggests that the bond between the older Endo and younger Philip may be understood within the terms of Japanese culture and history as *shudō,* an erotic relationship between a younger man and an older man widely accepted, practised, and represented during the Edo period in seventeenth- and eighteenth-century Japan (2011, 240).

One could also, I argue, appraise the pederastic relationship alongside the other, more "proper" student-sensei pairing in the novel, that of the character Kon and his Japanese teacher, Tanaka. A Chinese friend of Philip, Kon is the son of a powerful triad leader, who trains under Tanaka, himself an old childhood friend of Endo, to learn *aikijutsu*. Both teenage boys are prime candidates for recruitment as spies given their multilingual ability in English, Hokkien, Malay, and Japanese, but it is Kon who eventually joins the British-led counter-insurgency militia, Force 136, later working together with the Malayan Communist Party as well, to resist and thwart the Japanese through guerrilla warfare. Kon is a clear foil to Philip but also a surrogate, the one who would have been the main protagonist of the novel if it had been written as a purely realist and *straight* narrative. As Philip himself admits,

> More and more often now it occurred to me that Kon was living the life I should have lived, making the choices I should have made. He had taken the proper turnings, made the appropriate stand, while I had done otherwise.
>
> (Tan 2008, 362)

Philip foresees that his friend would be remembered as a national hero after the war, not him. Indeed, Kon dies a heroic death after fulfilling his sensei's wish by mercifully killing him. Tellingly, Kon is shot by his lover, a young woman and fellow communist guerrilla fighter, Su Yen, who snaps after having to abort their baby. Placed thus in parallel, where Kon's narrative trajectory may be seen as the heteronormative equivalent of Philip's queer tragic fate, the text brings to the fore not only the narrative elements required for a straight national history to serve as the norm but also the strategic silences and omissions required for its functioning.

The force of the counter-hegemonic move to queer the past in Tan's novel by the intertwining of reincarnation with the depiction of same-sex desire is diluted, however, by the problematic questions concerning agency, free will, and self-determination that are also raised as a result. Trapped within the karmic cycles of reincarnation, the historicity of Philip's and Endo's moral choices in the novel necessarily yields to apolitical abstraction and a disembedding from historical context. In knowing what must inevitably come to pass, Endo can thus only ever try his best to prepare Philip for executing his pre-determined path by training him physically and mentally for it. Adhering to the same logic, the manifestation of Endo's love for Philip must also necessarily assume such seemingly perverse acts as killing the latter's father, Noel, and sister, Isabel, since the only relief he can offer them is mercifully quick deaths. Despite the attempt to add a perspective about temporality and human agency from another cultural and religious tradition to complicate the more conventional understanding of a historical period in terms of cause and effect and linearity, this plot about reincarnated lovers appears overly romanticised and sentimental as it struggles to grapple with such politically fraught and complex questions about individual responsibility and moral obligation during a time of war.

In a similar way, another vector undercutting the queer dimensionality of the novel is the harmonising aesthetic of equilibrium and equipoise the text employs to effect closure. On one level, Philip's education and development in the novel may be seen in terms of a striving for "connection and conjunction" (227) as its telos. Thus his grandfather advises him in a way that is meant to be prophetic as well: "You have the ability to bring all of life's disparate elements into a cohesive whole" (234). Philip as the liminal and hybrid character must somehow reconcile and resolve the novel's opposing cultural and philosophical forces within his own person. When his grandfather Khoo shows him how he has carved his name "Khoo-Hutton" onto the family ancestral tablet, Philip reveals,

> I felt a shifting sense of being brought apart and then placed back together again, all by the single stroke of the hyphen. The hyphen was also similar to the ideogram for 'one' in Japanese and, as I discovered, Chinese as well.
>
> (227)

Even if one accepts Philip's embrace of a harmonising hybridity to resolve the felt dilemma of his fractured individual identity, it is a strain to apply a similar aesthetic to the novel's ambitious overall project of establishing a seemingly cosmopolitan ethos that links disparate spaces, cultures, as well as various time periods. The central dichotomy between fate and free will that informs the romantic relationship between Endo and Philip as well as their historical war-time actions remains intransigently unbridgeable, and any attempt at a resolution of these opposing forces, such as Philip's concluding and poetic-sounding explanation that "the inscriptions that dictate the directions of our lives merely write out what is already in our hearts" (431), feels tenuous at best. Indeed, one feels obliged to resist any move suggesting eventual harmony, given the Japanese state's continual refusal to fully confront and acknowledge the extent of its war-time atrocities in East and Southeast Asia. In this regard, perhaps the cautionary image that best reflects the politics of translating the past in this novel is the provocative, recurrent one of the eyelidless Daruma, the Zen Buddhist monk in Endo's painting, or the dead Wen Zu with his eyelids removed and eyes wide open, reiterating the need for constant and unwavering vigilance.

Conclusion

In their self-conscious translations of the past, both *This Place Called Absence* and *The Gift of Rain* pose important questions about the politics of historiography, dominant histories, and hegemonic cultural imaginaries. Both seek an articulation of the past in the narrative present and focus on the importance of language, narrative, and storytelling as part of their range of metatextual strategies that reflect upon the creative process itself. Kwa's role as author is mirrored by her main character's central act of imagination in creating a queer past in the story of two lesbian prostitutes, while Tan disrupts the historical realism of his novel by including beliefs from different Eastern cultural traditions and employing tactics from multiple visual as well as Asian genres to mediate the past. The former text, sticking more closely to social and psychological realism, engages explicitly in a queering of history to critique the default heteronormative frame for understanding colonial and national history in Singapore. By exploring the possibility of queer desire and of creating queer spaces in the historical past, Kwa seeks to disrupt hegemonic notions of reproductive time, family, the patriarchal social order, and nation. Similarly, the depiction of homoerotic attraction between Philip and Endo in *The Gift of Rain* serves to queer time since both characters are caught in a cycle of reincarnation and déjà vu that continually disrupts the linearity of historical time. The text exposes the heteronormative bias of national historiography through the symbolism of its main character—the queer, childless, lovelorn Philip Hutton—and the extinguished narrative of his straight double, Kon. Yet, Tan's novel ultimately sounds a more politically unsettling note because of the way Philip's relationship with Endo is tied to vexing questions about individual responsibility and agency within a war-time context where the stakes of either collusion or betrayal are especially high. In this regard, the harmonising aesthetic Tan pursues as a form of closure only serves instead to invite scrutiny of the irresolvable tensions the text raises.

This Place Called Absence and *The Gift of Rain* introduce us to heterogeneous possibility, asynchronicities, and diverse interconnections, to the possibility of life inflected by alternative histories, temporalities, cultural rhythms, and politics. In the process, we are also challenged to be critically mindful about what the past can mean as the translations these literary texts perform may carry different meanings, not least for multiply located reading audiences. Ultimately, these literary texts which (re)write history underline the need for a close reading practice grounded in historicity and informed by a critical national and transnational consciousness.

Notes

1 Although Holden's article deals only with the "global Malaysian novel," his conclusion also applies to the global Singaporean novel. For a discussion of the local and global contexts of Singapore fiction, see also Holden (2006).
2 The Federation of Malaya gained self-government in 1957 while Singapore was given limited self-government in 1959. Singapore merged with the Federation, North Borneo, and Sarawak Crown colonies in 1963 to form Malaysia. That arrangement lasted for two years before Singapore became sovereign and distinct from Malaysia in 1965.
3 The novels are *The Gift of Rain* (2008) and *The Garden of Evening Mists* (2013) by Tan Twan Eng; *The Harmony Silk Factory* (2005) by Tash Aw; *Breaking the Tongue* (2005) by Vyvyane Loh which is set in Singapore; and Rani Manicka's first and third novels, *The Rice Mother* (2004) and *The Japanese Lover* (2010).
4 For example, Kwa has two novels set in Singapore—*This Place Called Absence* and *Pulse*; the latter is published in 2010. Both of Fiona Cheong's novels, *The Scent of the Gods* (1991) and *Shadow Theatre* (2002), are also set in Singapore. Balli Kaur Jaswal's first novel in 2013, *Inheritance*, was published in Australia before it was published in Singapore.
5 For an illuminating historical overview of queer studies and queer history, see Weeks (2012).
6 Malaysia and Singapore continue to keep on the books a British colonial-era law against male homosexual sex.

7 See also Ellis-Petersen (2018).
8 Lydia Kwa was born and raised in Singapore before she left for Canada in 1980. She trained as a psychologist and now lives in Vancouver. She has written four novels and two books of poetry.
9 Besides *The Gift of Rain*, Tan has also published a second novel in 2012, *The Garden of Evening Mists*, which was shortlisted for the Man Booker Prize and won the Man Asian Prize and the Walter Scott Prize for Historical Fiction. *The Gift of Rain* was longlisted for the Man Booker Prize. Tan was born in Penang and trained as a lawyer. He now divides his time between Malaysia and South Africa.
10 Numerous scholars and commentators have discussed the novel's multiculturalism and neo-Orientalism especially its depiction of Penang as a farrago of races and cultural influences and its portrayal of Philip's hybridity. The discussion has been decidedly mixed, comprising praise and withering criticism. Well-known Malaysian dramatist Kee Thuan Chye, for example, has impugned the novel, declaring, "Tan exploits his [cultural heritage] for surface adornment. It is selling exotica to find favour with Western readers. It is a practice that is demeaning, somewhat akin to harlotry" (Kee 2010, 33). Indeed, it is hard to avoid the sense that much of the local detail provided seems staged and overly convenient as when a young, impressionable Philip shows Endo around Penang. Weihsin Gui, on the other hand, reads Tan's exoticising style differently, observing that "we should understand the overwrought and ostentatious parts of the novel as disarticulations or interruptions in the textual body of the Orient created in the imaginations of metropolitan readers" (Gui 2013, 191). To Gui, Tan is being deliberately self-conscious and strategic in his use of Oriental detail, producing a "super-exotic novel" (Gui 2013, 190) precisely as a form of critique of the desire for cultural authenticity.
11 In this interview, Tan notes, "The relationship [between Endo and Philip] is more about ignorance and knowledge, youth and experience. And sacrifice, of course" (Lim 2017, 16).

References

Belsey, Catherine. 2000. "Reading Cultural History." In *Reading the Past*, edited by Tamsin Spargo, 103–17. Basingstoke: Palgrave Macmillan.

Ellis-Petersen, Hannah. 2018. "Malaysia Accused of 'State-Sponsored Homophobia' after LGBT Crackdown." *The Guardian*, August 22. https://www.theguardian.com/world/2018/aug/22/malaysia-accused-of-state-sponsored-homophobia-after-lgbt-crackdown.

Eng, David L., Judith Halberstam, and Jose Esteban Munoz. 2005. "What's Queer about Queer Studies Now?" *Social Text* 23, no. 3–4: 1–17.

Freccero, Carla. 2007. "Queer Times." *South Atlantic Quarterly* 106, no. 3: 485–94.

Freeman, Elizabeth. 2010. *Time Binds: Queer Temporalities, Queer Histories*. Durham, NC: Duke University Press.

Gui, Weihsin. 2013. *National Consciousness and Literary Cosmopolitics: Postcolonial Literature in a Global Moment*. Columbus: Ohio State University Press.

Halberstam, Judith. 2005. *In a Queer Time and Place: Transgender Bodies, Subcultural Lives*. New York: New York University Press.

Holden, Philip. 2006. "Histories of the Present: Reading Contemporary Singapore Novels between the Local and the Global." *Postcolonial Text* 2, no. 2. https://www.postcolonial.org/index.php/pct/article/viewArticle/431/833.

———. 2012. "Global Malaysian Novels: Prospects and Possibilities." *Kajian Malaysia* 30, no. 1: 47–59.
Kee, Thuan Chye. 2010. "In Search of Good Penang Fiction." *Penang Economic Monthly*: 32–33.
Kwa, Lydia. 2000. *This Place Called Absence*. New York: Kensington Books.
Levine, Philippa. 2002. "The Cordon Sanitaire: Mobility and Space in the Regulation of Colonial Prostitution." In *Trans-Status Subjects: Gender in the Globalization of South and Southeast Asia*, edited by Sonita Sarker and Esha Niyogi De, 51–66. Durham, NC: Duke University Press.
Lim, David C.L. 2011. "Agency and the Pedagogy of Japanese Colonialism in Tan Twan Eng's *The Gift of Rain*." *Critique: Studies in Contemporary Fiction* 52, no. 2: 233–47. https://doi.org/10.1080/00111610903380162.
———. 2017. "On Art and Artifice: A Conversation with Tan Twan Eng." *SARE: Southeast Asian Review of English* 54, no. 2: 14–22.
Mantel, Hilary. 2017. "Lecture 5: Adaptation." *The BBC Reith Lectures*, 1–33. http://downloads.bbc.co.uk/radio4/reith2017/reith_2017_hilary_mantel_lecture%205.pdf.
Offord, Baden. 2013. "Queer Activist Intersections in Southeast Asia: Human Rights and Cultural Studies." *Asian Studies Review* 37, no. 3: 335–49.
Oswin, Natalie. 2014. "Queer Time in Global City Singapore: Neoliberal Futures and the 'Freedom to Love.'" *Sexualities* 17, no. 4: 412–33.
Patterson, Christopher. 2018. *Transitive Cultures: Anglophone Literature of the Transpacific*. New Brunswick: Rutgers University Press.
Tan Twan Eng. 2008. *The Gift of Rain*. New York: Weinstein Books.
Warren, James Francis. 1986. *Rickshaw Coolie: A People's History of Singapore, 1880–1940*. Oxford: Oxford University Press.
———1993. *Ah Ku and Karayuki-San: Prostitution in Singapore, 1870–1940*. Oxford: Oxford University Press.
Waugh, Patricia. 1984. *Metafiction: The Theory and Practice of Self-Conscious Fiction*. New York: Taylor and Francis.
Weeks, Jeffrey. 2012. "Queer(y)ing the 'Modern Homosexual.'" *Journal of British Studies* 51, no. 3: 523–39.
Williams, Walter L. 2010. "Islam and the Politics of Homophobia: The Persecution of Homosexuals in Islamic Malaysia Compared to Secular China." In *Islam and Homosexuality, Volume One*, edited by Samar Habib, 1–22. Santa Barbara, CA: Praeger.
Yue, Audrey. 2012. *Queer Singapore: Illiberal Citizenship and Mediated Cultures*. Hong Kong: Hong Kong University Press.

3 Performance and translation
Hang Li Po and the politics of history

Grace V.S. Chin

Introduction

In 2012, Malaysian historian Khoo Kay Kim caused a public stir by questioning the truth of historical figures like Hang Li Po, Hang Tuah, and Hang Jebat. Describing them as "myths and legends" (Kulasagaran 2012), Khoo claimed that there was no evidence that supported their existence in either the Malaysian or the Chinese Ming dynasty records (*Malaysia Today* 2012). At the time, Malaysian history textbooks recorded that the Chinese princess Hang Li Po was Sultan Mansor Shah's fifth wife during his reign in Melaka from 1456 to 1477, a period that ostensibly saw the rise of five famous Melakan warriors and brothers-in-arms: Hang Tuah, Hang Jebat, Hang Kasturi, Hang Lekir, and Hang Lekiu. Among them, Hang Tuah has been promoted by the state as the representation of the ideal Malay hero due to his unwavering and unquestioning loyalty to the Sultan.[1] These, then, were the stories that Malaysians had studied at school and grown up with, thinking they were part of the nation's history. While Khoo's revelation highlights the troubling ways in which fact and fiction are interwoven in the retelling of Malaysian history, it also brings into sharp relief the main purpose of history education: to build national identity and a sense of patriotism among students in accordance with the "nation-building agenda" (Kulasagaran 2012). It is this particular facet that I wish to examine in relation to the contentious figure of Hang Li Po, whose importance to the construction of national identity, culture, and history also bears significant implications for Chinese-Malay relations and for Malaysian Chinese identity in the nation space.

This chapter examines the ways in which the politics of history have been translated via state-constructed and creative appropriations and revisions of Hang Li Po, and how they throw light on evolving race and gender identities and relations in the multilingual and globalising landscape of postcolonial Malaysia, specifically from 1980s till late 1990s. As the representation of the Chinese woman in the Malay world, the figure and story of Hang Li Po have been explored by scholars in connection with Chinese-Malay relations (Kong 2001), gender perspectives (Ruzy Suliza 2008), Melaka's history and heritage (Suhaila Abdullah 2013; Worden 2001) as well as Malaysia-China relations (Ku 2016; Lee 2015). Such studies are, however, far and few, and none have yet considered the relevance of this racialised and gendered figure to the shaping of national history and public memory in Malaysia or its impact on both national and cultural imaginaries—gaps which I hope to address here. It should be noted that research into race and ethnicity is fairly well-established in the scholarship on Malaysian studies, based as it is on the sociopolitical reality of Malay/non-Malay hierarchies and divisions, which have increasingly been reinforced along the lines of religious differences between Muslim and non-Muslim, with the former as a defining feature of Malayness under the Constitution. Gender on the other hand has remained under-researched (see Chin and Kathrina 2018), and merits further investigation here. To understand how Hang Li Po has been ideologically deployed to position and articulate Chineseness and femininity in the nation space, my chapter traces her representation from the historical manuscript of *Sejarah Melayu* (Malay Annals) to the contemporary drama and performance texts situated within the changing spaces of postcolonial and globalised Malaysia.

Since the 1960s, the Malaysian interest in the Chinese princess has consistently manifested itself through drama and performance, two of which will be examined here: a Malay-language *bangsawan* (Malay opera) titled *Puteri Li Po* (Princess Li Po; performed in 1982, published in 1992) by Rahmah Bujang[2] and a multilingual monodrama, *Hang Li Poh—Melakan Princess* (performed in 1998, published in 2011), by Ann Lee.[3] While Rahmah's play reflects the political reality of the 1980s when Malay hegemony was firmly entrenched, Lee's play invokes the globalising decade of the 1990s, which witnessed the state's renewed interest in English and the widespread Malaysian Chinese diaspora. Both plays are therefore very different in their imagining of Chinese-Malay and local-global relations, and these differences are dramatised primarily through performance and language strategies. Also worthwhile bearing in mind is the manner in which both plays have been received in the public sphere. Rahmah's play was first performed in the early 1980s; it was revived in the 1990s and incorporated into the national curriculum in the study of Malay language in 2000. The same, however, cannot be said about Lee's play, which was only performed three times before live audiences in 1998. Despite these differences, both plays invariably tap into local and global ideologies and discourses on identity, revealing in the process a preoccupation with the idea of Malaysia as a nation, and what it means to be Malaysian.

In analysing the representations of race and gender in both plays, I consider too the significance of genre. Unlike prose or poetry, drama and performance engage the visual and auditory languages of body and performance, the process of which involves the interaction not only between actors and dramatic text/words but also between actors and audience. The multilingual, multi-textual, and multilayered world captured in performance and theatre in fact highlights the ways in which the "text-building" of the popular legend of Hang Li Po emerges from the translation and "rich interplay between words, music and movement" (Lindsay 2006, 14), an approach developed from the tradition of performance translation (Lindsay 2006). Employing this approach, I look not only at how translation takes place between multiple language structures—both verbal and non-verbal—operating within the genre itself but also at the levels of dialogue/text, performance (bodily movement and expression), music, and the audience. By drawing out the relations and interactions between body and text, I can consider the kinds of symbolic meanings and implicit messages that emerge from the processes of appropriating and revisioning the legend, particularly those involving the textual and performative engagements with the ideological discourses of language, race, and gender. Only then can we see how translation, or the lack of translation, becomes a political act of performing and articulating identity, and what it reveals about the politics of history in the postcolonial landscape of modernising Malaysia.

Hang Li Po: versions and visions

The stories of Hang Li Po and the five Melakan warriors originated from *Sejarah Melayu*, a fifteenth-century manuscript that recounts the story of Melaka's rise as a powerful sultanate and strategic trading post, and its eventual fall at the hands of the Portuguese in 1511. Widely regarded as a Malay literary masterpiece, the manuscript was commissioned by Johor's Raja Bongsu, a minor Malay ruler who wished to both preserve and exalt the glorious history of Malay royalty and its "semi-divine genealogical links to Palembang, India, Persia and Alexander the Great" (Cheah 2010, n.p.). Although its authorship has been disputed by scholars, *Sejarah Melayu* has nonetheless been praised for the seamless way in which the "different elements of historicity, fiction and imagination" (Cheah 1998, 11) are interwoven, so much so that its historical accuracy has been questioned and debated (Worden 2001). Originally penned in Jawi and titled *Sulalat-us-Salatin* (The Genealogy of Sultans), the text has since been translated into English and Malay, with at least thirty-two editions in libraries across the world, "each one different from the other" (Cheah 1998, 105) due to various recensions and translations. As a result, numerous inconsistencies in the narration of the Chinese princess can be found. In the editions by C.C. Brown (1952) and R.O. Winstedt (1938), she is known as Hang Liu. In W.G. Shellabear's version (1896), she is named Hang Li Po. Since Shellabear's edition is the most widely circulated and read at local schools and universities (Cheah 1998, 106), Malaysians primarily know the princess as Hang Li Po (汉丽宝 or Han Libao in Mandarin).

The story goes thus: Having heard of Melaka's importance, the Emperor of China sends forth his envoys and a shipload of needles as a symbol of his kingdom's infinite population numbers and, thus, immeasurable power.

In response, Sultan Mansor Shah sends Tun Perpatih Putih as an envoy to China together with a shipload of fried sago as a similar symbol of Melaka's greatness. The Emperor is so impressed that he decides to marry his daughter Hang Li Po (or Hang Liu) to the Sultan. Accompanied by Tun Perpatih Putih and the Chinese commander Ling Ho (or Di Po), the princess sails with a large retinue consisting of ladies-in-waiting and 500 handsome youths of noble birth (or 500 sons of ministers) to Melaka. The princess and her followers are received with pomp and ceremony, and the Sultan is "astonished by [her] beauty" (Brown [1952]2010, 91). After conversion into Islam, the princess and the Sultan marry, and an illustrious line of descendants is established from their union. The Sultan is so pleased with his new bride that he gives her and her followers a place of their own called Bukit China (Chinese Hill). Since then, both Bukit China and Melaka have been recognised as the birthplace of localised Chinese roots, notably represented by the acculturated *Peranakan* (local-born) Chinese or *Baba-Nyonya* community—who should be distinguished from the Chinese immigrants known as *sinkeh* or "new guest," who arrived in the late nineteenth and early twentieth centuries. Today, Bukit China houses the largest Chinese cemetery outside of China, and is a popular stop on the tourist trail in Melaka with Hang Li Po's Well—also known as the King's Well—featured as one of the main attractions. Hang Li Po has been prominently displayed as the Sultan's consort in the Melaka History and Ethnography Museum, which provides details of her arrival and even a diorama of her residence at Bukit China (Abu Talib Ahmad 2014), although this exhibition has likely contributed to the confusion surrounding her historicity in public memory.

To Malaysian Chinese, the story of the Chinese princess married to a foreign king is not an unfamiliar one. Many grew up hearing similar tales of Chinese princesses being married off to foreign kings from faraway lands, with the most famous being Wang Zhaojun of Han dynasty—also known as one of ancient China's Four Great Beauties—who was married to the "barbarian" Xiongnu chief in the north (Mongolia today). The trope of the Chinese princess is also known in neighbouring Indonesia (Sidharta 2007), where nineteenth- and early twentieth-century Malay translations of Wang Zhaojun's story have been found in the Sino-Malay literature of colonial Dutch Indies (Salmon 1987). Hang Li Po, however, is utterly unique to Malaysia and, in particular, to Malaysian Chinese identity, and thus speaks directly to Chinese-Malay relations in the country. Ruzy Suliza Hashim observes that the objectification of Hang Li Po as a material "gift" serves to reflect the Chinese Emperor's power in building strategic affinal and royal alliances; as a "wife-giver," the Emperor is able to establish his superiority over the Sultan (2008, 23). China in the fifteenth century was an unrivalled powerhouse in the region, and the Ming Emperor, identified by historians as Yung-lo, undoubtedly held the upper hand in the political alliance with Melaka. The story to an extent reflects this power hierarchy when the Emperor marries his daughter to the Sultan, an act designed to exact obeisance from the latter. Yet, what comes next in the story completely inverts the power relations between Melaka and China, and confers superiority to the Sultan. In the world of *Sejarah Melayu*, the Sultan's obeisance to the Emperor has an unexpected side-effect: the latter falls sick immediately and is "stricken with chloasma all over his body" (Brown [1952]2010, 95). The only cure is to drink and bathe in the water used by the Sultan to wash his feet. Once healed, the Emperor takes an oath to never again "demand 'obeisance' from the Raja of Melaka or those that come after him, but only friendship on equal terms" (Brown [1952]2010, 96). The story of Hang Li Po thus functions to reinforce the Sultan's supremacy and elevate his status to the point where he is acknowledged as equal to the Emperor. Significantly, there is no record of these events, not even of Hang Li Po's marriage to the Sultan, in *Ming Shi-lu* or the Ming Imperial Annals (Wade 1997)—an observation that, as noted earlier, had led Khoo to make his bold claim.

The story of revised China-Melaka relations in *Sejarah Melayu* therefore underscores the competing narratives at work in the reshaping of Malay—and, later, Malaysian—identity and history. According to Cheah Boon Kheng, the creation of *Sejarah Melayu* was thought to have achieved its ideological purpose in preserving the "traditional Malay ideal form of government—the 'traditional golden age' with its own concepts, beliefs, images, system of politics, laws and social behaviour" (1998, 111) based on Islamic principles of morality and justice as well as traditional Malay precepts like loyalty and face. It is also through *Sejarah Melayu* that Melaka has been validated as the "centre of the Malay world" (Worden 2001, 208), a representation that has been appropriated by the Malaysian government to support the "authority and authenticity [of] its current public history" (Worden 2001, 208). As the symbolic site where the precolonial Malay government (*kerajaan*) and Islamic traditions had flourished, Melaka has been reinvented by the Malaysian government as the "national birthplace, where the nationalist movement began" (quoted in Worden 2001, 210). However, this rhetoric also leaves little doubt that the public history being reconstructed here is one which mandates and upholds the representation of Malay Islamic masculinity as the source of national(ist) authority. Historically embodied by the Melakan Sultans whose lineage has been maintained by the royal houses of Malaysia today, the vision of a glorious Malay past has been used to defend the state's construction of a monocultural, monolingual, and Islamic "Malay Malaysia," rather than a multi-ethnic, multilingual, and multireligious "Malaysian Malaysia,"[4] especially in the 1970s and 1980s. By historicising the legendary figure of Hang Li Po in the formation of national discourse, the state also highlights the subordination of the Chinese as gendered and racialised other—an image that plays a central role in the shaping not only of Chinese-Malay relations but also of Malaysian Chinese identity and place in the revised narratives of the nation.

Chinese-Malay relations: roots and routes

Much has been written about Malaysia's neo-colonial politics of race and language following the race riots of 13 May 1969, the day when tensions erupted between the two biggest ethnic groups in the country: the Malays, who form the country's majority (currently at 50.1 percent), and the Chinese, who are the largest minority group (currently at 22.6 percent). Despite the pluralist character and composition of the country—one made up of Malays, Chinese, Indians, Eurasians, and indigenous tribes, the events following 13 May radically reshaped the sociopolitical landscape of the country, starting with the implementation of three pro-Malay policies in the early 1970s: the New Economic Policy (NEP), the National Education Policy, and the National Culture Policy. The NEP focussed on advancing the Malays economically to the point where they could be on par with the more affluent Chinese, while the National Education Policy established Malay language as the exclusive medium of instruction across national schools and universities; this policy also reinforced the role of Malay as the national language, known as Bahasa Malaysia. The National Culture Policy, however, would affect Malaysian drama and theatre most. Proposed in 1971, the policy defined national culture on the basis of indigeneity, with Islam playing an important role in its development; as for other "foreign" cultures, only elements deemed suitable may be incorporated into the national culture (Carstens 2005, 150–51). This definition was used to shore up a Malay Muslim cultural scene in which the Malay arts, music, and literature were given prominence. With the valorisation of Bahasa Malaysia in the nation space, non-Malay languages like English and the mother tongues of the "immigrant" groups of Chinese and Indians were relegated to secondary status. Even literatures written in non-Malay languages were similarly affected and dismissed as "sectional" or "communal" literatures. Only Malay-language literature was accorded national status. To prevent "seditious" comments on the privileged status of Malay language, the Malays (also known as *bumiputera*, or sons of the soil), and the Malay monarchy, the government utilised existing draconian laws and implemented new repressive measures to place further limits on speech, publishing, movement, and assembly. As a result of these divisive politics, the post-1969 generations have grown up with a compartmentalised mentality—a state in which they view themselves as "racially distinct and culturally separate" (Kwok and Mariam 1998, 116).

Throughout the 1970s and 1980s, the government aggressively pursued an ethnocentric, monocultural agenda that promoted Malay language and "indigenous, largely Malay, symbols" (Carstens 2005, 154) in the development of national culture despite calls for the adoption of a more liberal policy that would better reflect Malaysia's rich cultural diversity (Carstens 2005, 157). One of these very important Malay symbols pertains to the Sultan's *daulat*, or the sovereignty and power of a ruler, a concept that is important to traditional Malay worldview. In *Sejarah Melayu*, the Sultan's *daulat* leans towards the supernatural and is defined as a "mystical power" (Cheah 1998, 113). According to Anthony Reid, *daulat* was believed to have been rooted in "spiritual sources" while the success of the rulers and warriors was due to "ascetic and ritual preparation, meditation, magical charms, and their own god-given sanctity, as much as through the strength of their armies" (1988, 125). While the mystical dimensions of *daulat* have been stripped in accordance with contemporary Islamic discourse, the ruler's *daulat* or sovereign power has nonetheless been legitimised by the Malaysian Constitution and maintained as part of indigenous Malay claims on and rights to their ancestral land as *bumiputera*. It is also in this manner that the precolonial Melakan sultanate has been "harnessed to a nationalism that promoted the symbolic powers of the Sultans and monarchy" (Worden 2001, 203). At the same time, the symbolic investment of *daulat* on royal Malay masculine bodies reinforces the marginality of the Chinese female body, which is placed on the lower end of both race and gender hierarchies.

The story of Hang Li Po travelling across the seas to marry the Melakan Sultan can be read as an allegory of the Chinese diaspora in Southeast Asia, and reflects the gendered dimensions involved in the migration process. There are striking parallels between the proverbial Chinese bride leaving her natal home to reside with her husband's family and the Chinese sojourners who leave their motherland for foreign climes where adaptation and assimilation can prove difficult and painful. Oftentimes, they are unwelcome in the new land where their immigrant status as foreigners or outsiders is emphasised. The feminisation of the Chinese immigrant is also powerfully visualised by the marginalised and powerless body of Hang Li Po; she is merely an "object of exchange" (Ruzy Suliza 2008, 24) through which the Melakan Sultan's obeisance to the Chinese Emperor can be exacted. When the Sultan's authority is reinstated by the act of bestowing his feet-washing water to his father-in-law, Hang Li Po's value as a Chinese princess, and as a woman, is significantly reduced: the "Raja's feet-washing water, normally useless and never a gift, becomes [more] precious than the princess herself" (Ruzy Suliza 2008, 24). Hang Li Po may have played a central role in transforming Melaka's status from "political insecurity into political authority" (Ruzy Suliza 2008, 30) but her enduring image has been one of marginality, silence, and submission. The representation of the oppressed and powerless Chinese female migrant body can be said to reflect, I argue, the beleaguered position and identity of the Malaysian Chinese in the aftermath of 13 May, when they were redefined as non-*bumiputera*—non-indigenous, foreign, and other; this subordinate status would later be reinforced by other labels: non-Muslim, non-halal. It is this representation that was promoted by official Malaysian discourse when the legend of Hang Li Po was historicised and produced as "fact" in the history syllabus.

Subjected to the homogenising forces of Malayisation and Islamisation in the 1970s, Chinese heritage and cultural sites began to be neglected, and even excluded, from national representations of history (Worden 2001).

The hardening stance of the government towards Malaysian Chinese culture peaked in the late 1970s and early 1980s, when a series of key events rocked the Chinese community and revealed the precariousness of their situation: first, the government rejected a Chinese-language university called Merdeka University; second, the Chinese cultural symbol, the lion dance—decried as "foreign" by the then Home Affairs Minister (Carstens 2005, 152)—was categorically rejected from inclusion into national culture; and, third, the iconic Chinese Kapitan Yap Ah Loy, long known as Kuala Lumpur's founder and the symbol of Malaysian Chinese contribution to the country, was replaced with a Malay figure named Raja Abdullah in history textbooks (Carstens 2005). Even Bukit China, the place long associated with localised Chinese roots, was not spared when it was gazetted for commercial redevelopment in 1984 by the state government. Fierce opposition in the end saved Bukit China from this fate but the general perception that there was an ongoing "direct assault on Chinese cultural heritage" (Worden 2001, 215) prevailed. The 1980s was a pivotal decade for Malaysian Chinese whose growing anxiety over their position and rights—and, increasingly, their children's future—in Malaysia was expressed through several public debates and protests over the government's attempts to erase or suppress cultural difference. Heightened ethnic tensions and the erosion of non-Malay rights and identities also led to record numbers of Malaysian Chinese migrating overseas between 1983 and 1990 (Cartier 2003).

Between the late 1980s and early 1990s, another milestone was discerned in Malaysian politics when the government's stance towards ethnic relations and language was increasingly mediated by the necessity of economic development and the forces of globalisation. Then Prime Minister Dr Mahathir Mohamad promised to end ethnic quotas by 2020 with his new ambitious manifesto, *Vision 2020*, which aimed to make Malaysia a fully industrialised nation by 2020. In 1991, the National Development Policy (NDP)—replacing the NEP that had ended in 1990—relaxed the pro-Malay quotas, a move seen by many as a step in the right direction. Other promising signs were observed during these years: Islamic fundamentalist groups and movements became more moderate while restrictions were lifted from the Chinese lion dance, which could be performed across the country with a "minimum of government interference" (Carstens 2005, 173). Meanwhile, globalisation was restructuring the order of world economies, and Malaysia wanted in on the action. It would carve for itself a space in the new global order by reshaping its identity as a modern, international, and progressive country that was open to foreign investment and trade relations. In line with this objective, the government launched the Multimedia Super Corridor (MSC) project in 1996, under which a series of important constructions, including the Petronas Twin Towers, Cyberjaya, Putrajaya, and the Kuala Lumpur International Airport (KLIA), were erected as the shining symbols of modern Malaysia. The government's additional recognition of English as a vital language of the global marketplace, communication, and technology also led to the strengthening of English as a second language in the national curriculum (Gill 2002). Despite these promising signs, race and religious barriers remained enforced by draconian laws as well as prejudicial policies and practices that had been in place since the early 1970s.

Against the changing sociopolitical backdrop of postcolonial Malaysia, the story of Hang Li Po has been revisited numerous times through drama and theatre, reflecting the Malaysians' long-standing fascination with the Chinese princess. Kong Yuanzhi (2001) notes at least five performances held from the 1960s until late 1990s, starting with *Drama Tarian Hang Li Po*, a dance drama that was popularly performed in Melaka in the early 1960s. In 1971, Chen Luohan's musical theatre titled *Opera Hang Li Po* was held in Kuala Lumpur; it enjoyed a revival from 1991 till 1993, and was performed in various cities across the peninsular. Rahmah's *Puteri Li Po* (henceforth *PLP*) was staged in 1982, and revived in the 1990s (more below). Although unmentioned by Kong, Lee's *Hang Li Poh—Melakan Princess* (henceforth *HLP-MP*) was performed in 1998 at the international Kuala Lumpur Monodrama Festival. In April 2004, Istana Budaya staged a lavish musical production titled *Puteri Hang Li Po* (Princess Hang Li Po) whose portrayal of "multi-racial harmony" as well as "trans-cultural and trans-national solidarities" (Shanon 2004) was conveyed through the dual languages of Malay and Mandarin. In 2015, yet another dance drama titled *Hang Li Po* was held by the National Academy of Arts Culture and Heritage (*Akademi Seni Budaya dan Warisan Kebangsaan*, or Aswara). Unlike previous productions, this one focussed on Hang Li Po's return to Beijing for a visit. Showcasing classic Chinese dances, Aswara's revisionist performance can be seen as a recuperative effort to see the world from a Chinese viewpoint. While promoting the "understanding and appreciation of other cultures and artistic traditions" (Gopinath 2015), Aswara's transnational take on the legend is also in tandem with improved Malaysia-China ties at the time.

As my analysis will show, the appropriative act of re-imagining and translating the Chinese princess through drama and performance is also one that is influenced by sociopolitical developments occurring on the ground. Both plays engage with the complexities and contestations that underline the translational politics of identity as the nation-state moved from a Malay nationalistic stance of the 1970s and the 1980s to a more moderate and international outlook in the 1990s, one influenced by global postmodernity and its economic benefits. By responding to the hegemonic local and global discourses of their time, both plays also become the bearers of specific ideologies and, as a result, carry politically inflected objectives and nuances. Language is key to both plays, as is history—or rather, the politics of history. Using the Chinese princess to query, critique, provoke, subvert, or even to conform to and uphold ideologies and discourses, both plays reveal what is at stake here: the idea of Malaysia as a nation, and what it means to be Malaysian. However, both notions are neither simple nor clear, as the ideology behind them can be at odds with the material reality.[5] Despite the divisive politics of race, religion, and language, and despite having developed a compartmentalised mentality with regard to their identity and position in the nation space, Malaysians as a people have nonetheless experienced some form of acculturation or hybridisation in their daily social contact and interaction with each other; striking examples can be found in the country's rich food culture (see Duruz and Khoo 2015) and multilingual scene. Furthermore, the changes or transformations in identity are influenced by not only local developments but also global ones. Saiful Anwar Matondang points out that the Malaysian Chinese had, during the repressive decade of the 1970s, negotiated their identity by observing the "harmonious ethnic frame" while "absorb[ing] the Chinese transnational cosmopolitan identity" (2016, 58), a process that "hybridized the Chinese Malaysian into a new cosmopolitan culture, especially among the middle class society" (2016, 59). In short, contemporary Malaysian politics of identity and nation do not always cohere, and the ways in which they are interpreted and translated through drama and performance may also reveal schisms through which social, cultural, and political ironies, incongruities, and disjunctions are highlighted. With these issues in mind, I now turn to the two plays.

Lost in translation: *Puteri Li Po*

In many ways, Rahmah's dramatic conception of *PLP* falls within the national and "historical" framing of the race relations between Malay/*bumiputera* and Chinese/non-*bumiputera* that had taken shape in the early 1970s and consolidated by the 1980s. *PLP* was performed in the tradition of *bangsawan*, a nineteenth-century popular and culturally syncretic opera form that had blended multicultural musical elements as well as multilingual lyrics and dialogue for a multi-ethnic audience; by the 1980s, however, it became a monolingual, monocultural form that predominantly showcased Malay culture (Tan 1993). Staged in Melaka in 1982, *PLP* was so popularly received that it toured several states in 1992 (Mohd. Effindi and Rahmah 2013, 134). In 1999, the play was revived to commemorate University of Malaya's fiftieth anniversary under the revised title *Puteri Cantikku Sayang Li Po* (My Beautiful and Beloved Princess Li Po); at least nine performances were held from 27 November till 1 December (Kong 2001). The script was published in 1992 and included in the 1994 anthology titled *Mustika Diri: Bunga Rampai Karya Penulis Wanita, 1930–1990* (Self-image: Potpourri of Works by Women Writers 1930–1990). In 2000, the national curriculum incorporated *PLP* as one of the literary texts studied under the core compulsory subject of *Bahasa Melayu* (Malay language) at the secondary school level. Students who studied *PLP* would have also watched the video of the staged performance of *PLP* on Eduwebtv,[6] an online portal set up by the Ministry of Education with educational video and audio materials for students in both primary and secondary schools.

Generally observing the outline and themes of the tale in *Sejarah Melayu*, *PLP* opens with the princess already married to the Sultan in Melaka and ends with her acceptance of her new identity and homeland. However, there is one significant difference: the originally silent, one-dimensional princess is fleshed out here. Given a voice and (limited) agency, Li Po is endowed with emotional depth. She is lonely and homesick, and also upset about her lower station as one of the co-wives in a polygamous marriage. Disappointed (*hampa*) and bitter (*pahit*) about her fate (Rahmah 1994a, 642), Li Po also views the Sultan with dread—an emotion powerfully evoked when the latter appears as a wicked genie (*jin afrit*) in her nightmare. As she tells the *jin afrit*/Sultan: "One look at you and I lose my appetite"[7] (*Sekali kupandang mu hilang seleraku*, 641). Li Po then falls for one of Melaka's mightiest warriors, Hang Jebat, who happens to be in love with her female attendant, Dang Wangi. When Li Po finds out about their relationship, she feels shamed (*malu*) and angry (*murka*, 665). She then realises she has no choice but to fill "the emptiness of my heart" (*kekosongan hati ini*, 667) by "learning to love my husband" (*belajar mengasihi suami beta*, 667).

The imbalances in race and gender relations are visualised when the princess's limited agency, marginality, and powerlessness are juxtaposed against the Sultan's masculine virility and superior power, or *daulat*. His possession of four wives from powerful countries and empires, including Raden Galoh of Majapahit and Li Po of China, "prove Melaka's unparalleled greatness" (*membuktikan kebesaran Melaka jua adanya*, 647). Throughout the play, Li Po and the audience are repeatedly reminded about the Sultan's *daulat*, or that Melaka is blessed by his *daulat* (645, 649, 650, 661). Raden Galoh even cautions Li Po with the story of her own father who, stricken with illness as a result of the Melakan Sultan's obeisance, had to be cured with the water blessed by the Sultan's *daulat* (650). The play ends with a pregnant Li Po who finally accepts her new identity as a "co-wife and naturalized Malay—Sultan Mansor is her lawful spouse and Melaka is now her home" (Mohd. Effindi and Rahmah 2013, 135). Li Po's final submission—denoted by her willingness to wear clothes befitting "a Malay princess" (*seorang puteri Melayu*; Rahmah 1994a, 668), her mastery of Malay *adat* (customary law) as well as her desire to please her husband by sitting at his feet—is further reified by the Sultan's masculine and sexual potency in this scene; he is twice victorious for having conceived a son with Li Po and for healing the Emperor with his "curative [feet-washing] water" (*air penawar*, 669). By reasserting the Sultan's powerful *daulat* and Li Po's subordinate albeit rightful place in the Melakan court, *PLP* ends on the note of interracial unity and heterosexual harmony in which both race and gender hierarchies are maintained. By staying within the narrative confines of the original legend, *PLP* implicitly upholds the Malay Islamic glory represented in *Sejarah Melayu* and whose vested symbols of Malay power—the precolonial Melakan *kerajaan* and the Sultan's *daulat*—have since become part of the nation's foundation, and historicised in the narration of post-independence Malaysia.[8]

Performance and translation 53

According to Mohd. Effindi Samsuddin and Rahmah Bujang, the play questions whether Malaysian Chinese "should think of themselves as Chinese or Malaysian first" (2013, 135). They further state: "While her female desire and Chinese identity are treated sympathetically, Li Po, as is requisite in *bangsawan*'s heroic order, chooses loyalty to family and national unity in her adopted home. The general good and not her personal wishes must be served" (2013, 135). This interpretation of *Puteri Li Po*'s ending, while consistent with the sociopolitical climate and ideological prerogatives of the time, does not, however, acknowledge what has been lost in translation: the erasure of Chinese racial and cultural identity, strikingly projected by Li Po's transformation into a "Malay princess" in the play's final scene. By suggesting that Chineseness, a foreign element, can only be accepted when it is fully assimilated into the dominant Malay Muslim culture, the play also appears to uphold the conservative stance on race relations, with the most desirable outcome being the "'natural' assimilation[9] of Malaysia's minority cultures into the dominant (Malay) culture" (Carstens 2005, 155). In short, it is the Malayised (and not Malaysianised) Chinese who can be identified as part of the imagined community.

Significantly, my reading of the loss of identity is also reflected in another critical way: the use of the *bangsawan* form. Developed in the late nineteenth century, *bangsawan* was originally eclectic and non-traditional, and attested to the organic processes of cultural syncretism and hybridity on the ground (Tan 1993). By the 1980s, however, *bangsawan* was Malayised in accordance with the goals outlined by the National Culture Policy, and produced as part of the national arts heritage. By categorising *bangsawan* as *"teater tradisional"* (traditional theatre), the state reinvented *bangsawan* as an indigenous and historical Malay form that had been in existence for many generations. This official view has been supported by Rahmah, who considers *bangsawan* as a *"drama Melayu tradisional"* (traditional Malay drama; 1994b, 459) and lists it alongside *Wayang Kulit* (shadow puppetry), *Mak Yong* (a form of Malay dance drama), and *Boria* (comic skits accompanied by song and dance), among others. While classified as *Melayu*, many of these forms are, in fact, characterised by hybridity and syncretism as a result of contact with, or influence from, other cultures (Matusky and Tan 2004).[10] Influenced by the discursive forces of Malay nationalism, *PLP* ultimately supports the vision of Malay Malaysia, rather than a Malaysian Malaysia. Through the monolingual *bangsawan* performance, the play's translation of the legend stays firmly within the prescribed limits of the hegemonic discourse upheld by the state, and in so doing invalidates cultural difference, even hybridity, in national representation.

The play's refusal to accommodate difference and hybridity can be seen in the use of Malay monolingualism in *PLP*. Code-switching and code-mixing are not employed; even the songs—unlike those of the earlier *bangsawan* (see also Tan 2006)—are performed entirely in Malay. The verbal structures of the play not only establish *PLP* as *drama Melayu tradisional*, but they—and the form itself—also work to contain Li Po's cultural and racial difference, which is represented at the non-verbal level through visual cues, particularly in the opening scene: Li Po is seated on a long Chinese sedan chair that is decorated with red cushions, and dressed in the style befitting "a Chinese princess" (*seorang puteri China*; Rahmah 1994a, 638), with her hair done in the Chinese aristocratic fashion. She is, moreover, in a Chinese-themed garden setting that features Chinese bamboo, a fishpond filled with red and white lotus flowers, and a rock-garden in the corner. When she speaks, however, we find that she is already well-versed in Malay, and a formal court discourse at that. Li Po's speech lines suggest that she has, to some degree, adapted to her new country by "master[ing] the language" (*menguasai bahasa*, 643), but her refusal to let go of her Chinese identity and roots—translated through the non-verbal language of the performance—has nonetheless contributed to the barriers between her and the people of Melaka. Indeed, Hang Jebat criticises Li Po's resistance, arguing that she must "let go all her memories of and regard for her country of origin" (*melepaskan segala ingatan dan penghormatan kepada negara asalnya*, 645); only then can she "truly submit to the authority of His Majesty the Sultan, her husband" (*benar-benar berajakan ke bawah Duli Sultan, suaminya*, 645). In the end, Li Po does submit, both as a Chinese princess and as a woman, and her conflicted state is resolved through complete assimilation: she speaks, acts, and dresses in a way befitting a Malay princess.

By examining the translational processes of interaction and exchange, or, in this case, the lack thereof, between the verbal and non-verbal language structures of the performance, we find that *PLP*'s refusal to accommodate difference and hybridity can be said to both reflect *and* enact the divisive forces and cultural barriers operating among Malaysians. This is found in the scene when Li Po launches into a sad Malay song "ala Chinese music" (*ala-muzik Cina*, 641). The term "ala" is important here. Derived from the French "à la"—meaning "in the style or manner of," the term draws our attention to not only the imitative dimensions operating in the performance of Chineseness but also the ways in which they are influenced by essentialised ideas and stereotypes: Chinese bamboo and rock garden, lotus-filled ponds, Chinese furniture, clothes and hairstyle, and Chinese musical style. By translating race and ethnicity through the state-mandated framework, the play ends up reproducing racial stereotypes while also keeping intact the ideological boundaries and barriers between the two ethnic groups—an effect that can be attributed to the workings of a compartmentalised mentality.

On Eduwebtv, a digital portal watched by Malaysian educators and students, the stereotyped representations of the Chinese princess and her culture are even more glaring. Red—an auspicious colour in Chinese culture—dominates the opening scene of the performance: Li Po wears red clothes and headwear edged in gold; even her Chinese female attendant is dressed in red *samfoo* (a two-piece clothing consisting of a Chinese-style top and pants). In contrast, Li Po's Malay ladies-in-waiting are dressed respectively in cream and brown *baju kurung*, the traditional Malay female attire. Other costume changes also indicate the princess's cultural background: a Chinese bridal gown and beaded headwear in the Sultan's court and a green Chinese two-piece costume coupled with her red headwear from the opening scene. Meanwhile, soft background music "ala Chinese music" can be heard in many of Li Po's scenes. Another stereotyped marker seen in the play is the classic Chinese fan dance, which is also a staple performance in national representations of Chinese identity and culture.

Of interest here too is the casting choice, since the young actor playing Li Po is Chinese while the Malay characters are performed by actors of Malay ethnicity. In contrast to the fluidity and more natural rhythms of the dialogue lines spoken by Malay actors, the actor playing Li Po occasionally slurs and stumbles over her words, an unintentional performance of non-nativeness that nonetheless marks the space of racial difference. Jennifer Lindsay points out that "bodies *are* the language" (2006, 30), and that performativity is inextricably tied to the power structures of race and ethnicity; hence having "a Malay speak Chinese on stage or vice versa is no innocent artistic choice" (Lindsay 2006, 30). Different meanings can emerge from the translation between bodies and speech in performance, but when those meanings are anchored to the politically charged discourses of race and ethnicity in the nation space, the performance then becomes "a political statement, entering the highly sensitive area of potential racial stereotyping" (Lindsay 2006, 30). By casting a Chinese into a Malay monolingual show, Li Po's racialised otherness—embodied by the weaker vessel that is the female body—is doubly amplified on the online portal dedicated to the education of Malaysian youths.

The play's troubling performance of Chineseness additionally contradicts the lived reality of Malaysian Chinese identities, which are constantly evolving and adapting to both local and global conditions, and are "multiple, diverse, [. . .] both in official discourse and in the daily experiences of particular individuals" (Carstens 2005, 202). By endorsing the full assimilation of the Chinese minority as the desired outcome, *PLP* ultimately shows the lack of negotiation between monolithic state-defined notions of Chineseness and the ongoing transformation and hybridisation of Malaysian Chinese on the ground, revealing in the process gaps and cracks between the ethnic communities, or, indeed, how little they know of, or even understand, each other. It is at the level of the subtext that the play ironically taps into the profound sense of loss and displacement experienced by Malaysian Chinese, whose racialised and feminised position as non-*bumiputera* other is one that has been upheld in the national curriculum and taught across the country.

However, it is also important to point out that the Chinese characters are not the only ones being subjected to essentialised discourses of race and culture. The imagining and representation of Malay identity too are influenced by an idealised past found in the pages of *Sejarah Melayu*, a text supported by the state as an authoritative source for the understanding of Malay Muslim identity, culture, and history. As Judith Nagata argues, "Malay culture and identity are a product of centuries of hybridization" (2011, 15), a view supported by my earlier discussion of syncretic Malay dramatic and cultural forms. Marked by diversity, multiplicity, and fluidity, Malayness as an evolving and hybrid identity in Malaysia has, throughout history, developed through contact with as well as influence from Indian, Arabic, Chinese, and other regional sources, not to mention the changes and transformations engendered by generations of intermarriage and intermingling with other races and cultures. It was only after independence was achieved in 1957 that a more rigid concept of Malayness came into existence, one "distilled into constitutional and legal formulae, and subject to being 'remade' by the Malaysian constitution" (Nagata 2011, 4). The state has, furthermore, "narrowed its vision to one based on conformity to a political party and agenda," the result of which is that "the official range of expression of Malayness is now one of the narrowest in history" (Nagata 2011, 4). Through the nationalist processes and discourses of racialisation, both Malay and Chinese identities have been locked into inflexible and reductive binaries of *bumiputera* and non-*bumiputera* and their attendant associations—a situation mirrored to an extent in the play. In short, the performance of identity in *PLP* is based on essentialised ideas of race and ethnicity, albeit in differing ways that highlight not just the problematic construction of identity in the nation space, but also the manner in which they reinforce notions of and perspectives on race and ethnicity as historicised discourses in the shaping of Malaysia as a modern nation-state.

Hang Li Poh—Melakan Princess: multilingual translation and subversion

Deconstructing the Chinese princess in critical ways, the postmodernist monodrama *HLP-MP* is at once subversive inasmuch as it is new and exciting in its unabashed celebration of multiplicity, hybridity, and difference in Lee's reinterpretation of the legend. Notably, Hang Li Poh is recognised as a "Melakan princess," with the emphasis on her Melakan/Malaysian identity rather than her ethnicity. Other popular ideas about the princess are further unsettled when she refuses to stay put in Melaka or the fifteenth century; instead, she travels across time and space to different parts of the world. Temporal, spatial, and linguistic boundaries are blurred as the character traverses past and present as well as multiple locations (as indicated by the accents used) and languages. Hang Li Po's identity is rendered rich, multiple, and, more importantly, it defies labels and stereotypes; there are, after all, not one but *eight* versions of the princess in the play. Drawing on differences based on age, class, location, occupation, and status, the play conveys her multiple and shifting identities via the titles of the eight scenes: (1) Princess; (2) Courtesan; (3) Instrument of Trade; (4) Child Bride;

(5) Warrior; (6) Tourist guide; (7) Astronaut; and, finally, (8) Migrant. Each scene also functions as a critical commentary on the politics of language, race, and gender in society, both in the past and in the present. The character's subversive difference is further conveyed by the linguistic and phonetic play on the name used in *Sejarah Melayu*. Instead of "Po," the romanised Chinese "Poh" that is common among Hokkien and Cantonese speakers in Malaysia is used. At once an act of subversion and resistance, this small deviation from the original opens up a gap where difference comes into play; this time, the legend is retold from the viewpoint of the racialised and gendered other, with multilingualism as the key strategy in the narration.

Performed entirely by one actor who plays all eight versions of the Chinese princess (HLP 1–8; these acronyms are used from hereon), *HLP-MP* significantly demonstrates the concept of "multilingualism in one body" (Krishen Jit in *Coping*, 2004, quoted in Lindsay 2006, 16), which involves the body's familiarity with multiple languages and their "different physical embodiments" (Lindsay 2006, 16), such as code-mixing, code-switching, bilingualism, and multilingualism. Having grown up with multiple language patterns and speech varieties, Malaysians possess the innate ability to juggle and mediate two or more codes in everyday communication and interaction—a linguistic phenomenon termed "polyglossia." Taking this concept further in performance translation, *HLP-MP* translates the heterogeneity of Malaysian social reality through the multilingual body—a strategy that enables the critical analysis of the constructed hierarchies and historicised discourses of race and ethnicity (which are linked to language use). The multilingual performance thus becomes a theatre of resistance that not only critiques the politicisation of race and ethnicity, but also challenges the homogenising forces of Malay monoculturalism as the *only* representation of national culture. To a lesser degree, though no less important, *HLP-MP* also confronts and dismantles traditional gender stereotypes by tapping into the female body's agentic potential and possibilities, including its capacity for resistance, transgression, and insubordination.

Within the polyglossic contexts of postcolonial Malaysia, the legendary princess is represented as the embodiment of "multilingualism in one body," a concept that is dramatised from Scene Three onwards. In this scene, the cultural hybridity of HLP 3 is spotlighted when she speaks in impeccable "Quee[n's] English" (Lee 2011, 139). By alluding to Melaka's *Peranakan* Chinese community who, during the British occupation, had embraced the English language and culture, and regarded themselves as the Queen's Subjects, the play undermines the state-defined notion of identity as static and fixed, suggesting instead that identity is subject to flux, change, and transformation—a process that reflects the reality of evolving Malaysian Chinese identities. In the next few scenes, the individual body's culturally hybrid—and distinctly Malaysian—identity is further underscored by the actor's ability to speak and code-switch between four different languages: English, Malay, Mandarin, and Cantonese. While English constitutes the dominant linguistic code in the play, there are two scenes where the actor switches to Malay, Cantonese, and Mandarin; interestingly, subtitles in English and Malay are brought in whenever the dialogue lines are in Cantonese or Mandarin. Occasionally too, bilingual code-mixing between English and Malay is used. The actor, moreover, performs English in different accents in several scenes: Queen's English, Melayu—refined and rough, Malaysian Chinese, Bostonian, Sydney "neutral," and Glaswegian. The strategic use of translation and subtitles also affirms the power hierarchies among languages, with Cantonese—a Chinese dialect, and thus different from Mandarin, the medium of instruction in Chinese vernacular schools and the language by which Chineseness is often defined—placed at the bottom of the linguistic hierarchy; it is the only language that requires translated subtitles in both English and Malay. At the same time, the use of English as the dominant code reflects the politics of the performance, which situates itself firmly within an English-speaking, urban, and cosmopolitan Malaysian as well as international audience and setting.[11]

In a reversal of power positions, Malay not only becomes secondary in *HLP-MP*, but is actively resisted against, even destabilised. This can be seen in Scene Five when the play makes fun of formal Malay discourse—representing official Malay usage during state functions and in the media. Titled "Warrior," the scene depicts HLP 5 in a showdown with the legendary Malay woman warrior, Tun Fatimah, who, in Malaysian history was the fifth wife of Sultan Mahmud in the sixteenth century. Engaged in a "tense dance" (145) based on the martial arts movements of Malay *silat* and Chinese *wushu*, the two characters conduct a verbal exchange in their respective mother tongues. HLP 5 speaks formal Mandarin while Tun Fatimah speaks court Malay, with English subtitles used for both, albeit in unsettling ways. The English translation does not follow the formal structures of Mandarin and Malay; instead, it is "contemporary and informal, disconcerting and/or comic" (145). The discrepancy is even more noticeable when formal Malay is translated into English. For instance, when Tun Fatimah uses a rhymed quatrain to address HLP 5—"My country is of the Malay world / Renowned, prosperous, peaceful / To your eyes and heart / How is Melaka?"[12] (146), the English subtitles state: "So how?" (146). Another example is the irreverent subtitle—"What's the diff?" (146)—to Tun Fatimah's formal question, "What is the difference, to you?" (*Apa bezanya, pada adinda?*, 146). To the Malaysian audience who could understand the complex interplay between Malay and English, the out-of-synch meanings emerging from the in-between space of utterance and translation—while disconcerting—are nonetheless a timely reminder of how the "journey of a sign from source to target language [. . .] involves an *imposition*" (Alfian 2006, 283), which is reminiscent of the authoritative manner in which the state discourses of language and race have been imposed upon the plural Malaysian society. Hence, the strategic use of "bad" translation can also serve the crucial purpose of "empower[ing] the audience member into examining cultural incompatibilities and political incongruities" (Alfian 2006, 283) present in their social reality.

It is also important to note that the performance of multilingualism relies not only on the actor's facility with languages but also on the audience's ability to pick up and translate the different linguistic codes. Such a performance can "create communities of understanding and of non-understanding," an experience that "can validate and challenge an audience's communal sense as cosmopolitan, or as part of the nation" (Lindsay 2006, 20). This observation is particularly true for Malaysia, where language—inextricable from the politics of race and ethnicity—is subjected to stringent state regulation. As post-1969 Malaysians have developed a compartmentalised mentality based on their status as *bumiputera* or non-*bumiputera*, watching a multilingual performance can be challenging, even discomfiting—an experience that mirrors, to an extent, the disjunctions and divisions among Malaysia's ethnolinguistic communities.

Race, however, is not the only political construct under scrutiny here. As noted earlier, gender identity, too, is of consideration in *HLP-MP*. The play's structural divisions, in fact, tell a story about the changes in gender identity and roles across the ages inasmuch as they undermine prevailing stereotypes and ideals of femininity, showing in the process that gender is as much an ideological construct as race is. The opening scene features the original Chinese Princess (HLP 1), who enters the stage lighted by "garish gold and red" (Lee 2011, 139)—echoing the stereotypical colours used in Rahmah's play—and is accompanied by "stunning entrance music, fit for an Emperor's daughter" (139). No words are spoken in this scene or the next, when the stately Princess—stripped of her outer ceremonial garment—is transformed into a "coquette-ish" (139) Courtesan (HLP 2). If these two scenes play to the audience's sense of comfort and familiarity with the stereotyped images of the Chinese princess/woman as a silent, marginal (and where HLP 2 is concerned, sexual) object of the male gaze, the next scene subtly undermines this when HLP 3, showing off her intelligence in impeccable Queen's English, launches into a "dry" talk that weaves past and contemporary histories of maritime Southeast Asia in relation to trade and economy, while referring to her function as a "trade instrument" (139) in the fifteenth century. History is also called into question when she points out the systematic devaluation of the Princess, to the point of erasure: "There is no known record of me in Chinese history. I did not exist" (143). By naming contemporary regional organisations that include ASEAN (Association of Southeast Asian Nations) and APEC (Asia-Pacific Economic Cooperation), HLP 3 shows that things, really, have not changed all that much: economic and diplomatic relations are still relevant, even more so, in view of globalisation. Moreover, women's bodies are still being produced, circulated, and marketed as migrant labourers, including domestic helpers and sex workers, in the patriarchal contexts of the global labour and service economy; this point is brought home in the last scene, which features HLP 8 as a "humble migrant" who is "here to do a job nobody wants" (154).

The audience is further unsettled by the story in Scene Four, titled "Child Bride," which touches on an all too familiar tragedy still occurring in conservative patriarchal societies in third world countries around the world.[13] What is disturbing here is the portrayal of extreme powerlessness though the representation of an eleven-year-old HLP 4, who plays with a doll (and a golden ball later) and sings traditional songs in Cantonese addressed to her mother and father. The scene ends with her terrifying abduction, when "hooded figures appear and drag her away" (145) while she screams. It is no coincidence that the scene is performed in Cantonese, the language lowest on the linguistic ladder here, paralleling the vulnerable status of a young girl who is disadvantaged not only by gender but also by age. Scene Five, titled "Warrior," however, marks the turning point as the performance shifts its focus to female empowerment. As noted earlier, HLP 5 and Tun Fatimah— the wives of two different Melakan Sultans—face off each other in an apparent contest of power that is represented by their dance of *silat* and *wushu*. For all the linguistic subversion occurring at the subterranean level of the performance, the scene nonetheless ends with the characters sharing a wary acknowledgement of each other's status; both, after all, come "from thousands of years of culture" (146). With the English subtitles acting as a linguistic and cultural bridge, the women's acceptance of each other is at once a rebuke against the ideological imperatives of Malay monoculturalism inasmuch as it sheds light on women's untold herstories, "thousands of years" old. By highlighting their intelligence, martial movements, and flair with words, this scene also discredits historical images and stereotypes of women as passive, silent, and subservient.

Espousing the themes of female agency and liberation, the last three scenes signify the radical turn in gender identities in the past century, with each title spotlighting the gendered body's multifaceted potential and possibilities through identities that are associated with mobility, exploration, and discovery: a local tourist guide (HLP 6) from Johor who works in Melaka and speaks "malaysian english" (149) with a Chinese accent; a transnational astronaut-to-be (HLP 7) who reflects the widespread Chinese diaspora and transnationalism with her multiple accents—Bostonian, Sydney "neutral," Melayu (rough and refined), and Glaswegian; and, finally, a migrant worker (HLP 8) or, simply, a "citizen of earth" (154). Translated through the frames of multilingualism, transnationalism, globalisation, and glocalisation, these identities tap into contemporary, liberal discourses of global postmodernity and human rights that uphold multicultural diversity and their attendant freedoms. However, these positivist representations are checked in the final scene when HLP 8 sounds a note of caution in the evolving narrative of HLP/woman's struggle for equality and liberation. Performing a "Broadway-type song and dance" while miming the words to the song, titled "The Song of the Migrant" (153), HLP 8 repeatedly emphasises the disenfranchisement, dispossession, and powerlessness of migrant workers the world over: "Without a single high hope / I'm here to do a job nobody wants / This is the work I really need / Got my three kids to feed, so / whatever, I'll do what you want" (154). It is a timely reminder that exploitation on a global scale still remains while the oppression of the weak and vulnerable, especially women, is an ongoing phenomenon. The final verse simultaneously critiques the original legend of Hang Li Po and challenges Malaysia's divisive politics of race and ethnicity: "For thousands of years / Migrants have evoked such fears / For place of birth? / Try 'citizen of earth!'" (154). The play's criticism against the state is inescapable, as non-*bumiputera* Malaysians are denied their rights as citizens to full equality and freedom of expression. Implicitly admonishing the state and Malay nationalists for giving in to prejudice and "fear" of the foreign other, the song ends with a rousing call for the recognition of equality, regardless of race or gender.

Conclusion

The distinctive ways in which Rahmah's *PLP* and Lee's *HLP-MP* appropriate and revise the legend of Hang Li Po tell us a story of racial and cultural ironies, incongruities, and disjunctions that are anchored in ideological disparities. Rahmah's *PLP* translates the legend according to the hegemonic state imperatives of monoculturalism and monolingualism, through which the idea of Malay Malaysia undergirds the construction of the nation. In this translation, difference and hybridity become "lost," effectively excluded or erased from the narrative. Lee's *HLP-MP*, on the other hand, employs the idea of "multilingualism in one body" and translation to articulate a very different vision of Malaysia as a nation: multi-ethnic, multilingual, and multicultural. While Rahmah employs key symbols and figures of Malay history, culture, and language to represent the glorious past of the Melakan sultanate, Lee deconstructs legend and history by moving forward into the future to embrace modern Malaysia, one that is connected to the new age of diaspora, transnationalism, and globalisation. In the process, the textuality of history is made emphatic, as are the many ways in which it is subjected to the politics of appropriation, manipulation, and revision.

Another critical difference is the way the two plays imagine, represent, and perform identity. *PLP* draws on essentialist state-mandated discourses of race and ethnicity to construct Chineseness and Malayness, and in so doing reveals a compartmentalised mentality at work in the imagining of the princess. In contrast, *HLP-MP* crosses boundaries and breaks stereotypes with its performance of identity, which is rendered rich, hybrid, multiple, and different. Similarly, the treatment of gender is also distinctive in both plays. Whereas Li Po in Rahmah's play begins as a vocal character with (limited) agency, she nonetheless reverts to the silent and submissive type in the concluding scene. Meanwhile, *HLP-MP* reflects on gender experiences through depictions of female powerlessness and empowerment while also illuminating woman's inner potential and agency by showing the protagonist's strength, intelligence, independence, and, above all, mobility—linguistically, socially, and geographically.

While the two plays underscore the many ways in which race and gender mutually reinforce each other in the analysis of Malaysian politics, there are also moments in which they do not cohere. Race and ethnicity are much more visible as contested tropes in the nation space, whereas gender is of secondary importance. The story of Hang Li Po is often read in terms of interracial Chinese-Malay relations, while gender takes a backseat. Still, bringing a gendered approach to the texts can reveal the different yet related hierarchies and intersections of power that have helped reify the subordinated position of the Malaysian Chinese in the postcolonial Malaysian narrative. In representing and articulating the issues of their times, both plays ultimately show how the literary and dramatic act of translating the legend of Hang Li Po is a politically charged process in the evolving landscape of modern Malaysia, one that involves the complex negotiation of historicised knowledges that are anchored by the identity discourses of race, gender, and language.

Notes

1 For an interesting analysis of "multicultural" Hang Tuah, see Rusaslina Idrus (2016).
2 Rahmah Bujang is a well-known Malaysian playwright, scholar, and (retired) academic who used to be affiliated to the Academy of Malay Studies at University of Malaya, Kuala Lumpur. Rahmah specialises in *bangsawan* and has written at least seven plays, including *Puteri Li Po*.
3 Ann Lee is a Malaysian playwright and director. In 1994, she co-founded Kuali Works, an all-women's production company that specialises in theatre, television, and publications. Lee has written (or co-written) at least seven plays for Kuali Works. In 2010, Kuali Works closed down. Since then, she has directed, among others, *The Vagina Monologues* (2002), a controversial play that was banned in Malaysia. (Ann Lee, email correspondence, 4 March 2019).
4 The terms "Malay Malaysia" and "Malaysian Malaysia" were used by Lee Kuan Yew and his People's Action Party (PAP) after joining the Federation of Malaysia in 1963. The PAP objected to the creation of a Malay Malaysia that supported the special rights and position of the Malays, calling instead for equal rights for *all* Malaysians regardless of race and ethnicity under the banner of "Malaysian Malaysia." Communal tensions between Malays and non-Malays, however, intensified, culminating in the 1964 race riots in Singapore. To prevent further bloodshed, Singapore seceded from the Federation on 9 August 1965 (Lee 2001). A few years later, unresolved racial tensions and hostilities resulted in Malaysia's 13 May tragedy.
5 See Homi K. Bhabha (1990) on the split between ideology and material practice, described as a "particular ambivalence that haunts the idea of the nation" (1).
6 The official website (http://www.eduwebtv.com) no longer has the video performance of *PLP* but, as of 18 March 2020, it can still be found—in three parts—on YouTube: https://www.youtube.com/watch?v=rIIhm4gllGw (Part 1), https://www.youtube.com/watch?v=j6orCKFtsHw (Part 2), and https://www.youtube.com/watch?v=ta__ZTIZtuA (Part 3).

7 All translations are mine.
8 This narration has been incorporated into Malaysia's history syllabus, which emphasises Malay and Islamic history. See Samuel and Meng (2013) for more information.
9 "Assimilation" is often used interchangeably with "acculturation," but, in fact, they carry different meanings. Assimilation describes the process when the minority group is "absorbed" into the dominant culture and becomes indistinguishable from it, whereas acculturation involves a two-way process in which the cultural group adopts the values and customs of another culture while still maintaining its distinct identity. See Tan (2018) for more on these processes in relation to the Chinese overseas.
10 According to Matusky and Tan, syncretic music forms include *bangsawan* and *boria*, while *wayang kulit* and *mak yong* are of the classical and folk arts tradition. However, these delineations are not clear-cut as the latter forms can also have syncretic features (2004, 8). Certainly, *wayang kulit* and *mak yong* can be seen as unique, hybridised forms as they have, for centuries, incorporated or adapted "outside influences" and "foreign features" from other parts of Southeast Asia, India, and the Middle East (Matusky and Tan 2004, 10).
11 According to Lee, the audience was "[b]oth local and international, but I think mostly local" as "not many companies/government agencies can pay for audiences to come along" (Ann Lee, email correspondence, 4 March 2019).
12 *"Negeri kekanda rumpun Nusantara / Ternama, makmur, aman sentosa / Pada mata dan hati adinda / Bagaimanakah pula negeri Melaka?"*
13 The website, *Girls Not Brides*, has estimated that twelve million girls under the age of eighteen are married off each year, with the highest numbers recorded in Africa as well as parts of Asia and South America. For details, see https://www.girlsnotbrides.org/about-child-marriage/.

References

Abu Talib Ahmad. 2014. *Museums, History, and Culture in Malaysia*. Singapore: NUS Press.
Alfian Sa'at. 2006. "Out of Sych: On Bad Translation as Performance." In *Between Tongues: Translation and/of/in Performance in Asia*, edited by Jennifer Lindsay, 272–83. Singapore: NUS Press.
Bhabha, Homi K. 1990. "Introduction: Narrating the Nation." In *Nation and Narration*, edited by Homi K. Bhabha, 1–7. London and New York: Routledge.
Brown, C.C., trans. (1952) 2010. *Malay Annals*. Translated from MS Raffles no. 18. Kuala Lumpur: MBRAS.
Carstens, Sharon A. 2005. *Histories, Cultures, Identities: Studies in Malaysian Chinese Worlds*. Singapore: NUS Press.
Cartier, Carolyn. 2003. "Diaspora and Social Restructuring in Postcolonial Malaysia." In *The Chinese Diaspora: Space, Place, Mobility, and Identity*, edited by Laurence J.C. Ma and Carolyn Cartier, 69–96. Lanham, MD: Rowman & Littlefield Publishers, Inc.
Cheah, Boon Kheng. 1998. "The Rise and Fall of the Great Melakan Empire: Moral Judgement in Tun Bambang's 'Sejarah Melayu'." *Journal of the Malaysian Branch of the Royal Asiatic Society* 71, no. 2 (275): 104–21. http://www.jstor.org/stable/41493366.
———. 2010. "A 17th Century Drawing and Description of RAJA BONGSU, the Owner of MS. Raffles No. 18 of the SEJARAH MELAYU—An Explanatory

Note by Dr Cheah Boon Kheng, Editor of JMBRAS." In *Malay Annals*, translated by C.C. Brown. Kuala Lumpur: MBRAS.

Chin, Grace V.S., and Kathrina Mohd Daud. 2018. "Introduction." In *The Southeast Asian Woman Writes Back: Gender, Identity, and Nation in the Literatures of Brunei Darussalam, Malaysia, Singapore, Indonesia and the Philippines*, edited by Grace V.S. Chin and Kathrina Mohd Daud, 1–17. Singapore: Springer.

Duruz, Jean, and Gaik Cheng Khoo. 2015. *Eating Together: Food, Space, and Identity in Malaysia and Singapore*. Lanham, MD: Rowman and Littlefield.

Gill, Saran Kaur. 2002. "Language Policy and English Language Standards in Malaysia: Nationalism versus Pragmatism." *Journal of Asian Pacific Communication* 12, no. 1: 95–115.

Gopinath, Anandhi. 2015. "Redefining Hang Li Po." *The Edge Financial Daily*, May 7. https://www.theedgemarkets.com/article/redefining-hang-li-po.

Kong, Yuanzhi. 2001. "Cerita Hang Li Po: Ode Persahabatan Kedua-dua Bangsa China-Malaysia." *Sari* 19: 179–87.

Ku, Boon Dar. 2016. "Preserving the Cultural Bond towards Strengthening Sino-Malaysian Friendship." *International Journal of the Malay World and Civilisation* 4, no. 3: 87–96. http://doi.org/10.17576/IMAN-2016-0403-09.

Kulasagaran, Priya. 2012. "Prof Khoo: No Record of the Existence of Princess Hang Li Po; It's a Myth." *The Star Online*, January 16. https://www.thestar.com.my/news/nation/2012/01/16/prof-khoo-no-record-of-the-existance-of-princess-hang-li-po-its-a-myth/.

Kwok, Kian Woon, and Mariam Ali. 1998. "Cultivating Citizenship and National Identity." In *Singapore: Re-Engineering Success*, edited by Arun Mahizhnan and Lee Tsao Yuan, 112–22. Singapore: Oxford University Press.

Lee, Ann. 2011. "Hang Li Poh—Melakan Princess." In *Sex, Stage & State: Kuali Works Plays*, by Ann Lee, Shahimah (Charmaine W) Idris, Sue Ingleton, Jo Kukathas, and Foo May Lynn, 136–55. Jakarta: Parama Adhi Perkasa.

Lee, Hock Guan. 2001. *Political Parties and the Politics of Citizenship and Ethnicity in Peninsular Malay(si)a, 1957–1968*. Singapore: Institute of Southeast Asian Studies.

Lee, Kam Hing. 2015. "Images and the Shaping of Malaysia's China Policy: 1957–1974." *International Journal of China Studies* 6, no. 2 (August): 107–27.

Lindsay, Jennifer. 2006. "Translation and/of/in Performance: New Connections." In *Between Tongues: Translation and/of/in Performance in Asia*, edited by Jennifer Lindsay, 1–32. Singapore: NUS Press.

Malaysia Today. 2012. "Hang Li Po, Hang Tuah Did Not Exist." January 16. https://www.malaysia-today.net/2012/01/16/hang-li-po-hang-tuah-did-not-exist/.

Matusky, Patricia, and Tan Sooi Beng. 2004. *The Music of Malaysia: The Classical, Folk and Syncretic Traditions*. Aldershot: Ashgate.

Nagata, Judith. 2011. "Boundaries of Malayness: 'We Have Made Malaysia: Now It Is Time to (Re)Make the Malays but Who Interprets the History?'" In *Melayu: The Politics, Poetics and Paradoxes of Malayness*, edited by Maznah Mohamad and Syed Muhd Khairudin Aljunied, 3–33. Singapore: NUS Press.

Mohd. Effindi Samsuddin, and Rahmah Bujang. 2013. "Bangsawan: Creative Patterns in Production." *Asian Theatre Journal* 30, no. 1 (Spring): 122–44. https://doi.org/10.1353/atj.2013.0020.

Rahmah Bujang. 1994a. "Puteri Li Po." In *Mustika Diri: Bunga Rampai Karya Penulis Wanita, 1930–1990*, edited by Ahmad Kamal Abdullah and Siti Aisah Murad, 637–71. Kuala Lumpur: Dewan Bahasa dan Pustaka.

———. 1994b. "Drama Malaysia 40 Tahun." In *Mustika Diri: Bunga Rampai Karya Penulis Wanita, 1930–1990*, edited by Ahmad Kamal Abdullah and Siti Aisah Murad, 457–74. Kuala Lumpur: Dewan Bahasa dan Pustaka.

Reid, Anthony. 1988. *Southeast Asia in the Age of Commerce 1450–1680: Volume 1—the Lands Below the Winds*. New Haven & London: Yale University Press.

Rusaslina Idrus. 2016. "Multicultural Hang Tuah: Cybermyth and Popular History Making in Malaysia." *Indonesia and the Malay World* 44, no. 129: 229–48. https://doi.org/10.1080/13639811.2015.1133135.

Ruzy Suliza Hashim. 2008. "Gender on the Agenda: The Story of Hang Li Po Revisited." *Malay Literature* 21, no. 1: 19–34.

Saiful Anwar Matondang. 2016. "The Revival of Chineseness as a Cultural Identity in Malaysia." *Khazar Journal of Humanities and Social Sciences* 19, no. 4: 56–70.

Salmon, Claudine. 1987. "Malay Translations of Chinese Fiction in Indonesia." In *Literary Migrations: Traditional Chinese Fiction in Asia (17–20th Centuries)*, edited by Claudine Salmon, 395–440. Beijing: International Culture Publishing Corporation.

Samuel, Moses, and Meng Yew Tee. 2013. "Malaysia: Ethnocracy and Education." In *Education in South-East Asia*, edited by Lorraine Pe Symaco, 137–55. London: Bloomsbury.

Shanon Shah. 2004. "From Melaka With Love." *MY Art Memory Project*. Accessed April 14, 2019. https://myartmemoryproject.com/articles/2004/05/from-melaka-with-love/.

Shellabear, W. G., ed. 1896. *Sejarah Melayu*. Singapore: American Mission Press.

Sidharta, Myra. 2007. "The *Putri China* and Their Daughters." In *Chinese Diaspora since Admiral Zheng He with Special Reference to Maritime Asia*, edited by Leo Suryadinata, 267–77. Singapore: Chinese Heritage Centre.

Suhaila Abdullah. 2013. "Effect of Malay-China Trade Relations during the Malacca Sultanate on the Emergence of Chinese Peranakan Community." *World Journal of Islamic History and Civilization* 3, no. 4: 143–49. https://idosi.org/wjihc/wjihc3(4)13/1.pdf.

Tan, Chee-Beng. 2018. "Localization and the Chinese Overseas: Acculturation, Assimilation, Hybridization, Creolization, and Identification." *Cultural and Religious Studies* 6, no. 2: 73–87.

Tan, Sooi Beng. 1993. *Bangsawan: A Social and Stylistic History of Popular Malay Opera*. Singapore: Oxford University Press.

———. 2006. "Performing the Language of Inclusion: Multilingualism and Humour in Malay Comic Songs." In *Between Tongues: Translation and/of/in Performance in Asia*, edited by Jennifer Lindsay, 224–41. Singapore: NUS Press.

Wade, Geoff. 1997. "Melaka in Ming Dynasty Texts." *Journal of the Malaysian Branch of the Royal Asiatic Society* 70, no. 1 (272): 31–69. http://www.jstor.org/stable/41493322.

Winstedt, R. O. 1938. *The Malay Annals, or, Sejarah Melayu: The Earliest Recension from MS No. 18 of the Raffles Collection in the Library of the Royal Asiatic Society, London*. Singapore: Malayan Branch of the Royal Asiatic Society.

Worden, Nigel. 2001. "'Where It All Began': The Representation of Malaysian Heritage in Melaka." *International Journal of Heritage Studies* 7, no. 3: 199–218. http://doi.org/10.1080/13527250120079300.

4 Were-tigers in were-texts

Cultural translation and indigeneity in the Malay Archipelago

Nazry Bahrawi

Introduction

The venture of translation studies has been described as first emerging from translators vying to identify best practices of actual translations with the objective of "explaining, justifying or discussing their choice of a particular translation strategy" (Munday 2009, 1), in the words of Jeremy Munday from the revised edition of *The Routledge Companion to Translation Studies*. Since then, translation studies as a discipline has made great strides to establish itself as more than just a vocational field especially if one were to consider advancements in the sub-field of translation theory. Yet, for a discipline that is centred on the study of multilingual and intercultural exchanges, translation studies can be said to be starkly lacking in one particular element: Southeast Asia (see also Chapter 1 in this volume). More precisely, the discipline has not quite incorporated the study of Southeast Asian translation practices, traditions, and theories into its fold. This accounts as a significant gap because Southeast Asia figures as one of the most diverse regions in the contemporary world in terms of language (Bahasa [Malay], Tagalog, Thai, and Mandarin, for instance), political system (such as representative democracy, socialist republic, and absolute monarchy) and religion (Buddhism, Islam, Christianity, and Hinduism, to name a few).

The reasons for the region's exclusion in translation studies are hazy. There is, for instance, the critique of whether one can even speak of a unified region precisely because of the multiplicities that it contains. Here, the scholarly tradition has been to subdivide Southeast Asia into two components. One is the Buddhist-oriented, largely former French colonies of "mainland Southeast Asia," and the other is the primarily Islamic-oriented, former Dutch and British colonies of "maritime Southeast Asia." Victor Lieberman, for instance, points out that the two groupings differ in the latter half of the seventeenth century because "the chief mainland states were too removed from the chief sea routes, too immune from naval pressures and too well integrated to exhibit the same sensitivity to European pressure as their archipelagic counterparts" (2003, 20). Outlining another major distinction difference, Ooi Keat Gin and Hoàng Anh Tuân point to the spheres of inter-state relations that saw "the mainland world" move towards "a greater centralisation of authority which essentially laid the foundation for political unification in the nineteenth and twentieth centuries" while Southeast Asia's "island world" continued to be "fragmented both politically and culturally" (2016, 4). Amidst these is the Philippines, a Southeast Asian nation that does not fit neatly into the category of maritime Southeast Asia given its distinct experience as a Spanish and American colony, unlike the others in the region, making it the only Christian-majority state there. Rommel A. Curaming points out the absence of the Philippines in several academic works about the Malay world such as Timothy Barnard's *Contesting Malayness: Malay Identities across Boundaries* and Anthony Milner's *The Malays* while arguing for the merit of factoring the Philippines into the Malay world in order "to broaden further the spectrum of ideas on or approaches to the analysis of Malayness" (2012, 265).

As Chin argues in her Introduction to this volume (see Chapter 1), one could speculate that the basic reason for the exclusion of Southeast Asia is the dominance of Euro-American epistemology, or systems of knowledge. A similar debate has already taken place in the field of sociological theory. According to Syed Farid Alatas and Vineetha Sinha in *Sociological Theory beyond the Canon*, there has been a "neglect of non-Western sources and female voices in the formative period of the development of sociological theory" (2017, 1). This is premised on the charge that the knowledge manufactured in the Western hemisphere has been implanted in non-Western contexts and passed off as universal. They argue that this also takes the form of a gendered preference for male-produced over female-produced knowledge, resulting in students primarily studying the writings of dead white males in such classes. There is therefore a need to "decolonise" the current state of how knowledge has been assembled.[1] Alatas and Sinha issued this call with regard to sociological theory, but the same injunction has been made earlier by Walter Mignolo in the field of world history. For Mignolo, the example that best encapsulates the attempt to generalise the European experience comes in the form of G.W.F. Hegel's *Philosophy of History*, which postulates the theory of a universal Spirit common to all civilisations. Mignolo does not share this benign view, preferring to describe Hegel's Spirit as "a totalising force appropriating all knowledges under 'Absolute Knowledge'" (2000, xi).

We could ask the same of translation theory. What are the texts that have defined this discipline? Some candidates include early modern works such as Walter Benjamin's *The Task of the Translator* (1923) or George Steiner's *After Babel* (1975) as well as more recent ones like Lori Chamberlain's essay "Gender and the Metaphorics of Translation" (1988) or Emily Apter's *The Translation Zone* (2006). These are indubitably insightful works that students in the field need to read, but their insights have also been drawn from a close engagement with Euro-American texts and contexts. Should they be passed off as universal? There is validity in Alatas and Sinha's argument, in that theory should be contextualised and not generalised, so as to reflect the authentic experience and thought of others, typically the non-West. However, this does not mean that "Western" texts are unworthy of study. To be fair, there have been recent works that do draw from non-European, even Southeast Asian, sources. Here, we can point to Ronit Ricci's seminal work *Islam, Translated* (2011) though the author did not position her book as "decolonial." Works like Ricci, however, are few and far between.

Having identified this epistemic gap in translation studies, this chapter will respond to it by attempting to "decolonise" the discipline of translation studies. Its aim is not to replace or discredit seminal texts drawn from the Eurocentric sphere, but to complement them with texts that exist outside that normative. In other words, it is informed by the urgent question of what insights we might gather if we were to engage with non-Western translational praxis in Southeast Asia. Taking into account my linguistic repertoire and cultural expertise, I limit the term "non-Western" here to Malay-language literary texts in the Malay Archipelago, which encompasses both Malaysia and Indonesia. This qualification is important as it distances this study from the "postcolonial" perspective on the ground that its exploration of cultural transformations within a single culture (i.e., the Malay literary sphere) is not informed by the coloniser-coloniser binary. I also specify "translational praxis" here to the study of cultural translation, which I define as the non-linguistic transformation of cultural tropes across and within cultures, a specific area of study where I have published. Two essays worthy of mention here are "A Thousand and One Rewrites: Translating Modernity in the *Arabian Nights*" (Nazry 2016), which I will revisit below, as well as "Not My Bible's Keeper: Saramago's *Cain* Translate Postsecular Dissent" (Nazry 2014), which analyses how the biblical story of Cain was made to express postsecular ideas in Jose Saramago's last novel. This time though, I will focus on the literary representations of a specific mythological trope in the Malay world: *harimau jadian*, or were-tigers.

In this chapter, I will first consider the expressions of were-tigers in oral folklore before moving on to modern literary texts as a means of mapping how this trope has changed. This method of tracing the evolution of a specific trope falls squarely within the practice of cultural translation, which resulted from the "cultural turn" in the late 1980s and early 1990s in translation studies to shift the discipline away from the study of formalist approaches to the study of "extra-textual factors" such as "context, history and convention," according to Bassnett (2007, 13). She postulates that much attention in the study of cultural translation has been directed at unveiling how texts move between cultures, with postcolonialism shifting the attention from linguistic strategies to the study of unequal power relations expressed as textual transformation, or manipulation, between colonial and colonised cultures (Bassnett 2007, 21). It can be inferred here that less focus has been directed at exploring transformations that transpire within a single culture across time and context, something that this chapter hopes to accomplish by mapping the evolution of were-tigers as a cultural trope based on oral folklore and textual narratives in the Malay Archipelago. Specifically, it will consider the myths of Dato' Paroi and Dato' Gunung Ledang of peninsula Malaysia as well as the *macan gadungan* (the Javanese term for "tigers from the Gadungan village"[2]) of East Java in relation to the modern literary prose of *Sitora Harimau Jadian* (Sitora, the Were-Tiger) by the iconic Malaysian actor-director P. Ramlee, which was made into a movie in 1964 and published as a book, first in 1965 and then again in 2012, and *Lelaki Harimau*, which was published in 2014 and translated into English as *Man Tiger* in 2015, by Indonesia's rising literary star, Eka Kurniawan. Spatially, the two authors hail from different nations though they settle comfortably within the Malay literary sphere that I have stated above. Chronologically, the original versions of the texts are forty-nine years apart. Despite this considerable gap, the two texts are modernist in the way they tweak traditional were-tiger narratives, as will be discussed. That P. Ramlee's *Sitora Harimau Jadian* was reproduced in 2012, just two years prior to the publication of Eka Kurniawan's *Lelaki Harimau*, lends further credence to the argument of its pertinence to modern concerns.

Yet, this chapter also concurs with Bassnett's (2007) critique of postcolonial translation theory, in that it would be insufficient to interpret such cultural changes as merely a function of colonial capital (which she sees as an extension of Pierre Bourdieu's notion of cultural capital), particularly in the way European colonisation had led to literary translations that affirm the supremacy of the coloniser over their colonised subjects. Exercising caution against such a view, she argues that colonial capital could not *fully* explain why F. Scott Fitzgerald's English translation of *Rubaiyat of Omar Khayyam* in 1859 was well-received, and even considered part of the English literary canon, as opposed to the works of other passionate Orientalist translators like Sir William Jones at around the same period. She believes that we need to consider other factors such as reader expectations, the norms, and the broader cultural context in which the translation was taking place, among others. Bassnett concludes:

> To attempt an understanding of this phenomenon we have to go more deeply into how taste is constructed in a culture, how publishers market their authors in accordance with those changing patterns of preference and how one culture invents the myth of another.
>
> (2007, 21)

Indeed, unequal power relations alone cannot explain the transformation of were-tiger narratives in the Malay Archipelago. Questions of taste, market demand, and myths are just as relevant here. In its limited scope, this chapter is particularly interested in the role of myth and its reinvention, because were-tigers can be considered as an indigenous Malay myth that had arguably existed before the region was Islamised in the fifteenth century. It is also important to reiterate an important element of this study that has already been raised—that is, this chapter aims to interpret cultural transformations that occur within a single linguistic culture (the Malay literary sphere) and not between two cultures, which renders the postcolonial angle somewhat moot. Surely, unequal power relations matter in these narratives, but this will not take the form of the coloniser-colonised dichotomy since modern renditions of were-tiger narratives were penned by native writers themselves. Indigeneity thus takes centre-stage. It is clear that a new theoretical frame is required to fully understand the phenomenon. As we are dealing with the theme of inter-species relation, it is apt to refer to the theoretical developments on the intersection between animal studies and indigeneity. One work that is particularly relevant here is *Indigenous Creatures, Native Knowledge and the Arts* (2017), which features a series of essays focussing on non-Western cultures beyond sub-Saharan Africa that have been carefully compiled and edited by Wendy Woodward and Susan McHugh. This chapter shares the editors' objective to "explore the frictions as well as crossovers between indigenous beliefs and those of modernity" in culture so as to "situate how old ways are [. . .] being adapted to modern conditions in ways that make vital contributions toward the future of life shared across species lines" (Woodward and McHugh 2017, 2–3). This re-channelling of the old as modern as it relates to were-tigers in Malay literature will become clearer when we move into the analysis proper.

For now, Alexandra-Mary Wheeler's essay from this volume resonates strongly with the points I intend to raise. Focussing on Neil Gaiman's adaptations of African animist gods in his novels *American Gods* and *Anansi Boys*, Wheeler argues that these should not be condemned as insensitive cultural appropriations, but better seen instead as efforts to "make interventions in the present" (2017, 120). These "interventions" take the collective form of Gaiman's literary animism, which serves to challenge "the widely-held truth of Cartesian dualism" (Wheeler 2017, 135), most famously expressed as the Latin expression *cogito ergo sum*, or "I think, I am." This constitutes the self/other dichotomy in Euro-American epistemology, which has inadvertently led to our modernist conception of the human-nature dichotomy and informed our practice of anthropocentrism. In support of her claim, Wheeler cites Graham Harvey's reading of animism as cultivating a sense of mindfulness that humans exist "within diverse communities of persons of many species or nations" (quoted in Wheeler 2017, 124). The same can be said of the Malay novels *Sitora Harimau Jadian* and *Lelaki Harimau*, as I argue below. In so doing, Wheeler unwittingly lends credence to Bassnett's caution against reductive conclusions that might result from an overzealous application of the postcolonial lens in translation studies. To recap, this is the view that colonial capital alone can explain why Indian writers in English are more popular than those who write in their native languages. Instead, Bassnett recommends a cultural deep dive. What better way to begin than to revisit old myths?

Lore of yore

Oral folktales of were-tigers were common to parts of the precolonial Malay Archipelago, an area that encapsulates what is today Malaysia, Indonesia, Brunei, and Singapore.[3] A comprehensive survey of were-tiger narratives from the Malay Archipelago by Robert Wessing divides archetypes of were-tigers roughly into two primary groups: tiger-spirits and those who transform into tigers by magic. While there are variations within each group, Wessing comes to the conclusion that the first group are benevolent, while the second group can be dangerous (1986, 74, 103). While the populace of precolonial Malay Archipelago was then unfettered by the limits of nation-states, borders still bothered them. This is true of one of the most famous were-tiger myths of peninsula Malaya (known as Peninsular or West Malaysia today). This is the tale of an epic battle between two were-tiger villages at Bukit Putus, a hill in the present-day state of Negeri Sembilan, according to Zainal Abidin bin Ahmad (1925). One of the factions is led by the fierce and pious Dato' Paroi of Gunung Angsi, a mountain located in the same state. The other faction is commanded by Dato' Gunung Ledang, who hails, as his name suggests, from Gunung Ledang, or Mount Ophir, in the present-day state of Johor.

Before getting into the cause of the battle, it is important to note that the two clans represent two types of were-tigers. Dato' Paroi and his followers are spirit-tigers. Dato' Paroi himself only became one upon his death. At their village at Gunung Angsi, they engage in banal human activities like farming and studying. They are also good Muslims who diligently read the Qur'an and perform prayers. To hone their fighting skills, the Angsi were-tigers practise fencing and the Malay form of martial arts known as the *silat*. It is also noteworthy that the personage of Dato' Paroi is highly revered at the time of Zainal's article. It is said that the earth contained within Paroi's footprints can be "dug up, and kept as a protective talisman against all demons, sickness, misfortunes and especially temporal tigers" (Zainal 1925, 75). Meanwhile, his grave is taken as a sacred shrine of sorts (*keramat*). Located near a stream "on the left of the road between Seremban and Kuala Pilah," it is littered with offerings like joss sticks and toasted rice, indicating the performance of rituals of reverence at the site from "Malays, Chinese and Tamil alike" (Zainal 1925, 77).

On the other hand, the were-tigers of Gunung Ledang are shape-shifters, not spirits leading second lives. Even though Dato' Gunung Ledang is their commander, this clan is ruled by the Puteri Gunung Ledang, the princess and sorceress of Mount Ophir who was unsuccessfully wooed by the last Sultan of Malacca, Mahmud Shah, according to the classical text, *Sejarah Melayu* or the *Malay Annals*, of which the oldest copy known as Raffles Manuscript 18 dates back to 1612. Similar to the Angsi clan, the Ledang were-tigers farm, plant, and fish when in their human form. But, they are ferocious and wild in their tiger form, and have the habit of wreaking havoc in surrounding villages. This is why they have to be magically chained up, earning them the moniker *harimau berantai*, or enchained tigers. Zainal writes:

> . . . the moment they or any of them take on the shape of a tiger they become vicious and dangerous again; and so to save the surrounding country from their depredations their movements become automatically restricted as heavy chains are by some mysterious power clamped round their necks.
>
> (1951, 87)

Despite this cautionary measure, there are occasions where the Ledang were-tigers have broken free. One such escapee causes destruction for months within the territory of Dato' Paroi, who punishes the intruder severely. That intruder then returns to Dato' Gunung Ledang "with broken limbs and exhausted strength" (Zainal 1925, 76). Taking this as an insult, Dato' Gunung Ledang leads a party of his were-tigers to confront Dato' Paroi. At Bukit Putus, they encounter a tiny wildcat and interrogate him as to the whereabouts of Dato' Paroi. Responding to their threats, the wildcat miraculously gains in size to a height transcending the tallest trees, before finally revealing itself to be Dato' Paroi. A fierce battle ensues, which sees Paroi overpowering the Ledang were-tigers. As they run back to Mount Ophir, they cleave a hill that is today known as Bukit Putus, translatable as "Sundered Hills." Since then, the Ledang were-tigers do not dare venture to Gunung Angsi, a tale that Zainal acknowledges as sounding one-sided on the basis that it glorifies Dato' Paroi over Dato' Gunung Ledang (1925, 77). In the absence of other competing oral narratives, it appears here that Paroi's supremacy was premised on his ability to manipulate matter as an unperishable spirit. Despite their ferocity, the Ledang were-tigers could only shape-shift between two forms—human and tiger—and could theoretically die. This myth suggests the superiority of otherworldliness over this worldliness, or abstraction over materiality. It ensues from the view that the Angsi were-tigers are spirits first, and tigers second, while the Ledang were-tigers are tigers disguised as humans.

A third type of were-tigers can be found in the oral folklore of Java. Known as *macan gadungan*, these shape-shifters are humans with the ability to transform themselves into tigers by way of magic. They are neither tiger-spirits like the Angsi were-tigers, nor naturally born shape-shifters like the Ledang were-tigers. The mythic quality of the Javanese tale is heightened by the haziness of the *macan gadungan*'s location. On the one hand, they are thought to have originated from the Gadungan village, supposedly located in the Lodoyo district of East Java. However, Peter Boomgaard in his book *Frontiers of Fear* found no evidence of such village on the map of Lodoyo. Instead, he locates another village of that name somewhere north of Mount Kelud in the neighbouring Blitar district, some fifty kilometres from the Lodoyo region. While there is little geographic accuracy, it must be noted that both locations still fall under the Kediri Residency. In the case of the *macan gadungan*, the place itself becomes a central part of their myth. Boomgaard points to Lodoyo's longstanding reputation as a typical tiger country prior to 1800, when it was "a wild, almost uninhabited area, entirely covered with forests and swarming with tigers" (2001, 198). The area was home to the kingdom of Kadhiri, a Hindu-Buddhist state, which reigned from eleventh to late sixteenth century, when it was ransacked by Muslim forces from the north coast. According to Boomgaard, it was at the height of the Kadhiri reign, somewhere in the twelfth century under the rule of the seer-king Jayabaya, that a man there first mastered the art of morphing into a were-tiger, living with his family in the Lodoyo forest (2001, 199). Another form of uncertainty concerning the *macan gadungan* highlighted by Boomgaard (2001, 199) and Wessing (1986, 101) relates to the etymology of the word "*gadungan*" itself. Basically, the root word "*gadung*" refers to a type of yam that can intoxicate its users, while the word "*gadungan*" bears the connotation of deceit or disguise. Combined together, it can be taken to mean that the Lodoyo were-tigers are "mock tigers," as Boomgaard puts it (2001, 199). This again enhances the artificiality of this type of were-tigers, one that can only be achieved through sorcery. Quoting an 1899 article by Knebel, Wessing points to another interesting aspect of the Lodoyo were-tigers that connects them to the practice of inheritance—it is said that were-tigers often help members of the village to recover their lost sacred heirloom weapon, either returning them the day after or making a meal out of the thief who stole it (1986, 101).

In summary, these oral narratives point to three types of were-tigers: spirit-tigers, naturally born tiger shape-shifters, and humans who use magic to become were-tigers. In fact, there are more types if we take into account Wessing's study of were-tiger narratives. He points to other types of were-tigers, such as tiger-familiars, which are animals who have a strong connection with a human and perform his or her bidding (1986, 63–5), as well as tigers who came to be through the transmigration of the human soul into a body of a tiger, as in case of the were-tigers of Lamongan village of East Java (1986, 99). For the purpose of this chapter though, these three narratives can help us map the textual transformation of the were-tiger trope into postcolonial Malay Archipelago, and what it says about indigeneity.

Modern man-animals

In the twentieth century, were-tigers continue to hold sway over the cultural imaginary of natives of the Malay Archipelago as the region modernised. By "natives," I am referring here to the Malays and Javanese, though the term can also be taken to refer to the Sea-Dyaks, who are not without their own narratives of were-tigers, the most famous being "Danjai and the Were-Tigers' Sisters" (Gomes 1904). It is also important to note that the trope has fired up the literary imagination of colonial writers too. The colonial administrator Hugh Clifford, for instance, writes of a were-tiger in Slim Valley (located between the Malaysian states of Pahang and Perak), who originated from Korinchi, Sumatra, in his collection of short stories, *The Further Side of Silence* (1916), which suggests a distrust of immigrants. This fear of outsiders is also the premise of the were-tiger story of the Malaysian actor-director P. Ramlee's film, *Sitora Harimau Jadian* (1964), which was reproduced as a novel in 1965 by Zakaria Mohd Yassin, and again in 2012 with minimal edits by the Malaysian publisher, Buku Fixi. The novel recounts the tale of a fictional Malaysian village called Kampung Kiambang, whose residents are being terrorised by a mysterious were-tiger named Sitora. Hope comes in the form of Effendi, a medical doctor from the city, who is sent by the government to the village to introduce to the rural villagers the marvels of modern science and, at the same time, act as a sort of myth-buster to dispel their superstitious belief in the were-tiger. While Effendi is not successful at quelling superstition, he does manage to capture Sitora with the help of some villagers. Sitora is seemingly killed by one of the elder villagers, Pendekar Amin, who is a teacher of *silat*. Miraculously, Sitora's body disappears, and Effendi later finds himself transformed into a were-tiger following an ambush and the performance of a ritual by Sitora, who turns out to be none other than the village shaman, or *dukun*. The excerpt reads:

> The Were-Tiger takes the knife from his waist. He nicks the young doctor's neck. Then, he makes a small cut on his own hand. He places the wound on his hand on the young doctor's bleeding neck. Blood flows between Sitora's hand and the Dr. Effendi's neck. The blood between Sitora's hand and the young doctor's neck intermingles with each other.[4]
> (Ramlee 2012, 143)

This scene that describes Effendi's "becoming," from man to monster, suggests an important change in the trope of the were-tiger of yore. Here, the process is clinical, almost reminiscent of a blood transfusion between donor and patient. That Effendi himself is a medical doctor strengthens the irony of this affair. Seen this way, the origin of the were-tiger is depicted as a process of science, making the were-tiger a creature of modernity. Another aspect of the scene entrenches this process. That is, the scene places emphasis on the material, and not the abstract. In the past, were-tigers came into being through death as spirits, the use of magic, or the transmigration of soul or magic. In lore, there is an absence of a living, breathing body as a core element of their transformation. Rather, bodies are used tangentially. For instance, Wessing describes how shamans use parts of a tiger's body to develop cures and amulets (1986, 51–3), though this did not lead to an actual transformation. The preference for body over soul is a modernist turn reflected in Euro-American philosophy through the inception of Marxist ideas on the centrality of material conditions and the theory of evolution conceived by both Charles Darwin and Alfred Russel Wallace. On the latter, it is apt for us to take a slight detour into British science fiction and consider H.G. Wells's novel, *The Island of Doctor Moreau* (1896). Said to have been inspired by Charles Darwin's claim that humans are descended from the apes, Wells's novel speculates a radical future of speciesism, or the idea that the species on Earth can be ranked hierarchically. The book's focus on speciesism is radical because it does not imagine human beings as the apex creature in this hierarchy, as is the norm in the real world. In fact, it treats humans as an "uncompleted" species that might further evolve. On the island of Doctor Moreau, human beings can become man-animals, or were-beasts. But, there is nothing magical about this becoming. It is all the result of the crazy doctor's experimentation. Steven McLean compares Wells's were-beasts to other monsters that are the "creations of scientists remorselessly indulging in his 'passion for research'" (2009, 56) in two literary texts, which are Mary Shelley's *Frankenstein* and Robert Louis Stevenson's *The Strange Case of Dr. Jekyll and Mr. Hyde*. P. Ramlee's were-tiger narrative shares similar elements to this recurring trope, with some slight differences. His protagonist is a passionate scientist, though he is also a believer of the supernatural. His were-tiger is not directly the product of a scientific experiment gone wrong as its "birth" can, in part, be explained scientifically as I have observed above, marking a change in its origin story within the genre of Malay were-tiger narratives.

Yet, one modern work by a native Malay-language writer goes against this Marxist-Darwinist materialism, though it is important to note that my survey of Malay literature does not suggest that there are many modern works that feature were-tigers in the first place. I am referring to Kurniawan's *Lelaki Harimau*, an even more recent work of postcolonial fiction from Indonesia. When the English translation was launched as *Man Tiger* in 2015, it was met with positive market response. Critics were quick to compare Kurniawan's fantastical prose to Gabriel Garcia Marquez's and Salman Rushdie's.[5] Kurniawan was hailed as the latest non-Western storyteller in the tradition of magic realism. Yet, when I asked him whether he was indeed inspired by Marquez at the 2016 Singapore Writers Festival, Kurniawan diplomatically replied that he was merely channelling traditional Indonesian narrative forms. Herein lies the conundrum of world literature. Global South writers are often made to fit certain moulds invented by literary centres of the Global North. Critics are quick to hail Kurniawan as the new Marquez, but his narrative form in *Man Tiger*—as in the original, *Lelaki Harimau*— did indeed draw from an indigenous narrative form. That particular form is the established tradition of were-tiger lore, as I will demonstrate, based on the translated version, *Man Tiger*.

By way of a short synopsis, this story opens in an Indonesian village with news of the horrific murder of Anwar Sadat, a married but amorous man, by the hot-headed young villager Margio. Authorities are perplexed that

Anwar's body seems to be ravaged by a wild animal, and the reader is led to believe that this is the doing of the were-tiger that resides within Margio. Through flashbacks, the reader begins to understand the events leading up to the murder. Anwar gets Margio's mother, Nuraeni, pregnant, and when Margio decides to speak to him about it one fateful day, Anwar becomes agitated and proclaims that he does not love Nuraeni, which triggers Margio's spirit-tiger to attack him. While Margio has forgiven Anwar for getting his mother pregnant (seeing that Nuraeni is in an abusive marriage and appears to be happy with the affair with Anwar), the latter's proclamation nonetheless busts that belief, unleashing the beast within Margio. Unlike Sitora, the were-tiger in *Man Tiger* is not *quite* the typical shape-shifter. Rather, it appears that Margio's were-tiger is a spirit-tiger, a being that is part of him and yet separate. Through Margio's conversation with his grandfather, we learn that the were-tiger is female and has stayed with his family over generations, acting as a "wife" to the men in his family. The excerpt reads:

> One evening, on Margio's last visit before his grandfather's death, the old man said firmly: "The tiger is as white as a swan."
>
> He wanted Margio to recognise the tigress if she came to him. Grandpa added that if the beast wished it, she might go to Margio's father and become his. Margio would then have to wait until his father died to take possession of the tigress. But if she didn't like his father she would someday come to Margio, and she would be his.
>
> "And if she doesn't like me?" Margio asked anxiously.
>
> "She will go to your son, or your grandson, or she might never reappear if our family forgets her."
>
> (Kurniawan 2015, 43)

Indeed, the were-tigress has decided not to appear to Margio's father, Komar, in the novel. Though no reason is given, we can infer that this is probably because he is an abusive man who has taken to beating his wife, Nuraeni. Komar is a dishonourable man, whom Margio loathes and dreams of murdering. Still, the novel has also outlined Komar's sufferings, complicating any easy conclusion readers might have that the character is a two-dimensional antagonist. Most importantly, it can be inferred from the above that the were-tigress is capable of making her own decision. That agency, coupled with the fact that it is female, accords the novel another form of modernist twist to the were-tiger lore of yore. It speaks to the contemporary issue of unbalanced gender relations, particularly patriarchy. We see in *Man Tiger* that while the two (Margio and the tigress) are intertwined, power resides with the tigress. Not only is she the one to choose her vessel, she is also able to appear at will, leaving Margio susceptible to her whims. In fact, the primary male characters in the novel are shown to be defective in some ways. This lends voice to the idea of toxic masculinity, though it also resists the need to categorise man as the "typical" enemy by showing up the complications. Anwar may be a good father, but he cheats on his wife and takes advantage of women for his own sexual gratification. Komar beats his wife, but he is also the product of his poverty. Even Margio, the protagonist, who is protective of his mother, is shown to be brash and thuggish. While the novel appeals to the lore of spirit-tiger that is similar to Dato' Paroi, it also modernises were-tiger narratives by way of reversing the gender binary that privileges man over woman. Here, it is symbolic that Anwar Sadat, arguably the very epitome of male privilege, is killed off by the feisty and independent were-tigress. Despite channelling modernist turns concerning science or toxic masculinity, parallels can be drawn between *Sitora Harimau Jadian* and *Man Tiger*, with implications for the theory of cultural translation.

Theorising were-texts

They may speak of were-tigers of varying stripes, but P. Ramlee's *Sitora Harimau Jadian* and Eka Kurniawan's *Man Tiger* share one thing in common. They modernise what used to be authorless oral tales of the were-tiger, while adhering to tradition to a certain extent. With *Sitora Harimau Jadian,* this comes in the form of fidelity to the trope of shape-shifters that is reminiscent of the Ledang were-tigers of Malaya and the *macan gadungan* of East Java. Unlike these two myths though, the were-tiger in *Sitora Harimau Jadian* is not created through magic, but by way of something closer to the scientific process of biological infection in the form of blood transfusion. Meanwhile, Kurniawan's *Man Tiger* appeals to the lore of spirit-tigers the like of Dato' Paroi. Yet, while magic still prevails in Kurniawan's novel, it renders the spirit-tiger feminine and independent-minded. It also leads readers to think that it might be the beast that controls its human host and not the reverse, as is traditional. If so, this challenges prevailing ideas of the Anthropocene, which positions humans at the top of the hierarchy of species on Earth. Relatedly, it is important to note here that the Malays have long practised a form of animism that establishes a certain symbiotic relationship between humanity and nature. This too subverts the primacy of humans and the Cartesian mind/body duality in its recognition that non-human objects like rice can have soul (or, *semangat*), as highlighted by Elizabeth Allard (1946). More pertinently, animism makes an appearance in the traditional *mak yong* dance-performance as a healing ritual in Kelantan, where it sees participants channelling the temperament (or, *angin*) of the were-tiger (Hardwick 2014, 43).[6]

In essence, both novels have transformed prevailing old myths by introducing tweaks to an existing cultural trope. Linking this back to the idea of cultural translation, what insights might be gathered from engaging with this trope of Malay literature? I would like to suggest here that the trait of in-betweeness has spilled over from trope to texts in our case studies. Much like the were-tigers, the literary texts that contain them are just as transformative without discrediting tradition. *Sitora Harimau Jadian* straddles between superstition and science while *Man Tiger* speaks to the grey zone between feminism and patriarchy. This process is what Karin Barber in *The Anthropology of Texts, Persons and Publics* (2008) refers to as "instauration," or, the idea that the text can be taken as a medium through which "[p]eople innovatively establish social forms and attentively maintain them" (4). For instauration to happen, Barber points to yet another process known as "entextualisation," in which new "forms emerge from everyday life" (2008, 207). A simple example provided by Barber is the way letters and newspaper columns generate epistolary novels. In our case, the premodern oral myths of the were-tiger (such as Dato' Paroi) can be said to have been manifested in the modern forms of the novel (*Man Tiger*) and film (*Sitora Harimau Jadian*). We can therefore position these two modern narratives of were-tigers (*harimau jadian*) as were-texts (*teks jadian*). Produced by native writers and therefore indigenous, they lend voice to some aspects of tradition while making subtle yet critical interventions that make them not quite original, but not quite archetypal either. To give this theory further shape, "were-texts" can be described as fictional works in modern formats like novels or films, and quite possibly, digital narratives, that transform and recycle primordial cultural tropes to express contemporary concerns. In essence, they straddle between modernity and mythology. Given that this arises from the study of a specific trope from one part of the world, it is worthwhile to ask the extent to which we can "apply" the notion of were-texts to other contexts.

A quick reference to other deeper scholarship of non-Western contexts suggests that theoretical generalisations can be drawn to a certain extent. Take, for instance, the postulation that the nation is an imagined community, based on Benedict Anderson's deep engagement with Indonesia. If this is a possibility, then how can were-texts exist in cultures beyond the Malay Archipelago? I would like to refer to my previous article on cultural translation "A Thousand and One Rewrites" (2016), which explores modern renditions of *The Arabian Nights* in Edgar Allen Poe's *The Thousand-and-Second Tale of Scheherazade*, Naguib Mahfouz's *Arabian Nights and Days*, and Hanan Al-Syakh's *One Thousand and One Nights*. Similar to *Sitora Harimau Jadian* and *Man Tiger*, these three texts have also transformed and recycled an old narrative to express modern concerns. They too can be figured as "were-texts." There is some scope to explore the applicability of were-texts elsewhere. One possibility is to turn one's gaze to Sinic cultures, especially if we consider Byung-Chul Han's work, *Shanzai* (2017). Han argues that unlike Western cultures, imitations or copies are common practice in Chinese art, differentiating between two types: *fuzhipin*, which are "exact reproductions of the original," and *fang-zhipin*, where "the difference from the original is obvious" (2017, 60). One might explore here the possibility of literary *fang-zhipin* as were-texts. Lu Xun's prose that re-reads Confucianism might be a good start. In summary, this chapter has attempted to factor in Southeast Asia in translation studies by way of drawing insights from the evolution of were-tiger narratives in the Malay Archipelago. It identifies a trend in the form of texts that straddle modernity and mythology, which I call "were-texts," proposing further studies of cultural translation in other cultures to test the validity of this frame.

Acknowledgement

This chapter was finalised at the Toji Cultural Centre, South Korea.

Notes

1 This is not to say that Southeast Asians have been passive recipients of European knowledge. Rather, I am referring here to formal education in universities concerned with global rankings. In the sphere of informal knowledge, there are instances in which Southeast Asians have exercised some agency in engaging and transforming knowledge they have encountered elsewhere. One example is the development of "Islam Nusantara" fashioned by Indonesian clerics like Nurcholish Madjid and Gus Dur and supported by the current Indonesian president Jokowi to distinguish the Indonesian practice of Islam from Middle Eastern expressions of Islam. Another example is the Balinese practice of Hinduism, which is a distinct form that has incorporated Hindu doctrines with local practices of animism.
2 This is the most popular definition, though this chapter later also points to another possible definition that has to do with the Javanese root word "*gadung*," or a type of yam that can induce a state of intoxication when taken by humans.
3 In fact, tales of were-tigers are also common in parts of China, India, and other parts of Southeast Asia. See, for instance, Patrick Newman's *Tracking the Were-tiger: Supernatural Man-Eaters of India, China and Southeast Asia* (2012).
4 The translation is my own. The Malay text reads:

   Harimau Jadian itu mengeluarkan sebilah pisau dari pinggangnya. Leher doctor muda itu ditorehnya. Kemudian, tangannya pula ditoreh. Tangannya yang luka itu dilekapkannya ke leher doktor muda yang berdarah itu. Antara tangan Sitora dan leher Dr. Effendi mengalir darah. Dan darah itu saling mengalir ke dalam tangan Sitora dan ke leher doktor muda itu.

5 See, for instance, Deborah Smith's review of *Man Tiger* (2015).
6 Across the Malay Archipelago, *mak yong* was once performed "throughout the southern Thai provinces of Yala, Narathiwat, and Pattani, the northern Malaysian states of Kelantan, Terengganu, and Kedah, the Riau Islands of Indonesia, and briefly on the Indonesian island of Sumatra" (Hardwick 2014, 40). According to Ghulam-Sarwar Yousof, it is today primarily performed in the Kelantan, Pattani, and the Riau Islands to some extent (2017, 1).

References

Alatas, Syed Farid, and Vineetha Sinha. 2017. *Sociological Theory beyond the Canon*. Cham: Palgrave.

Allard, Elizabeth. 1946. "Animistic Beliefs and Rites in the Malay Archipelago (Continued)." *Oceania* 17, no. 1: 79–91.

Apter, Emily. 2006. *The Translation Zone: A New Comparative Literature*. Princeton, NJ: Princeton University Press.

Barber, Karin. 2008. *The Anthropology of Texts, Persons and Publics: Oral and Written Culture in Africa and Beyond*. Cambridge: Cambridge University Press.

Bassnett, Susan. 2007. "Culture and Translation." In *A Companion to Translation Studies,* edited by Piotr Kuhiwczak and Karin Littau, 13–23. Clevedon: Multilingual Matters.
Benjamin, Walter. (1923) 1989. "The Task of the Translator." In *Readings in Translation Theory,* edited by Andrew Chesterman, 13–24. Helsinki: Oy Finn Lectura Ab.
Boomgaard, Peter. 2001. *Frontiers of Fear: Tigers and People in the Malay World, 1600–1950.* New Haven, CT: Yale University Press.
Chamberlain, Lori. 1988. "Gender and the Metaphorics of Translation." *Signs* 13, no. 3 (Spring): 454–72.
Clifford, Hugh. 1916. *The Further Side of Silence.* New York: Doubleday.
Curaming, Rommel A. 2012. "Filipinos as Malay: Historicising an Identity." In *Melayu: The Politics, Poetics and Paradoxes of Malayness,* edited by Maznah Mohamad and Syed Muhd Khairudin Aljunied, 241–74. Singapore: NUS Press.
Ghulam-Sarwar Yousof. 2017. "The Mak Yong Dance Theatre as Spiritual Heritage: Some Insights." *SPAFA Journal* 1, no. 1: 1–9.
Gomes, Edwin H. 1904. "Two Sea-Dyak Legends." *Journal of the Straits Branch of the Royal Asiatic Society* 41 (January): 1–29.
Han, Byung-chul. 2017. *Shanzai: Deconstruction in Chinese.* Cambridge, MA: MIT Press.
Hardwick, Patricia. 2014. "The Body Becoming: Transformative Performance in Malaysian *Mak Yong.*" *Music & Medicine* 6, no. 1: 40–8.
Knebel, Josef. 1899. "De Weertijger op Midden-Java, den Javaan Naverteld." *TBG* 41: 568–87.
Kurniawan, Eka. 2015. *Man Tiger.* Translated by Labodalih Sembiring. London: Verso.
Lieberman, Victor. 2003. *Strange Parallels: Southeast Asia in Global Context, c.800–1830. Volume 1: Integration of the Mainland.* Cambridge: Cambridge University Press.
McLean, Steven. 2009. *The Early Fiction of H.G. Wells: Fantasies of Science.* Basingstoke and New York: Palgrave Macmillan.
Mignolo, Walter. 2000. *Local Histories/Global Designs: Coloniality, Subaltern Knowledges, and Border Thinking.* Princeton, NJ: Princeton University Press.
Munday, Jeremy. 2009. "Issues in Translation Studies." In *The Routledge Companion to Translation Studies.* Revised Edition, edited by Jeremy Munday, 1–19. London and New York: Routledge.
Nazry Bahrawi. 2014. "Not My Bible's Keeper: Saramago's *Cain* Translates Postsecular Dissent." In *Reading the Abrahamic Faiths: Rethinking Religion and Literature,* edited by Emma Mason and Nazry Bahrawi, 255–66. London: Bloomsbury.
———. 2016. "A Thousand and One Rewrites: Translating Modernity in the Arabian Nights." *Journal of World Literature* 1, no. 3 (January): 357–70.
Newman, Patrick. 2012. *Tracking the Weretiger: Supernatural Man-Eaters of India, China and Southeast Asia.* Jefferson, NC: McFarland.
Ooi, Keat Gin, and Hoàng Anh Tuân, eds. 2016. *Early Modern Southeast Asia, 1350–1800.* London and New York: Routledge.
P. Ramlee. 1964. *Sitora Harimau Jadian.* Malaysia: Shaw Brothers.
———. 1965. *Sitora Harimau Jadian.* Edited by Zakaria Mohd Yassin. Kuala Lumpur: Penerbitan Angkatan Baru.
———. (1965) 2012. *Sitora Harimau Jadian.* Kuala Lumpur: Buku Fixi.

Ricci, Ronit. 2011. *Islam Translated: Literature, Conversion, and the Arabic Cosmopolis of South and Southeast Asia.* Chicago, IL and London: Chicago University Press.
Smith, Deborah. 2015. "The Animal Within." Review of *Man Tiger*, by Eka Kurniawan. *The Guardian*, November 28.
Steiner, George. 1975. *After Babel: Aspects of Language and Translation.* Oxford: Oxford University Press.
Wells, H.G. (1896) 2002. *The Island of Doctor Moreau.* New York: Modern Library.
Wessing, Robert. 1986. *The Soul of Ambiguity: The Tiger in Southeast Asia.* DeKalb: Center for Southeast Asian Studies, Northern Illinois University.
Wheeler, Alexandra-Mary. 2017. "The Porosity of Human/Non-human Beings in Neil Gaiman's *American Gods* and *Anansi Boys*." In *Indigenous Creatures, Native Knowledge and the Arts*, edited by Wendy Woodward and Susan McHugh, 119–36. Cham: Palgrave.
Woodward, Wendy, and Susan McHugh. 2017. "Introduction." In *Indigenous Creatures, Native Knowledge and the Arts,* edited by Wendy Woodward and Susan McHugh, 1–9. Cham: Palgrave.
Zainal Abidin bin Ahmad. 1925. "Dato' Paroi, Were-Tiger." *Journal of the Malayan Branch of the Royal Asiatic Society* 3, no. 1 (April): 74–8.
———. 1951. "Some Malay Legendary Tales." *Journal of the Malayan Branch of the Royal Asiatic Society* 24, no. 1 (February): 77–89.

5 Translating the ideal girl
Female images in Khmer literature and cinema

Daria Okhvat

Introduction

Khmer literature has traditionally played an important role in shaping the images and representations of women in society. It is worth noting that female images in the colonial and postcolonial literature of Cambodia are generalised and belong to Khmer literary tradition as a whole. According to Khing Hoc Dy, there are three main periods in the history of Khmer literature: "ancient" (twelfth–fourteenth centuries), "middle" (fifteenth–nineteenth centuries), and "new" (nineteenth century–present) (1997, 5). The border between "ancient" and "middle" periods is marked by the change in religion: Theravada Buddhism was established by the fourteenth century; it rapidly spread among the general public and had a strong influence on the Khmer perception of the world. By the end of the middle period, female images influenced by Theravada Buddhism in traditional poetry texts were established. Despite the passage of time, the influence of these historical texts—and the female images within—have remained strong in the present day. As such, Khmer literature can be considered as one of the main broadcasters of women's images and gender stereotypes. It is also important to observe that Khmer literature was closed off to the world and isolated for many years, and, as a result, writers did not have the opportunity to become acquainted with new literary genres and forms. Consequently too, the first prose works in Khmer literature only appeared in the first half of the twentieth century.

In this study, I examine how the translation process affects the images and representations of Khmer women from the past to the present by focussing on prose fiction and film texts, respectively, from the colonial and postcolonial periods: two classic colonial novels, *The Faded Flower* ([1949]1960) by Nou Hach and *Sophat* ([1942]2014) by Rim Kin, and two postcolonial film texts, *Apsara* (1966) by Norodom Sihanouk and *Lost Loves* (2010) by Chhay Bora. I've decided to restrict my study of colonial literature to novels as they were the first prose works to appear in Khmer literature; besides, other genres such as the short story and drama only appeared after the country achieved independence in 1953. For the postcolonial period, I've selected film texts which interpret gender identity and roles against the backdrop of a changing society. Although the films depict updated images of Cambodian femininity, they still reflect women's traditional roles in society as well as their reality. Through the two genres of novel and film, I will analyse how the traditional images and representations of Khmer women have been translated into the "new" languages of modern prose and cinematography.

In translating female images from the past to the present, I do not refer to the translation of one language into another, but rather, the translation process within the same language system: Khmer. In *Intersemiosis and Intersemiotic Translation* (2003), Peeter Torop states that all types of communication in culture can be seen as a process in which texts (or fragments) are translated into other texts, and that culture itself is "an infinite process of total translation" (2003, 271). Based on Torop's concept, I argue that the images and representations of women in Khmer novels and films are formed through intralingual translation. In short, translation is carried out within the frame of a single language and cultural field. According to this concept, the female images and representations formed in traditional poetry texts from the middle period are considered the "source" element or language, which is then subjected to the intralingual process through which the images are translated via the "target" language of modern prose and cinema. At the same time, the intralingual process also serves to transmit cultural memories as well as the ideological position of the translator—in this case, the Khmer author or film-maker who wishes to convey certain ideas and messages to the reader or viewer.

The term "ideology" is based on Basil Hatim and Ian Mason's definition, which draws on the linguistic perspective in that "all use of language reflects a set of users' assumptions which are closely bound up with attitudes, beliefs and value systems" (1997, 120). Khmer literature thus constitutes an important cultural medium through which the collective experiences and memories are transferred or translated from generation to generation within a society; in this case, the images and representations of Khmer women have been translated from the past to the present through prose and cinema, both of which are considered "new" or "modern" forms and languages in twentieth-century Khmer society, whether in the colonial or postcolonial period.[1] Although they constitute "new" or "modern" forms and languages, both Khmer prose and cinema have nonetheless been influenced by the gendered representations of the middle period. As a result, the translation of historical female images into the modern literary and cinematic languages still conveys the gendered archetypes of the Khmer woman to both readers and viewers, and it is in this manner that the traditional gender ideology has been maintained in society.

Female images in Khmer novels of the colonial period

The literature of the colonial period, specifically, of the first half of the twentieth century, serves as a reference point in this study. It was during this time that very significant changes occurred to Khmer literature. Before the first prose works appeared in the late 1930s, all Khmer literary works were exclusively poetic in form and focussed mainly on didactics (Chigas 2005), with plots borrowed from the *Jatakas*, which are moral tales about the previous earthly incarnations of Buddha, also known as Siddhartha Gautama.[2] Khmer writers of the colonial period adopted the novel as a literary form from French literature. The Khmer novel grew in popularity during the colonial period as it was widely circulated among the masses. Printing, which appeared in Cambodia at the end of the nineteenth century, undoubtedly played a critical role in boosting the popularity of the novel.

During the colonial period between the 1930s and 1954, a well-formed system of characters—which can be called a "traditional" system—first appeared in literary works. In the Khmer novel, the system can be seen in the gendered representations. The protagonist, for instance, is always a young man (often an orphan too) who finds himself in very difficult circumstances but by the end of the story, he is usually rewarded for his suffering and travails. As for the female characters, they are often represented through two stereotypes: (1) the ideal Khmer girl and (2) the mother. While the male character's appearance or personality features are rarely described, the same cannot be said about the female heroine, whose description (often focussed on her physical attributes) is more detailed and vivid; the attention on Khmer femininity reveals how she is exclusively the object of male gaze and admiration. This is not surprising given that the majority of the authors were men whose ideas of women reflected the patriarchal standards of its time.

The stereotyped ideal Khmer girl is the most important gendered representation in the novels of the colonial period and is based on two female archetypes formed, respectively, by cultural tradition and the literary texts of the middle period. In order to understand how and when these archetypes were formed in Cambodia's literary tradition, it is necessary to examine the middle period of Khmer literature. Khing divides all the poetic works of the middle period into two key sections: religious literature and entertainment literature (1997, 23). The latter is deemed entertaining because the poems are supposed to please the readers. In this case, entertainment is understood not as a form of amusement but as an aesthetic enjoyment that is derived from reading a literary work. As the works of this period have been characterised as didactic in orientation, they are expected to follow the moral and ethical standards of Theravada Buddhism (Chigas 2005). Within the present study, the "religious literature" section is of interest as it includes a particular genre of medieval literature called *Chbap*, which are brief instructions and regulations written in verse and addressed to the common people. Works of this type are based on binary oppositions: rich/poor, smart/foolish, and so on.

All *Chbap* are divided into *Old Chbap* and *New Chbap*, with the former produced from fifteenth to seventeenth century while the latter were created from eighteenth to mid-nineteenth century. One of the most famous and important *Chbap* collections of this period is *Chbap for Women* or *Women's Law*; more importantly, they are the first works of the written literary tradition that established woman's ideal behaviour. In these collections, the archetypal Khmer woman is portrayed as having certain characteristics that include obedience, kindness, a gentle quiet voice, and an easy gait. Because of *Chbap for Women*, this female archetype was already firmly established in Khmer literature by the time the first prose works appeared in Cambodia. As a result, Khmer prose writers simply transferred this archetype to their works, filling it with *Chbap* content. Furthermore, the *Chbap for Women* collections have remained influential as they have been reprinted on a regular basis up to the present day. Until 2007, studying these collections formed part of the compulsory state-approved school curriculum. We should therefore consider *Chbap* as one of the main source languages used by writers to translate the female archetypes that had been formed in cultural tradition into the modern language of colonial prose and, subsequently, postcolonial cinema.

Influenced by the *Chbap* collections, the archetypal image of the ideal girl became a dominant stereotype in the colonial novels. This stereotype refers to a very beautiful girl whose appearance, as stated earlier, is not only depicted in detail but also based on standardised features that comply with traditional perceptions of ideal beauty; this beauty, moreover, functions as one of the ideal girl's merits. Mandatory attributes of this type include long shiny hair, an oval face, thick eyelashes as well as light, radiant skin. For example, the traditional epithet "crocodile's egg" is often used when describing the shape of the face; another common symbol in the works of Khmer authors is "girl-flower." Such symbolic images and traditional representations are important elements of the source language. During the process of intralingual translation, writers make active use of symbols rooted in Khmer cultural tradition and which are easily understood by readers who are already familiar with their meanings and associations.

The same standardisation can also be found in the descriptions of the heroine's character as it is always based on a set of qualities that defines her as a stereotyped ideal. Let us consider some of these qualities in detail. The heroine of the colonial novel is distinguished by humility and modesty. She has to respect her elders and unquestioningly obey her parents' will, even if it goes against her own opinion. She must not challenge her parents, no matter what. All of the above also applies to her relationship with her husband. No matter how destructive the relationship is, the heroine has no right to express her opinion or complain about her husband. At the same time, the authors describe their heroines as being "strong in spirit." This is reflected in how bravely the heroine endures all hardships and suffers in stoic silence. Another important quality for the heroine is loyalty—mainly to the beloved who has been separated from her. Devotion to Khmer traditions is also important and the authors express this value by describing everyday habits, traditional rituals, and manner of dressing. For example, the ideal Khmer girl usually wears the traditional costume; if she wears more modern kinds of clothing, they are always decorated with Khmer national ornaments. By using such key Khmer symbols to tap into the source language, the authors emphasise the heroine's connection to cultural and traditional values.

The representation of the ideal Khmer girl thus appears to fulfil a didactic purpose, for she is shown as a positive model to follow.[3] It is important to note that didacticism is one of the main features of Khmer literature in general (Iv 2013). By defining all of the above-mentioned qualities as feminine, the authors also distinguish the different social roles between women and men in their novels. Historically, women were not involved in public life; their role in Khmer society was limited to the domestic sphere as they conformed to the traditional gender scheme: obedient daughter–wife–mother. The heroine in the novels of the colonial period is thus based on this traditional scheme as her "ultimate goal" is a happy marriage.

As previously mentioned, the ideal girl is not the only female stereotype in colonial-period works. There is also the mother of the main heroine or protagonist, who is typically divided into two types: despotic mother and good mother. The mother figure adheres to a certain pattern, in that the mother of the heroine is despotic, while the mother of the hero is good. The figure of the despotic mother is used by authors to create conflict based on the idea that the heroine has no choice and it is her mother who determines her fate. The mother of the protagonist, on the contrary, is the ideal model of a "mother-woman"—a central figure in Cambodian culture (Ledgerwood n.d.) whom children must honour and listen to. In Khmer literature, it is the "mother-woman" who inculcates moral standards in her children and whose opinion cannot be challenged. Inscribed in Khmer literary canon and often represented as the carrier of traditional values in society, the idealised "mother-woman" is often represented as someone who is no longer alive; she lives in the memories of the protagonist or is described through the events that occur after her death.

Having identified the common female images and stereotypes, I shall now examine two classic novels of the colonial period more closely: *The Faded Flower* by Nou Hach and *Sophat* by Rim Kin. They are among the most famous and beloved traditional novels in Cambodia and have been included for study under the national education curriculum. More importantly, the character types outlined above are represented in both novels and, as such, they are of great interest for the study of women's images and representations in Khmer literary tradition.

The Faded Flower: the ideal Khmer girl

First published in 1949, the novel *The Faded Flower* became popular very quickly. Till today, its author Nou Hach (1916–1975) is very well-known and his works have retained its popular appeal; they include *Garland of the Heart*

(1972), *Life* (1973), and *Beloved Girl* (1953). *The Faded Flower* ([1949]1960) is a love story between a seventeen-year-old girl, Vitheavy, and an eighteen-year-old boy, Bun Thoeun, who is also the protagonist. Both have known each other since childhood. They later fall in love and their parents give their consent to the marriage. However, they have to wait until Bun Thoeun graduates from a prestigious college in the capital. When Bun Thoeun's family suddenly becomes bankrupt, Nuan, Vitheavy's wealthy mother, decides to find a new fiancé for her daughter. The potential fiancé, Naisot (who acts as the antagonist), does not care about Vitheavy; he is only interested in her beauty. Meanwhile, Bun Thoeun writes a letter to Vitheavy, asking her to follow her mother's will. After all, he is poor and, in his opinion, does not deserve such a bride. As preparations for the wedding are in full swing, Nuan notices that her daughter is grieving and decides to take her to Siem Reap, where the magnificent temples of Angkor help to calm her. Caught in the rain, Vitheavy falls sick and dies soon after coming home. Before dying, she writes a letter to Bun Thoeun, in which she declares her love and gives him her ring.

Representing the ideal Khmer girl, Vitheavy is very beautiful. She is described as having a well-defined facial shape, a delicate figure, and shiny black hair that flows over her shoulders. It seems that Nou Hach has translated the image of the gorgeous Apsara that has adorned the walls of Khmer temples for centuries into prose. However, the author writes not only about her appearance, but also about her intellect and cleverness. Before reaching adulthood, Vitheavy attends school where she studies the Khmer and French languages, history, and geography; additionally, her mother hires a Siamese language teacher so that Vitheavy can read books in Siamese. However, we can clearly see how gender norms are complied with when Vitheavy leaves her studies at her mother's insistence; education only serves the purpose of helping her to marry well. By establishing the traditional family ideology in which the child is subordinate to the parent, the author reinforces the conventional value system, which is an aspect of the source language.

Nou Hach also emphasises the ideal heroine's loyalty and obedience, both of which are important qualities. In the novel, Vitheavy swears loyalty to her beloved Bun Thoeun by promising that she will never marry another man. Furthermore, she is also portrayed as being loyal to Khmer traditions: she wears national clothing, reads Khmer poems with pleasure, and loves visiting old temples. At the same time, she dare not disobey her mother, nor can she express her anger and indignation. Although Vitheavy does not want to marry a man she does not love, she does not dare to be angry with her mother, even in her heart; instead, she transfers all her resentment to the man whom she is engaged to. When her old nanny asks what is wrong with her new fiancé, Vitheavy stays silent, even though she knows that he has been gambling, drinking heavily, and spending time in suspicious company. Such talk, however, is completely inappropriate for the ideal Khmer girl.

As the central female figure in the novel, Vitheavy fully reflects the idealised Khmer girl, fixed not only in cultural tradition but also in prose. By adhering to traditional precepts of Khmer femininity, Nou Hach ultimately depicts Vitheavy as a hostage to the archetype.

The second classic image in the novel is that of the despotic mother, Nuan. Although Nuan loves her daughter very much, she is not concerned about Vitheavy's wishes in the matter of the arranged marriage. Nou Hach in fact uses the character of Nuan to criticise old or archaic traditions. Two striking moments can be used to illustrate this point. When thinking about accepting the Naisot's proposal, the mother consults not with her daughter, but with the astrologer, whom she trusts unconditionally. And when Vitheavy becomes sick, instead of calling for a doctor, Nuan invites a traditional healer who treats the girl with ice-cold water.

Other minor female characters in the novel also adhere to prescribed feminine types, including Vitheavy's old nanny, Phai, and Bun Thoeun's young sister. Phai, who knows Naisot's personality, pities Vitheavy but cannot do anything for her. Bun Thoeun's sister is also mentioned several times, but very little is said about her, except that her hair reaches her shoulders and that like Vitheavy, she is also obedient, kind and hard-working. Apart from these minor female characters, there is another group of female characters who play supporting roles; however, they function as the antithesis to Vitheavy: Tho and Chan. Tho is Naisot's mother and wants him to marry Vitheavy very much. It is she who advises Nuan not to listen to the doctor and to seek help from healers and sorcerers. Chan is Nuan's friend; she acts as a matchmaker and advises Nuan to refuse the marriage offer from Bun Thoeun's family. All of these female characters are defined as villains whose primary function is to reinforce the image of the ideal Khmer girl. This gendered binary opposition is in fact based on traditional images of womanhood found in the *Chbap for Women* collections.

Based on the established gender archetype, the ideal Khmer girl is presented as the ultimate role model for Khmer women. However, despite the textual attention given to Vitheavy and despite the fact that the novel's title refers to her, the main protagonist of the novel is nonetheless a man, Bun Thoeun. This distinction in gender roles is in line with the patriarchal views of the colonial period, when a woman was perceived and positioned as secondary, or, "behind the back" of the man (Ledgerwood n.d.). Despite the differences in time and context, it can be seen that the source language of the *Chbap* collections has been retained in the process of translating Khmer femininity into the "modern" prose language of the colonial novel—a recurrence that can again be seen in my analysis of the following novel, *Sophat*.

Sophat: the deceived girl and the good mother

The novel *Sophat* ([1942]2014) is written by Rim Kin (1911–1959) who, like Nou Hach, is also very famous in Cambodia. Within the context of colonial

Translating the ideal girl 89

literature, this novel is extremely important for the study of the source language because it introduces the representation of the single mother for the first time. The novel's treatment of the single mother not only reveals the social attitudes of the time towards women who gave birth to and brought up children out of wedlock, but it also reflects the traditional gender ideology that can be considered as the source language. At the same time, the ideal Khmer girl is brought in as a contrast to the "deviant" figure of the single mother.

Sophat, the protagonist and titular character, is the son of a poor country girl named Soya. She falls in love with a young clerk from Phnom Penh, Suan, who is travelling on business, and soon becomes pregnant. But her beloved cannot marry her because his bride is waiting for him in Phnom Penh. Before leaving Soya, he leaves his ring with her as a keepsake. Soya later gives birth to her son and names him Sophat. When she finds out that Suan has married, she is unable to take the news and eventually dies of grief as a result of his betrayal. The orphaned Sophat is raised in a monastery, but his mother's neighbours bring him her ring and tell him her story. When he is older, Sophat decides to search for his father in Phnom Penh. There, he meets Man Yang, the foster daughter of a rich official in the capital where he stays and runs errands. Man Yang is very beautiful, modest, and obedient, and is much loved by her foster father.

A few years pass before Man Yang accidentally discovers Sophat's ring and gives it to her foster father as she does not know who it belongs to. It is then revealed that the foster father is Suan, who recognises the ring as the one he gave to his beloved Soya many years ago. Although he realises that Sophat is his son, Suan does not say anything to the young man; however, his attitude towards Sophat changes: he allows Sophat to eat at the family table and sends him to study together with his own son. Suan does not reflect on his guilt towards Soya and Sophat; he simply decides to take care of the young man. Then Man Yang and Sophat fall in love. However, when Man Yang suspects that Sophat is having an affair with another girl, she ends their relationship and distances herself from him as much as possible. The protagonist decides to leave the house, thinking that Man Yang does not love him anymore. Then Man Yang's parents decide that she should get married, as they believe that Sophat is already dead. Shortly before her marriage, however, Man Yang sees Sophat by accident. Thinking it is his ghost, she is unable to calm down and feels as though she is betraying her beloved. Unable to handle the situation, she decides to commit suicide by jumping into the river. She survives but her family thinks she is dead. Due to a chance meeting, the main characters are reunited, first with each other, then with the family.

It is the image of Soya—a young girl who is seduced, impregnated, and abandoned by her beloved—that is of interest to us. During the colonial period, the life of a single mother was incredibly difficult in Cambodia as she and her child would have been exposed to stigma and mockery.

The Cambodian society has remained conservative about gender relations and roles. Having a child out of wedlock was, and still is, considered a source of shame for the girl and the whole family; this prevailing view is reflected in the literary treatment of single mothers who usually suffer a tragic fate. It should be noted that while Soya is not blamed for being a single mother, her actions are not justified either. This "neutral" attitude is reflected in Sophat, who does not show any obvious sympathy towards his mother. He also does not blame his father for his mother's hardships or death. All he wants is to find his father and live with him. As a result, there is no conflict between father and son in the novel. Suan is furthermore portrayed as a victim of circumstances. He left his beloved Soya because he was already engaged to another woman and had to fulfil his duty; besides, his family would never accept a poor peasant woman—a theme important to the literature of the period, as social inequality was a key topic then.

Juxtaposed against the shameful and tragic figure of Soya is Man Yang, the ideal Khmer girl who, with her perfect behaviour and gentle nature, can do no wrong. Like Vitheavy in *The Faded Flower*, she is under-developed as a character. We are given little information about her background in terms of education, interests, and passions as the descriptions are focussed mainly on her modesty. All we know is that her behaviour is beyond reproach, even when she ends her relationship with Sophat. From the perspective of Khmer tradition, it is correct that Man Yang does not speak to Sophat or reveal her doubts to him as conversations of such kind were deemed improper for Khmer girls. Additionally, Man Yang follows all the established rules. When Sophat leaves, she grieves for a long time but does not tell anybody about her feelings; and when her parents decide she should get married, she agrees, being unable to oppose. Like Vitheavy too, Man Yang is torn between her sense of duty towards her parents and her love for Sophat. In fact, this internal conflict highlights two key features of the stereotype: an ideal Khmer girl should be obedient to her parents' will, but, at the same time, she must also be loyal to her beloved.

The works analysed above show how women are stereotyped during the colonial period. The authors applied the characteristics based on the classic feminine archetype as well as traditional gender precepts and views to every female character they created, which can be seen in the appearance of the heroine as well as her personality. Reflecting woman's status in Khmer society, these socially prevalent "ideals about the proper behaviour for women are elaborated in great detail through codes of moral conduct" (Ledgerwood n.d.) and can be found in the novels' descriptions of the ideal Khmer girl or woman. As noted earlier too, the ideal girl appears to be the living embodiment of Apsara, which follows Elizabeth Chey's observation that the "image of the Cambodian woman has always been compared to the celestial goddess on the walls of great temples Angkor Wat. Apsara represents water and purity and the fluidity of the virtuous female" (n.d.). Then there's the fact that the main protagonist of the colonial novel is always a man, even when the title may allude to the heroine. All these characteristics underscore the woman's subordinate position in Khmer society, which is defined according to the status of the man in her family (father, husband, or brother) (Ledgerwood n.d.).

Having examined the representations of Khmer women in colonial novels, I conclude that the authors of the time combined and translated into prose language two traditional characteristics—also elements of the source language—that came to define Khmer femininity: first, the mythological Apsara, who is linked to the heroine's beauty and grace; and, second, the female behavioural norms prescribed by the *Chbap* collections since the middle period. Based on the fusion of these characteristics, a unified image of ideal femininity is produced and translated via the target language of prose novels, and through which the prevailing gender ideology and stereotypes have been reinforced. The novel's plot structure and development—which were restricted in traditional Khmer poems—are also vital to the intralingual translation process. An essential part of the target language of modern prose, the popular plots of colonial novels form an important site that connects the readers and cultural memory, and through which the traditional image of the ideal Khmer girl is voiced.

Female images in Khmer cinema of the postcolonial period

Khmer film-makers began to master the language of cinematography only in the 1950s. The first film-makers were young men who studied this art in France at the bidding of the monarch, King Norodom Sihanouk, who was himself a passionate admirer of the cinema. He dreamt of developing this industry in Cambodia, and spared neither trouble nor expense on his passion. A film-maker, director, producer, screenwriter, and even an occasional actor, Norodom Sihanouk has produced popular films in the 1960s, including *Apsara*, *The Little Prince*, *Shadow over Angkor*, and others. The period of 1960s–1970s is considered the Golden Age of Khmer cinematography. By some estimates, more than 300 films were produced during this period (*Golden Slumbers* 2012); they include adaptations of some of the most popular novels of the colonial period, such as *The Rose of Pailin* and *Sophat*, as well as films based on folk stories, like *The Snake King's Wife*. What's interesting here is that the female images in these postcolonial films are fairly similar to those featured in the colonial novels which, as previously noted, have been translated from Khmer cultural tradition. However, my analysis of Chhay Bora's *Lost Loves* (2010) and Norodom Sihanouk's *Apsara* (1966) will also show that there are important differences in women's representations in cinema due to changes in Khmer society.

Apsara: the ideal heroine in the postcolonial world

Before entering the analysis of Norodom Sihanouk's *Apsara*[4] (1966), it is necessary to turn our attention to the film's ideological motives, which form the source language in the translation of traditional female images into cinematic representation. There is very little plot development in *Apsara* as much of the film is focussed on showing idealised images of the country. We see rather long scenes that dwell on modern Phnom Penh and its suburban areas, or the military aerodrome and pilots defending the country's borders. These idealised images of Cambodia not only frame and reinforce the stereotyped ideal Khmer girl but also connect the nation to womanhood, in that both must be protected.

It is against this backdrop that the narrative unfolds, starting with a meeting between the elderly General Rithi and his young mistress Rathana. Together they attend a performance of the Khmer Royal Ballet, where the General happens to meet the ideal Khmer girl and main heroine, Kantha, who is also the troupe's principal dancer. After the performance, Rithi expresses his gratitude to the performers and makes a speech about the importance of national art, its preservation and development. At the same time, we are introduced to Kantha's beloved Poly, a young military pilot, who watches the performance with his younger brother from behind the scenes. After some time, Rithi asks for Kantha's hand but, before he does so, breaks up with his mistress. Kantha's mother gives her consent to the marriage and soon Rithi arranges an elaborate wedding. The next day, Kantha tells her husband that she was once betrothed to Poly, whom she has known from childhood, but her mother opposed their marriage as Poly is an orphan who has been raising his younger brother. Rithi promises his wife that he will help her to reunite with her beloved Poly, and then goes on a business trip. Several days later, Poly becomes seriously injured during an operational sortie and is hospitalised. Rithi informs Kantha what has happened and keeps his promise: he "grants her freedom." Kantha is reunited with Poly, and at the end of the film, Rithi goes back to Rathana.

In *Apsara*, we see two heroines who are given almost equal attention: Kantha and Rathana. Both women are quite similar in that they wear European-type clothes that accentuate their modernity, and have been given European education. Both women can understand the French language, but they themselves speak the Khmer language exclusively; in contrast, the male characters often use the French language in their speech. As such, the film attempts to link women to the preservation of culture—a link made more prominent through the characterisation of Kantha, the protagonist.

The ballet dancer Kantha, who is also a working woman, is undoubtedly a modern translation of the traditional figure of the Apsara, with the visuality of cinema as the target language. Although the film deviates from the classical image in certain ways, it is nonetheless interesting that the director tries to balance each deviation by relying on the source language. For example, although Kantha is a dancer in the Khmer Royal Ballet, she is nonetheless associated with "Apsara"—the title of the film. This allusion to the heavenly dancer is the most important aspect of the source language, and shows that Kantha still adheres to the traditional identity. As such, the director uses the same source language as the prose writers of the colonial period by representing Kantha as beautiful, kind, and gentle. In this way, the Kantha's representation links both modern heroine and the traditional ideal girl. Other aspects of the tradition can be seen when Kantha submits to her mother's wishes and agrees to marry a man whom she does not love, saying nothing about her true feelings. During the betrothal, she behaves exactly as the stereotyped ideal should behave. She is quiet, modest, and polite. She talks to the guests with a smile on her face during the wedding even though she has been forced into a marriage with a man she does not love. Similarly, in one of the final scenes when her husband "grants her freedom," Kantha warmly thanks him and expresses "her profound gratitude" (*Apsara* 1966). Any deviation from the classical image is therefore compensated by the girl's perfect behaviour.

As in the colonial Khmer novel, the film contrasts the idealised Kantha and her antithesis—Rithi's mistress, Rathana, who acts as the "villainess." Rathana talks about her rival scornfully and makes fun of her "righteousness." She also attends Rithi and Kantha's wedding without an invitation. She acts defiantly, thereby openly expressing her discontent to her lover. However, she is deeply attached to Rithi and is sincerely upset about their break-up. Because of her anger, Rathana even invites a man whom she has just met at the wedding celebration to her home. As she is a widow, however, this brief relationship does not attract as much criticism as an unmarried girl's would in her place. Still, Rathana is also a modern translation of the traditional "villainess" figure. Through the target language of film, her physical sensuality is displayed when she and Rithi embrace and kiss each other passionately.

Indeed, *Apsara* is the first film in which such images are presented. Constituting a key modern element, the film's representations of women's bodies also address the sensitive issue of physical intimacy between the characters. Given the context of its time, these few scenes are, of course, rather decent. Nonetheless, the portrayal of the physical body—seen in how characters embrace and touch each other—should be considered an important milestone in Cambodia's postcolonial cinematography. Apart from the sensual kissing scene stated above, the scene where Kantha and Poly are swimming in the river is also very illustrative: Kantha wears a strapless low-cut dress and enjoys her beloved's touch. Additionally, the director demonstrates physical contact as a manifestation of love, with no hint of condemnation towards the women. Such scenes are an important aspect of the target language, especially as sexual descriptions of the woman's body are exceptionally rare in modern Khmer literature and cinematography, even in the present day. Such scenes would, of course, have been absolutely impossible in the colonial novel as authors in general do not describe moments of physical intimacy between the ideal girl and her beloved; instead, they focus on ideal relationships in the spirit of Khmer tradition.

Despite these innovations, however, both female characters and their fates depend completely on Rithi who is always in power. And even though

Rathana openly expresses her discontent to her lover during his wedding, she—like Rathana—can only obey the General's will. It is worth mentioning too that Rithi's role is performed not by a professional actor but by a serving General in the Khmer army, Nhiek Tioulong. His image is important to the film as he projects the "authentic" image of a man who is fair and devoted to his country. Rithi regularly gives speeches about protecting the country, thereby reinforcing a sense of national identity and devotion to traditions.

Female images in contemporary Khmer cinema

During the Democratic Kampuchea period and the Pol Pot Cultural Revolution (1975–1979), the normal life of the whole country was disrupted. Most of the film-makers and actors died, and around 400 films were lost or liquidated during this period (Chou 2012). After the fall of the Khmer Rouge regime in 1979, Cambodian cinematography began to recover. However, the topics and storylines remained conservative, even in films produced in the 1990s; as a result, female images and role models were largely unchanged. Throughout the 1980s and 1990s, the country experienced great sociopolitical changes. Khmer culture was greatly influenced by Vietnam and the USSR, the countries that provided the greatest assistance in restoring the country. Active ideological work was carried out in order to integrate Cambodia into the socialist camp. During this period, works by Khmer authors began to reappear in Cambodia. According to estimates by researchers, several hundred works were written in the period between 1980 and 1989; some were published in Cambodia while others were published outside the country (Ebihara et al. 1994, 34).

The main feature of this period is its ideological orientation, which was influenced by the politicised literatures of socialist countries and reflected in the dominant themes of patriotism and nationalism in Khmer literature, which often features a patriotic hero who is ready to give his life to the struggle for the liberation of the motherland (Foshko 1986, 252). However, such works have no place for female characters as their stereotyped images do not fit into the new plots, while the love stories in which the ideal heroine usually appears have also lost their relevance. At the same time, these works exclude Cambodian women from representation as they were historically not allowed to participate in politics or its processes (Frieson 2001). In other words, women were not considered as civic-minded members of society, and therefore cannot participate as active members or as citizens as such roles do not conform to established gender norms. The lack of female characters in literature is reflected in the films of this period, which were also subjected to state censorship due to a policy influenced by socialist Vietnam. As a result, a new target language that could accurately describe the heroine was never formed in the Khmer literature and cinema of the 1980s.

In recent years, however, Cambodian film-makers experimented with and created new or different female images that have moved away from the usual stereotypes found in colonial and postcolonial literature. Several films show how women lived during the period of the Khmer Rouge, and, as a result, a new target language emerged, one that endorses non-traditional female images through the representations of women as heroines of Democratic Kampuchea. Undoubtedly, this development is due to the strengthening of women's position in contemporary Khmer society, which has encouraged film-makers to reconsider the images of the past and find new ways of representing and expressing the new or contemporary Khmer woman. I will now examine Chhay Bora's *Lost Loves* (2010), an important film for studying the new images of women and, thus, the target language of postcolonial Khmer cinema.

Lost Loves: the mother-woman in Democratic Kampuchea

Inspired by true events, *Lost Loves* (2010) by film-maker Chhay Bora had its premiere at the Cambodia International Film Festival in 2010. The film revolves around Amara, the female protagonist and heroine of *Lost Loves*. Although Amara is one of thousands of village women who suffers from being separated from her loved ones, she is not a passive and submissive heroine. She does not surrender to frustration and tries her best to save her children.

The film opens with a scene in which an elderly nun, revealed as Amara, is staying near a pagoda. Memories take her to the past. Amara lives in a big and happy family. Her father is a retired army general while her husband is an active officer with the Lon Nol army. Then the Khmer Rouge seizes power in Cambodia. In the days following the capture of the capital, Amara experiences a series of tragedies: the execution of her father, followed by the execution of her husband who had been fighting the Khmer Rouge in one of the provinces with other supporters of Lon Nol. Uprooted from their home, Amara and her children as well as brothers are evacuated from Phnom Penh. Despite the deaths of her father and husband, and despite the overall atmosphere of chaos and panic, Amara remains strong. She tries to keep her children alive, using all possible means to get more food and medicine. She also tries to support the people around her. According to the new rules of the Khmer Rouge, children have to live apart from the adults (in general, relatives were usually separated and settled in different camps), and, as a result, Amara is separated from her brothers and eldest daughter. One day, the daughter obtains permission to visit Amara but the latter has been sent to work and so they miss each other. The boat carrying Amara's daughter unfortunately flips over and she drowns. Although the overseers could have helped save her, they decided not to because she is deemed a "useless" person who is not worth their time. Meanwhile, Amara's brothers also die. In the end, she manages to keep only her younger daughter and son alive.

One of the most important narrative peculiarities of *Lost Loves* lies in its different approach to creating and expressing women's images, which are non-standard[5] for Khmer literature and cinematography. Narrated in the first-person female voice, the film expresses Amara's viewpoint, thoughts, and emotions—a representational approach that would have been absolutely impossible in the colonial period as the female protagonists of literary works were simply based on stereotypes. In *Lost Loves*, the heroine not only gets the right to a voice; she can openly speak without handing this function over to the male characters. The female narration can be regarded as a new target language of postcolonial Khmer cinematography through which the traditional female image is transformed. However, it should be noted that the translation of a "new" female image still preserves certain aspects of the source language, seen when the characterisation of Amara draws on the idealised image of the mother-woman from colonial literature. This is especially apparent in the scenes that focus on her family life and children. As a loving mother, Amara not only feeds her daughter, but also helps her to cope with hard physical labour. She also speaks of how she "tried to understand the feelings of my daughter and give her strength" (*Lost Loves* 2010). In these scenes, we see in Amara the traditional image of the ideal mother-woman in colonial literature, albeit with one critical difference: unlike this figure who is usually already dead when the narration starts, Amara is alive and narrating her own story; she is not some mere minor character who lives on in the memories of the male protagonist.

Another important feature here is Amara's development as a female character. Although there are similarities between Amara and the stereotyped images of colonial literature—one of which is the mother-woman figure while another is her helplessness and obedience in the face of circumstances—what is also important here is how these typical "feminine" characteristics are replaced with images of self-confidence and resistance as the film develops. It should be noted that the heroines of colonial novels, when placed in difficult situations, usually bow to fate and even take their own lives when they are unable to find a way out. Amara, on the contrary, firmly withstands all travails in trying to save her family. She is not a passive ideal heroine, but a woman who fights for her children's lives while living in unbearable conditions. This radical break from tradition is emphasised when she cuts off her long hair, saying: "The first thing I had to sacrifice for Angkar[6] was my hair" (*Lost Loves* 2010). While this illuminating scene can be interpreted as a break from the traditional image of the ideal Khmer woman, whose long shiny hair is an important characteristic, it also shows how Amara represents a new type of female image in Cambodian literature and cinematography.

By resisting Khmer cultural traditions that dictate gender identities, Chhay Bora creates a new female image and female-centric narrative in the narration of a woman's turbulent life in Democratic Kampuchea. However, it must be said that such heroines are still very rare in modern Khmer cinema. One factor could be that Khmer cinema is still relatively undeveloped as it lacks both state and financial support. *Lost Loves*, for instance, was made without financial support from the government and could only be shown in a few cinemas in Cambodia. State censorship is another significant factor. All programmes on state TV channels have to undergo a vetting process and obtain permission before they can be aired (Sisovann 2002). As the same restrictions also apply to Khmer cinema, the viewer thus does not always have access to certain films.

Conclusion

Having considered the evolution of Khmer women's images and representations in the respective novels and films of the colonial and postcolonial periods, I conclude that the influence of the medieval Khmer literary canon is still very stable and strong. Throughout the twentieth century, Cambodia had experienced many changes, and the language of literary representation was similarly affected. This can be seen in the changing images of women in the postcolonial period, which have become more complex in contrast to the static or undeveloped female characters of the colonial period. Although there are more attempts by authors and film-makers/directors to modernise the representations of Khmer women in prose fiction and cinema, the orthodox ideas and perspectives on gender identity and roles have prevailed: many postcolonial works still depict the final goal of a woman as that of a happy marriage. The female character can have a good education and successful career but, in the end, she always rejects her achievements in favour of the traditional role of the mother.

Notwithstanding that Khmer literature has always been monolingual, the language has changed in accordance with the historical and sociocultural developments of the country. The language of the colonial novel, for instance, is abundant with Sanskrit loan words—also the source language that has been used to describe female archetypes like Apsara. Moreover, the authors rely on stereotypes to uphold the ideal image of the Khmer girl or woman. The popularity of the novel has also contributed to creating an essential dialogue between the author and the reader, through which the traditional female image or archetype—translated into the modern language of prose—is transferred. In postcolonial texts and films, modern language is mostly used, and these linguistic changes have coincided with the changes in the images and representations of Khmer womanhood. New genres and forms appear in which the authors and film-makers/directors transfer female images, sometimes describing them in a language that is new and unusual for Khmer culture.

Despite the promising changes in women's images and representations in the postcolonial period, they are still very slow in coming. This protracted development can be attributed to the isolation of Cambodian literature and cinema as well as to the contemporary authors' focus on didacticism (Iv 2013), an approach that has been maintained since the middle period of Khmer literature. Read in this context, the images and representations of women in modern literature can be said to reflect the entire literary process of Khmer cultural history. Despite the changes and developments in the literary and cinematic scene, female characters are still based on centuries-old gender archetypes. This is also why modern Khmer literature has remained as one of the main broadcasters of cultural tradition through which the ideal Khmer girl is upheld.

Notes

1 It should be clarified that Khmer literature has always been monolingual; in other words, authors have written only in the Khmer language, even during the French colonial rule. Although some works of French literature were available during the colonial period, few people had the opportunity to be acquainted with them; moreover, they resisted the adoption of the French language. Nevertheless, the target language of colonial prose was an entirely new language for Khmer literature which, historically, was written in verse. And it was exactly this language into which the first Khmer prose authors translated the traditional female archetypes and images.
2 *Jataka Tales* or *Jatakas* are included in *Khuddaka Nikaya*, the fifth collection of *Sutta Pitaka*—also, the second part of *Pali Canon*. The works in this section address not only the members of the religious community, but also the masses. *Jatakas* were very popular and exerted a great influence on Khmer literature in the middle period.
3 The following novels can be used as an example: *The Waters of Tonlesap* (1941) by Kim Hak; *The Spirit of Love* (1942) and *The Rose of Pailin* (1943) by Nhok Thaem; *The Story of Samapheavy* (1943) by Rim Kin; *The High Point of Love* (1946) and *The Sad Man* (1946) by Heng Yan; *Tong Chin* (1947) by Nou Kan; *Nakry's Destiny* (1952) by Suy Hieng; and *Blooming Flower, Fading Flower* (1952) by Ieng Say.
4 *Apsara* is Norodom Sihanouk's third film. At this time, he was not yet King of Cambodia. He abdicated in favour of his father, Norodom Suramarit, in 1955, and held the position of Head of State when the film came out. Even after regaining the throne in 1993, Norodom Sihanouk remained active in cinema not only as a film-maker and producer, but also as a screenwriter and actor. He directed approximately thirty films and his last work was screened in 2006. It is worth mentioning the main heroine in *Apsara*, Kantha, was played by Norodom Sihanouk's daughter, Norodom Boppha Devi.
5 One of the first works to feature the "new" Khmer woman is a novel, *Women's Fate*. Authored by a woman writer, Lyk Rary, and published in 1962, the novel is about the life of an orphaned girl Nieng who has been abandoned by her beloved and has a baby to take care of. The heroine, however, does not lose her faith: she becomes educated, opens her own small salon, and finally ends up married and living happily with the father of her daughter. As can be seen from the plot summary, despite the changes in the heroine's position, her image has not changed conceptually as her final goal is still a happy marriage. Still, the image of a financially independent single mother can be considered a positive development in the representation of the Khmer woman.
6 "Angkar" is the name of the Communist Party of Cambodia during the Democratic Kampuchea period.

References

Chey, Elizabeth. n.d. "The Status of Khmer Women." Accessed May 4, 2019. http://www.mekong.net/cambodia/women.htm.

Chhay, Bora. 2010. *Khliet Tow Saen Chhngay* [Lost Loves]. KH: Phnom Penh: Palm Film Production, 2010.
Chigas, George. 2005. *Tum Teav: A Translation and Analysis of a Cambodian Literary Classic.* Cambodia: Documentation Center of Cambodia.
Chou, Davy. 2012. *Golden Slumbers.* KH: Paris: Vycky Films; Phnom Penh: Bophana Production.
Ebihara, May M., Carol A. Mortland, and Judy Ledgerwood, eds. 1994. *Cambodian Culture Since 1975: Homeland and Exile.* London: Cornell University Press.
Foshko, Natalia. 1986. "Traditzionniy Folklor I Literatura Kampuchiyi I Ih Transformatziya V Sovremennyh Usloviyah [Traditional Folklore and Literature of Kampuchea and Its Transformation in the Modern Reality]." In *Artistic Traditions of Oriental Literatures and the Modernity: The Present-Day Traditionalism* [Hudozhestvenniye tradizii literaur Vostoka I sovremennost' tradizionalizm na sovremennom etape], edited by Vladimir Braginsky and Yury Chelyshev, 249–65. Moscow: Nauka.
Frieson, Kate G. 2001. *In the Shadows: Women, Power and Politics in Cambodia.* Occasional paper no. 26 (June). Victoria: Centre for Asia-Pacific Initiatives. https://www.uvic.ca/research/centres/capi/assets/docs/Frieson_-_Women_in_Cambodia.pdf.
Hatim, Basil, and Ian Mason. 1997. *The Translator as Communicator.* London and New York: Routledge.
Iv, Thong. 2013. *Aksasel Khmae* [Khmer Literature]. Phnom Penh: Int. Standart Books.
Khing, Hoc Dy. 1997. *Apercu General Sur La Literature Khmere* [General Overview of Khmer Literature]. Paris: Edition L'Harmattan.
Ledgerwood, Judy. n.d. "Cambodian Recent History and Contemporary Society: An Introductory Course." Accessed April 12, 2019. http://www.seasite.niu.edu/khmer/Ledgerwood/Contents.htm.
Norodom, Sihanouk. 1966. *Apsara.* KH: Phnom Penh: Khemara Pictures.
Nou, Hach. (1949) 1960. *Phka Sropoun* [The faded flower]. Phnom Penh: Vapathoa.
Rim, Kin. (1942) 2014. *Sophat.* Phnom Penh: Int. Standart Books.
Sisovann, Pin. 2002. "A Closer Look at the Troubled World of Modern Cambodian Cinema." *The Cambodia Daily*, June 29. https://www.cambodiadaily.com/news/a-closer-look-at-the-troubled-world-of-modern-cambodian-cinema-696/.
Torop, Peeter. 2003. "Intersemiosis and Intersemiotic Translation." In *Translation Translation*, edited by Susan Petrilli, 271–82. Amsterdam: Rodopi.

6 Gained in translation

The politics of localising
Western stories in late-colonial
Indonesia

Tom G. Hoogervorst

Introduction

Translation in (post)colonial contexts is inherently embroiled in power asymmetries, not least between the languages involved. One persistent legacy of Western imperialism is the disproportionate prestige and enhanced social status of languages associated with dominant societies—such as English—compared to those of dominated societies (Asad 1992). The translation of literary works into more powerful languages, therefore, has a history of serving political centres and imperialist agendas. In today's globalised era, the translated word frequently serves as a catalyst for Western epistemic dominance over people in its influence sphere and for hegemonic representations of the Other (Niranjana 1992; Sengupta 1995; Venuti 2008). As a consequence, translating—and then consuming—texts from the Global South into European languages typically renders the views and even linguistic structures of the former subordinated to those of the latter, which are considered "the norm" (Bassnett and Trivedi 1999; Gupta 1998). As the author and academic Shinji Yamashita put it crudely: "English translators are aggressive. They are like colonizers" (1997, 136).

Yet it must also be kept in mind that translation is imbued with a strong anti-colonial potential. It enables colonised peoples to recreate their image in the language of their colonisers (Tymoczko 1999) and access the literary products of other colonised people (Chandra 2016; Liem 2012). Moreover, translation enables marginalised people to reformulate texts written in dominant languages, thereby expropriating them and asserting power over their contents. For Southeast Asia, the emancipatory value of this strategy has been shown in the context of the Philippines, where early-colonial Spanish texts were reshaped rather than simply translated into Tagalog (Rafael 1988). As the present study demonstrates for late-colonial Indonesia, the translation of Western literature into Malay produced equally subversive and politically motivated outcomes; it helped facilitate a powerful counter-discourse to Europe's hegemony over language, knowledge, and information.

Indonesia under Dutch occupation, known as "the Netherlands Indies" or "Dutch East Indies," exhibited a somewhat unusual sociolinguistic history. Unlike anglophone, francophone, hispanophone, and lusophone colonies, the archipelago's educated middle classes had comparatively little access to Western literary discourses and other modes of knowledge production. What they had in common was a lingua franca, Malay, spoken as a second and sometimes first language by indigenous Indonesians, Chinese, Eurasians, Arabs, etc. Since the mid-nineteenth century, the emergence of a Malay-printing industry in the Latin alphabet revolutionised access to information and, hence, the cultural outlook of Indonesia's Malay-literate communities (Adam 1995). The incorporation of external knowledge into existing information structures was completely dependent on this vernacular type of Malay (Jedamski 2014). In the first decade of the twentieth century, the Malay press was gradually modernised, commercialised, diversified, and popularised. Newspapers, serialised stories, novels, and other books in romanised Malay became the primary source for non-Europeans to learn about and become part of the modern world (Hoogervorst and Schulte Nordholt 2017; Maier 2006). The market for Malay-language publications was exceedingly diverse, with their producers—who were often simultaneously authors, journalists, editors, and translators—and consumers hailing from various ethnolinguistic backgrounds.

While most readers of Malay had no direct access to European discourses, its writers were often remarkably cosmopolitan. Famous Eurasian authors and translators included Carel Frederik Winter (1799–1859), Adolf Friedrich von de Wall (1834–1909), Ferdinand Wiggers (1862–1912), Gijsbert Francis (c.1860s–c.1910s), and Herman Kommer (1873–1924). These author-translators, as I will refer to them in this study, must be seen as pioneers of the Netherlands Indies Malay press. Equally important were their colleagues of Chinese origins, including Lie Kim Hok (1853–1912), Gouw Peng Liang (1869–1928), Kwee Tek Hoay (1886–1951), Njoo Cheong Seng (1902–1962), Tio Ie Soei (1890–1974), and Kwee Kek Beng (1900–1975) (Salmon 1981; see Table 2 in Appendix for the orthographies of Chinese-Indonesian names). Indigenous Indonesian author-translators were considerably fewer in number, but European-educated journalists like Frederick Daniël Johannes Pangemanann (1870–1911), Abdoel Rivai (1871–1937), Tirto Adhi Soerjo (1880–1918), and the autodidact Parada Harahap (1899–1959) proved equally prolific and decisively crucial for the development of the early twentieth-century Indonesian press. Together, the Eurasian, Chinese, and indigenous inhabitants of Indonesia's late-colonial cities constituted what has been described as a "mestizo society," whose shared language, shared access to information, and shared consciousness stood at the foundations of an "imagined community" (Coppel 2002).

It is no coincidence that the author-translators of Western texts into Malay predominantly came from liminal communities that were fully part neither of the colonial elites nor of the indigenous masses. Initially, these in-between groups had to stick together to navigate the rocky landscape of the Malay-language press (Adam 1987, 1995). Both Eurasians and localised

Chinese (*Peranakan*) typically had indigenous female ancestors, binding them to the land through the ties of kinship. For this reason, both groups had access to multiple cultural repertoires and could quickly stake out their turf in popular music, theatre, and the Malay press (Adam 1995; Cohen 2016; Keppy 2008). The increasing number of indigenous consumers, too, came from various regional, ethnic, and religious backgrounds. Yet tastes—literary or otherwise—proved remarkably able to overstep demographic divisions. From the beginning of the twentieth century in particular, people from all nationalities enjoyed highly popular Malay pulp fiction centring on vice, extramarital affairs, scandal, and revenge (Chandra 2011; Hellwig 2002; Sutedja-Liem 2007). Such literary developments were intimately connected with the rise of colonial modernity, with its emphasis on visual culture, mass consumption, and Malay as a boundary-crossing language to articulate a new set of aspirations (Hoogervorst and Schulte Nordholt 2017).

Nevertheless, a shared vernacular language could never fully reduce interethnic distance, nor racial tensions. The Dutch were quick to realise the importance of Malay to restructure society in their own vision, including as a tool of law enforcement and cultural transformation (Mahdi 2006; Maier 2006; Jedamski 2014). Malay complemented Mandarin as a force for pan-Chinese nationalism and anti-colonialism by the early 1900s (Sai 2016). Soon afterwards, it became the vehicle of similar politics among indigenous Indonesians (Shiraishi 1990). As the Malay press diversified, starting in the 1910s but reaching its zenith in the 1930s, it accommodated competing and often conflicting intellectual discourses along the fault-lines of politics, ethnicity, and religion (Jedamski 2014). This made it lucrative for journalists to cater to the preferences of specific audiences—including Chinese chauvinists, communist intellectuals, local aristocrats, progressive Muslims, and pro-Dutch conservatives—and diverging ideological orientations eventually eclipsed overlapping ones on the battlefield of Malay printing. Indonesia's late-colonial cities gradually ceased to be "mestizo" in character, with growing numbers of Malay-literate authors starting to caution against the dangers of interracial relationships (Chandra 2011; Chin and Hoogervorst 2017; Salmon 1981). The translated Western novels into Malay likewise faced tribalisation, especially from the 1920s onwards, with communal interests increasingly determining the agenda. At the same time, maximising one's readership by appealing to broadly shared tastes, often at the expense of budding notions of copyright and intellectual property, remained important in spite of the colony's changing interethnic relations (Arens 1999; Jedamski 2014).

The present study compares three Malay translations to their Western originals, highlighting the specific linguistic choices through which their author-translators engaged with the complexities of race and ethnicity. The Malay translations of *De Dubbele Moord* (1855), *The Mystery of Dr. Fu-Manchu* (1915), and *My Chinese Marriage* (1922), which appeared, respectively, in 1900, 1925, and 1922, have been selected because they all contain illuminating passages on these issues. The first novel is set in Java, the second in the UK, and the third partly in the US and partly in China. This diversification of locations corresponds to an increasingly cosmopolitan outlook of Indonesia's indigenous and Chinese communities during the course of the early twentieth century, in which stories no longer needed to take place in recognisably local contexts in order to "make sense." The first novel was written by a Eurasian author, the second by a Chinese, and the third by an anonymous but presumably also Chinese author. All feature Chinese characters, while the first additionally exhibits indigenous Indonesians and the second and third Westerners. What was gained by translating them into Malay? In investigating how and why these stories were translated, I look into the heterogeneity of the Malay language itself, which in late-colonial times freely drew from the Dutch and the Hokkien variety of Chinese to designate concepts unfamiliar to its readership (see Table 1 in Appendix). As I hope to demonstrate, a printing tradition in the powerful Malay vernacular allowed for deliberate strategies to de-Europeanise popular literature, in particular by removing its racist characteristics and, in doing so, subverting the colony's racialised hierarchies.

A murderous plot and its translation

De Dubbele Moord (The Double Murder) is a story set in rural western Java at the beginning of the nineteenth century. It was originally written by Wilhelm Leonard Ritter (1799–1862) and published in the Dutch literary journal *Biäng-Lala*, which the author co-edited with his colleague Louis Jacobus Anthonie Tollens. Ritter had previously worked for the Netherlands Indies administration, first as a soldier and later as a civil servant. After losing his position in 1837 on account of his questionable financial integrity, he saw himself forced to make a living out of writing (Dornseiffer and Kate 1991; Sol 1991). Ritter's conservative attitude—even for his time—came to the fore in his writings. He repeatedly expressed approval of slavery, glorified the Dutch presence in the Indies, and linked ethnicity to a broad spectrum of negative characteristics including—in the case of indigenous Indonesians—laziness, subservience, vengefulness, cruelty, and the incapability to truly love others (Arens 1999, 33). Somewhat surprisingly, his stories nonetheless proved popular among Malay-literate audiences, yielding Malay translations of *Pieter Erberveld* ([1840]1924), *Sara Specx* ([1843]1926), *De Arme Rosetta* (The Poor Rosetta, [1852]1903), *Si Tjonat de Landrover* (Tjonat the Robber, [1855]1900), and *De Dubbele Moord* ([1855]1900) (Arens 1999; Toer 1982). Some of his translated works had further afterlives in other textual formats: *De Arme Rossetta* and *Si Tjonat de Landrover* were "translated" into traditional Malay poems (*syair*), whereas his short story *Toeloecabesie* (1844)—named after its protagonist—inspired parts of the orally transmitted *Hikajat Kotidjah* (Story of Kotidjah) (Arens 1999, 35–6, 46). In understanding the remarkable success of Ritter's oeuvre in Malay, it is important to point out that the author-translators involved in its translation had a tendency to transform the somewhat grandiose prose of the source texts into a more plain, no-nonsense idiom, typically by omitting his lengthy and hardly charitable portrayals of Asian people and concepts in the target texts (Arens 1999, 38, 41).

Herman Kommer's *Tjerita Njonja Kong Hong Nio* (The Story of Lady Kong Hong Nio), one of the first translations of Ritter's work into Malay, provides the ideal case study to highlight these translational politics along the lines of race and ethnicity. Published in 1900 by W.P. Vasques in Batavia, it follows essentially the same storyline as *De Dubbele Moord*: the widow and rich Chinese landowner Kong Hong Nio (Kong Honio in the original) tries to keep her family afloat amidst the copious malfeasances—including a surfeit of sexual affairs with indigenous women—of her greedy stepsons, who eventually conspire with corrupt aristocrats and local criminals to murder her. As a single mother skilled at armed combat, Kong Hong Nio is a somewhat unusual protagonist in the fictional landscape of late-colonial Indonesia. Born in Batavia of humble origins, her parents married her off at an early age to the China-born physician Tan Hap Pon (Tan Happon in the original), who died prematurely after the couple had one daughter. After some years, Kong Hong Nio remarried with the wealthy Chinese widower Liem Tek Kan, taking good care of his three sons and his large estate, for which purpose she mastered horseback skills and weaponry. After Liem Tek Kan too passed away, his oldest son, the story's main antagonist Liem Hok Kan (Lim Hokkan in the original), began to claim ownership of the family estate. The indigenous district head (*tjoetak*) Mas Albaram (Maas Albaram in the original) had his own reasons to clandestinely assert dominance over what he perceived to be his rightful ancestral grounds. After a failed attempt to convert Kong Hong Nio to Islam and incorporate her into his aristocratic lineage through marriage, he decided to assist with Liem Hok Kan's evil plan to murder the fearsome heroine. The story contains no important European characters.

Herman Kommer (1873–1924) was a Eurasian civil servant known for his social criticism and active career in the Malay press. Uncannily echoing the career of Wilhelm Ritter, Kommer resorted to writing only after losing his position in the Netherlands Indies administration (Berens 1991, 77). From 1902, he also edited the Surabaya-based newspaper *Pewarta Soerabaia*, where he worked with Chinese-Indonesian entrepreneurs and journalists. In many ways, Kommer seems to have been closer to the Asian part of his heritage than to his European (German, French, and Belgian) roots. He married an unidentified Chinese woman and—after ending his journalistic career in 1921—enjoyed no shortage of fame around Surabaya as a venerated snake hunter and animal collector (Termorshuizen 2009). The theme of strong women combating colonial injustice also runs through three of Kommer's original creations: *Tiga Tjarita* (Three Stories, 1897), *Tjerita Siti Aisah* (The Story of Siti Aisah, 1900), and *Tjerita Nji Paina* (The Story of Nji Paina, 1900) (Sutedja-Liem 2007, 45–7). Concubinage, corruption, and unaccountability among Java's rural administrators are additional thematic threads throughout his writings (Berens 1991). Not much else is known about Herman Kommer. The fictionalised journalist "Kommer" in Pramoedya Ananta Toer's renowned *Buru Quartet* (1980–1988) is obviously based on this Eurasian writer. In real life, it is likely that Kommer's ideological leanings and relations with Chinese and indigenous Indonesians had indeed influenced his literary writings, but he has never specifically stated so. His *Tjerita Njonja Kong Hong Nio* lacks an introduction and does not acknowledge Ritter as the original author, instead presenting itself as "A story that is very funny, beautiful and lively, and has really happened about a century ago in West Java" (Figure 6.1).[1]

Ritter's seventy-four-page source text, *De Dubbele Moord*, starts with a description of the local countryside, before proceeding with a "story within a story" narrating the exploits of protagonist Lady Kong Honio. Kommer's 105-page Malay translation, *Tjerita Njonja Kong Hong Nio*, omits this introductory chapter and starts directly with the main story. Descriptive parts with no direct bearing on the storyline—in particular those in which Asians were described in negative terms—were systematically omitted in Kommer's Malay version, while a number of subplots were added (Arens 1999, 38). Other effects of translation had to do with the nature of the Malay language itself. The initial description of the story's protagonist Kong Hong Nio is a case in point. While occupying several pages in both versions and being roughly similar, the Malay version comes with a much greater surprise effect. Readers of the Dutch original would have immediately realised that the story's protagonist was a woman through Ritter's use of female pronouns, yet readers of Malay—which lacks pronominal gender—discovered Kong Hong Nio's gender only after lengthy descriptions of her clothes, weapons, and horseback skills (Hoogervorst 2016, 287).

Ritter's source text is infused with hints of local flavour, including various Malay words followed by their explanation in Dutch: *baba* (Indies-born Chinese men; Dutch: *mannelijke Chinezen in Indië geboren*), *galangan* (dikes; Dutch: *dijkjes*), *gardoe* (guardhouses in which natives keep guard; Dutch: *wachthuisjes waarin de Inlanders de wacht houden*), *goedang* (storehouse; Dutch: *pakhuis*), *kemmit* (those destined to watch over houses, storehouses, cattle, etc.; Dutch: *zij die [. . .] tot het bewaken van huizen, pakhuizen, vee, enz. bestemd worden*), *oengoe* (violet; Dutch: *purperkleurig*), *penawar* (native painkilling remedies; Dutch: *Inlandsche pijnstillende geneesmiddelen*), *pondokh* (caretaker's shed; Dutch: *oppassersloots*), *samanka* (watermelons; Dutch: *watermeloenen*), *sinsang* (physician and pharmacist; Dutch: *geneesheer en apothecar*), *tjoetak* (native head of a district; Dutch: *inlandsch hoofd op een land*), *toedong* (headdress; Dutch: *hoofddeksel*), and *toewan tanah* (landlord; Dutch: *landheer*). Some Malay words were not glossed, implying a level of familiarity with them among the targeted readership: *anklong* (a kind of traditional music), *badjoe* (upper garment), *blanda* (European), *doekon blanda*

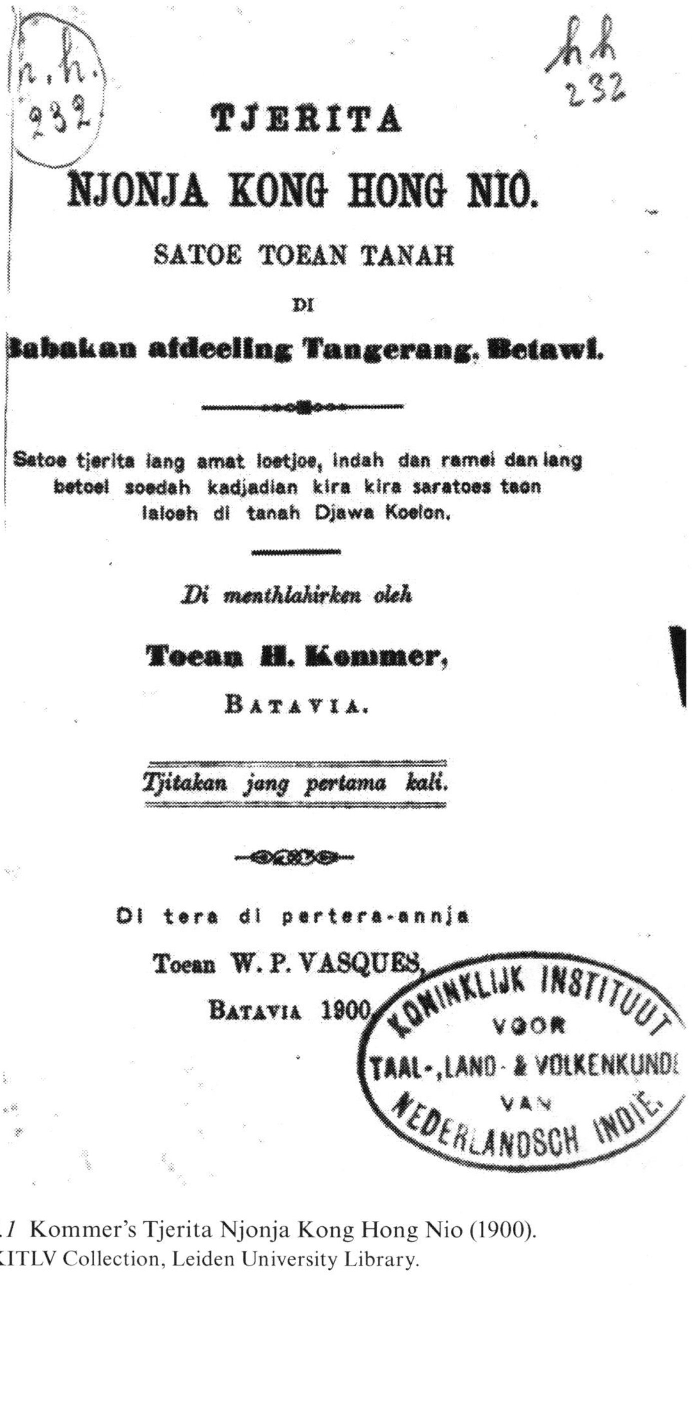
h.h. 232

TJERITA

NJONJA KONG HONG NIO.

SATOE TOEAN TANAH

DI

Babakan afdeeling Tangerang, Betawi.

Satoe tjerita iang amat loetjoe, indah dan ramei dan iang betoel soedah kadjadian kira kira saratoes taon laloeh di tanah Djawa Koelon.

Di menthlahirken oleh

Toean H. Kommer,

BATAVIA.

Tjitakan jang pertama kali.

Di tera di pertera-annja

Toean W. P. VASQUES,

BATAVIA 1900.

Figure 6.1 Kommer's Tjerita Njonja Kong Hong Nio (1900).
Source: KITLV Collection, Leiden University Library.

(European-trained doctor), *golokh* (machete), *kris* (a Javanese dagger), *mandor* (overseer), *nonja* (madam), *panton* (Malay quatrain), *roengging* (paid dancing-girl), and *sinké* (China-born immigrant). Unsurprisingly, most of these Malay words were left as such in Kommer's translation, save for some slight orthographical modifications. In some translated dialogues, Kommer furthermore attempted to highlight that the story took place in a Chinese milieu by deliberately adding ethnolinguistic nuances. The word *moeder* (mother), for example, was translated as *entjim*, a Hokkien loanword chiefly used in Chinese-Indonesian families. Some further insights in the politics of translation can be found in the pejorative domain. For Dutch *valschaard* (miscreant), *ellendeling* (wretch), and *schooijer* (derelict), the rather unimaginative Malay catch-all swearword *bangsat* was used. Interestingly, the Dutch insults *hoer* (whore) and *hoerekind* (whore's child) were censored in the original text ("h..r; h. . . .k..d"), whereas their Malay renditions *djingge* (second-in-rank concubine) and *anak haram djadah* (bastard) were not. In the case of *djingge*, Kommer again opted to use a word chiefly used by Indonesia's Chinese community to localise the story more convincingly, even though his targeted readership would have included Malay speakers of other backgrounds.

While containing several added layers to the storyline, the Malay "translation" similarly features numerous omissions of elements deemed irrelevant for its Malay-language readership, such as Eurocentric accounts of Asian things. One such omission is the protagonist's residence, which is described in the source text as being "one of those estates whose vastness surpasses many a German principality" (Ritter 1855, 171)[2] and "crammed with a series of Chinese statues, which could well be classified as belonging to the most hideous" (Ritter 1855, 180).[3] Likewise omitted were Ritter's many ungenerous descriptions of Chinese and indigenous Indonesians, a habit also picked up by other translators of his work (Arens 1999, 38). Some illustrative examples include "[. . .] as much as her beauty could not appeal to European tastes, displaying that stiff, cold, and expressionless look on the face" (Ritter 1855, 181)[4] and

> Whoever imagines how cold, cool, and indifferent a native is, at least outwardly, in even the gravest of affairs and circumstances, cannot be surprised that not the slightest expression on her face betrayed her murderous intention and her vengeful plans.
> (Ritter 1855, 227)[5]

Whenever such passages were essential to the storyline, Kommer took the liberty to reformulate them according to the (inferred) tastes of his target audience. The description of Kong Hong Nio's first husband is a case in point. Below, Ritter's original text is juxtaposed with Kommer's translation:

[Tan Happon] was a China-born immigrant and—being well in his 50s, with a big pince-nez on his nose, teary eyes, dirty infected teeth, and a greyed pigtail [. . .]—he seemed anything but an appealing match for our sixteen year old blossoming maiden, yet all the more for her parents, if only for the sake of dowry (Ritter 1855, 185).[6]	Therefore his proposal was accepted, even though Dr. Tan Hap Pon was almost 60 years. His short queue had turned grey and many of his teeth were gone, so that he wasn't the most appropriate husband for Kong Hong Nio, who was still young and very pretty, shining with a radiance similar to the full moon of fourteen days (Kommer 1900, 21).[7]

Besides the issue of racialised physical descriptions, Kommer also exercised caution with hard-to-translate sections that reflected a European rather than Asian worldview. The following passage was unceremoniously left out: "But it was nevertheless determined, perhaps in the heaven of the Chinese—if they have one—that she was to once again bear Hymen's yoke" (Ritter 1855, 187),[8] as it contained a disparaging comment about Chinese religiosity as well as a reference to Greek mythology that would have been insignificant to Malay-language readers. Also omitted were the following words of guidance on the best way to punish Indonesians who had come into conflict with the colonial law: "The people aren't afraid of all this hanging business, and a good thrust with the kris or a decapitation would instil more fear, since without their head nobody dares appearing in paradise before the prophet" (Ritter 1855, 234).[9] Indeed, religion proved a particularly fruitful theme for rewriting. While himself not a Muslim, Kommer obviously realised that his readers came from multiple ethnic and religious backgrounds. Whereas Ritter embarked on countless digressions to vent his condescension towards Asian religious practices, Kommer apparently preferred to err on the side of caution, if not conciseness. He was by no means alone in doing so. When *Njai Dasima*, a popular book written by Gijsbert Francis, was made into a film in 1929, the story's anti-Muslim aspects were likewise left out by the Chinese-owned film studio Tan's Film Company (Siegel 1997, 28). The following passage from *Tjerita Njonja Kong Hong Nio*, in which the crooked district head Mas Albaram attempts—without much success—to flatter the story's protagonist into converting to Islam, can be seen as exemplary for these translational politics:

"I love you too much and am too indebted to you, not to sincerely and affectionately wish for your eternal salvation and the preservation of your beautiful soul. You do not know God and what are your miserable gods compared to the Only One, to my God?—What are your pagan sacrifices compared to our prayers to Him and our Prophet. You don't know, Madam!" (Ritter 1855, 178)[10]	"It is a shame, that someone as kind-hearted as yourself does not know about Allah and the Prophet Muhammad. You don't know. . . " (Kommer 1900, 14)[11]

A similar avoidance of (potential) religious sensitivities can be seen when the story's antagonist, Kong Hong Nio's sinister stepson Liem Hok Kan, kidnaps an indigenous woman to satisfy his sexual pleasure. Abducting her to a cemetery, he orders her to proclaim her loyalty to him and forget about her husband. In the Malay translation, this forced oath is considerably shortened:

"Be silent about and stop thinking of him, but swear on this grave, by all that is dear to you, by your prophet—if need be, since you Muslims always boast about him anyway—by the shade of your mother—is she still alive?" "No, she is dead, Sir!" "Swear, I tell you, by the ghost of your mother, that you will forget your husband and will love, follow, and always be faithful to me—swear!" (Ritter 1855, 198)[12]	"Do not mention that husband of yours again; here on this grave, you must swear that you want to forget about your husband, and will follow me faithfully." (Kommer 1900, 40)[13]

Kommer, who used Malay (near-)natively, seemed unimpressed by Ritter's occasional forays into poetry. Neither Ritter's erratic attempt to compose a Malay quatrain (*pantun*) nor his Dutch couplet ("He who trusts a beautiful woman, has built all his hope on sand") made it into Kommer's translation (Ritter 1855, 199, 233).[14] Ritter's jokes, too, were deemed in need of improvement. When, near the end of the story, the death-sentenced antagonist Liem Hok Kan was reminded by his similarly gallows-bound companion of his substantial unpaid debt, the original version comments: "Perhaps he has settled it in the next world" (Ritter 1855, 235).[15] In the Malay translation, however, the unscrupulous stepson sardonically replies, "If you truly believe Hell exists, that is where I will pay you back the money" (Kommer 1900, 105).[16]

Tjerita Njonja Kong Hong Nio was published on the brink of the twentieth century, when commercialised literature in Malay was still in its infancy. It came out over a decade before the first anti-colonial mass-mobilisations, yet—as becomes clear from Kommer's other writings—dissatisfaction with colonial power hierarchies rested just beneath the surface. Kommer's Malay translation seized agency over its source text, with potentially sensitive phrases, especially in the domains of religion and race, being shorn of their edges. His reworking thus marks an important development in the history of Malay translational politics. Patterned after the classical Malay literary conventions, it was a rewriting more so than a strict translation (see also Maier 2004, 385–6), as Kommer freely added and removed parts of the story according to the perceived tastes of his readers. What was added in translation was the centrality of the strong, unyielding female role model. What was removed were colonially rooted racial stereotypes. What was gained was a new type of Malay literature that described colonial realities, warts and all, in a language largely ungoverned by European conventions. Kommer and his contemporaries had paved the way to later authors to do the same.

The next section, therefore, zooms in on the 1920s, in which interracial tensions and anti-colonial sentiments became commonplace in the Netherlands Indies. What, then, were the implications for the Malay translation of an even more sensitive story, *The Mystery of Dr. Fu-Manchu*?

Making Sinophobia acceptable again...

The Mystery of Dr. Fu-Manchu, first published in book form in 1913, is the debut of a series of thirteen popular thrillers. The infamous Fu-Manchu books, with their enormous success and gratuitous racism, have received considerable scholarly attention (Bloom 1996; Cogan 2002; Frayling 2014; Greene 2014; Seshagiri 2006; Taylor 2011). They were authored by the English novelist—some would say pulp writer—Sax Rohmer (Arthur Henry Sarsfield Ward, 1883–1959), who was famously and self-admittedly ignorant of all things Asian. Nevertheless, the publication of *The Mystery of Dr. Fu-Manchu* coincided with a crucial juncture in world history. It came out during the early period of the Chinese Republic and amidst the turmoil leading up to the First World War, with China's Boxer Rebellion and Japan's unbroken string of military victories still fresh in the West's collective memory. A range of conspiracy theories centring on the trope of the "Yellow Peril" prevailed around this time in the anglophone world and beyond. This upsurge of anti-Asian sentiments was further bolstered by the continued migration of East Asian men to a number of white-majority countries, not to mention lower middle-class anxieties in general. It is therefore no coincidence that Rohmer's books were quickly adapted into films, television series, and radio plays, which "turned Fu Manchu into a household name and distributed the stereotypes of Chinese torture, mercilessness, craftiness, and villainy across half the world" (Pan 1990, 89). Indeed, this particular epoch of translating popular literature to the medium of film, supported by Hollywood's powerful franchise system, was crucial in cementing a persistent and globally pervasive orientalist image of the evil Chinese male Other (Greene 2014).

Representing some the most fanciful flights of pulp fiction the English literary canon had to offer, the storyline of Fu-Manchu thrillers is relatively simple. Fu-Manchu—China's rather nonsensically named criminal mastermind—aims to overthrow the hegemony of the white race. Clever yet immoral, he does so not by military might, but through sophisticated methods of poisoning, enlisting dacoits, and biological warfare. Fu-Manchu's portentous combination of unfathomable occultism and apparent power over technology—and even over the streets of metropolitan London—marked him as the prototypical racialised arch-villain of Western popular culture (Seshagiri 2006, 164; Taylor 2011, 75). Set to stop this imagined incarnation of Asia's encroachment upon the West, the story's British protagonists Dr Petrie and Nayland Smith play a dangerous cat-and-mouse game with Fu-Manchu that continues throughout the book series. They are aided—at times—by the enslaved Karamaneh, an Egyptian woman who quickly becomes Dr Petrie's sexual obsession, thus tapping into a second thematic thrust of Western fiction about Asia: the exoticisation of "oriental" women. Dr Petrie, who provides the story's narrative voice, repeatedly describes Karamaneh in terms of her alluring yet dangerous otherness.

Rohmer's Doylesque brand of storytelling greatly appealed to Western and non-Western audiences alike, with translations appearing in a broad range of languages: "French, German, Spanish, Italian, Dutch, Portuguese, Swedish, Greek, Polish, Hungarian, Czech, Japanese and even Arabic" (Pan 1990, 89). The first Malay rendition, *Rasianja Dr. Fu Manchu* (Figure 6.2), appeared in 1925 and is remarkable in several regards. Foremost, it constitutes a noteworthy effort in a colonised society to assert agency over the literature of their colonisers through translational strategies. Not much is known about the book's translator, Tan Tjin Kang. Also known under the pseudonym Tan King Tjan, he was born in 1900 in Sukabumi and passed away in Batavia at a young age around the year 1932, having written several novels, serialised stories, and articles in the Chinese-Indonesian newspaper *Sin Po* (Salmon 1981, 331–2). Published by Surabaya's Chinese-owned publishing house Ang Sioe Tjing, Tan's *Rasianja Dr. Fu Manchu* appeared in five volumes consisting of eighty pages each, none of which had an introduction. No references to this publication in other Malay books or newspapers are known to me, but a comparison between the source text and the target text reveals that Tan Tjin Kang made a conscious effort to render this Eurocentric book palatable to a localised readership, as Herman Kommer did twenty-five years earlier with *Tjerita Njonja Kong Hong Nio*. As will be argued below, he did so by omitting a large number of adjectives which, cumulatively, pervaded the story with a deep sense of Asian otherness and racial inferiority. At the same time, however, Tan left intact most references to the story's antagonist Fu-Manchu as a potent and hostile counterforce to the white colonial order.

Tan's Malay translation of Rohmer's *The Mystery of Dr. Fu-Manchu* is quite literal, especially compared to Kommer's *Tjerita Njonja Kong Hong Nio* discussed previously. Nevertheless, it is probably not a direct translation from the English original. A Dutch translation of the novel—*Het Geheim van Dr. Fu-Manchu* (Figure 6.3)—was published in 1922 by the well-known translator Willem Jacob Aarland Roldanus Jr. As advertisements of this Dutch translation can be found in several Netherlands Indies newspapers as early as July 1922, we must assume that Tan Tjin Kang had access to it and probably used the Dutch rather than the English version as his source text. To see what was lost and gained in translation and at which stage this took place, I will compare all three texts in my analysis below. At times, Rohmer's histrionic prose proved difficult to translate even in Dutch, a language closely related to English. For example, the archetypically English construction "if you will excuse me, we will resume these gruesome inquiries after the more pleasant affairs of dinner" (Rohmer 2008, 38) was rendered

Figure 6.2 Tan Tjin Kang's 1925 Malay translation of The Mystery of Dr. Fu-Manchu.
Source: KITLV Collection, Leiden University Library.

Figure 6.3 Willem Jacob Aarland Roldanus Jr.'s 1922 Dutch translation of The Mystery of Dr. Fu-Manchu.
Source: private collection Tom Hoogervorst.

into Dutch as "if you approve, we will further discuss these terrible affairs after dinner" (Rohmer 1922, 73)[17] and in Malay simply became "if you like, we'll discuss everything after dinner" (Tan 1925, 94).[18] The Malay translation of the English sentence "Sir Crichton was addicted to cocaine, but there are indications which are not in accordance with cocaine-poisoning" (Rohmer 2008, 6) also reveals Dutch intermediacy; in Tan's target text it was rendered as "Sir Crichton had become a slave of cocaine, but there are indications conflicting with the indications of cocaine-poisoning" (Tan 1925, 12),[19] clearly reflecting the Dutch constructions *verslaafd* ("addicted," but also "enslaved") and *in strijd met* ("not in accordance with," but also "conflicting with") (Rohmer 1922, 14).[20] In other instances, loss of nuance took place only in Malay. A clergyman's insistence that "only One may deter my going" (Rohmer 2008, 41) was literally translated in Malay as "only one can prohibit me from going" (Tan 1925, 102),[21] apparently without noticing the sentence's religious connotations. In the Dutch translation, as in the English original, the use of a capital letter served to indicate that the reverend was talking about God (Rohmer 1922, 78).[22]

The politics of translating unfamiliar words adds another level of interest. Such terms as *dacoit, lascar,* and *thug* were left intact in the Dutch and the Malay translation alike, but were followed by an explanation when first introduced. Surprisingly accurate equivalents were found for "bacilli" (Dutch: *bacillen*), "dope-shop" (Dutch: *opiumkit,* or opium den), "phansigar" (Dutch: *godsdienstige worger,* or religious strangler), and "pseudogypsy" (Dutch: *pseudo-zigeunerin,* or female pseudo-gypsy), which Tan rendered into Malay as *koetoe-koetoe* (bugs), *petjandon* (opium den), *toekang tjekek* (strangler), and *zigeuner palsoe* (fake gypsy). Hokkien loanwords (see Table 1 in Appendix) were drawn from in a number of instances: *Pak Koen Thauw* for "Boxer" (Dutch: *Bokser*) and *thauwtjang* for "pigtail" (Dutch: *staart*). An example of a mistranslation is "hamadryads" (Dutch *hamadryaden,* or king cobras) into Malay as *semoet besar* (large ants). For a number of overly specific European terms, Tan opted for a more general Malay translation: "marmoset" (Dutch: *marmoset*) became *binatang* (animal), "oaten cakes" (Dutch: *gerstenkoekjes*) became *koewe* (cakes), "mastiff" (Dutch: *mastiff*) became *andjing* (dog), and "Assyrian hall" (Dutch: *Assyrische hall*) became *roeangan dalem* (inner room). This process of semantic broadening proved especially useful in translating the book's numerous ethnic references that would have made absolutely no sense to a Malay-literate readership. Hence, the "Dago seaman" (Dutch: *Dago-matroos*) became a *matroos* (sailor) and the "Yiddish theatrical bill" (Dutch: *Yiddish theaterbillet*) became *salembar soerat* (a piece of paper).

As the racism in *The Mystery of Dr. Fu-Manchu* was even more rampant than that of *De Dubbele Moord*, the tested strategy of "sanitising" unsavoury passages was used in extremely productive ways. Expressions of anti-Chinese sentiment in the source text ranged from dehumanising characterisations of Chinese people, including of their faulty English, to actual swearwords deployed against them by the story's Western protagonists.

Consider, for example, the following scene describing an invasion by Nayland Smith and Dr Petrie of a Chinese narcotics den. As the place is masqueraded as a barber shop, the story's protagonists encounter a Chinese employee who tells them that it is closed. In the original text, he does so in Pidgin English, serving as a confirmation of his portrayed otherness and inferiority. The passage is pervaded with racialised commentary ("simian," "squinting," "yellow scum"), both in the narrative voice and in dialogue. Already in Roldanus's Dutch translation, the Pidgin English was rendered into normally pronounced—yet still ungrammatical—Dutch, while the word "simian" was dropped. In Tan's Malay translation, none of the overt racism was kept in. The English original (left), the Dutch source text (centre), and the Malay target text (right) are juxtaposed below:

"No shavee—no shavee," he chattered, simian fashion, squinting from one to the other of us with his twinkling eyes. "Too late! Shuttee shop!"
"Don't you come none of it wi' me!" roared Smith, in a voice of amazing gruffness, and shook an artificially dirtied fist under the Chinaman's nose. "Get inside and gimme an' my mate a couple o' pipes. Smokee pipe, you yellow scum—savvy?" (Rohmer 2008, 29)

"No shaving—no shaving," he chattered, while he squinted with his twinkling eyes from one to the other of us both. "Too late! Shut shop!"
"That won't do with me!" roared Smith with an amazingly gruff voice while shaking an artificially dirtied fist under the nose of the Chinese. "Get inside and give me and my pal a pipe. Smoking opium, yellow scum—understood? (Rohmer 1922, 57)[23]

"I can't shave you! I can't shave you. It's already late, the shop is shutting down."
"That won't do to chase me away," shouted Smith with a theatrically gruff voice while sticking his fist, which he had deliberately dirtied, under the nose of the Chinese. "Get inside and give me and my friend a pipe. Smoking opium, understood?" (Tan 1925, 75)[24]

It is remarkable that the pidginised language of the barber was translated into perfectly grammatical sentences in the Malay target text. This conscious reworking implies a degree of equality between the Asian and the European character that was lacking in the source text. In doing so, Tan Tjin Kang confronted and rejected its colonial subtext. Furthermore, the above example does not stand in isolation. In other cases too, racist commentary was simply omitted from the Malay translation. The following excerpts juxtapose descriptions in the source text and the target text of, respectively, a South Asian dacoit, a Chinese assassin, and a Chinese assistant. Again, the gratuitous and dehumanising references to their race in the English and the Dutch versions are omitted in Tan's Malay rendition:

The dacoit swung himself below the window with the agility of an ape, as, with a dull, muffled thud, something dropped upon the carpet! (Rohmer 2008, 17; cf. 1922, 35)[25]

The dacoit threw something with high agility, and an object fell in the water container (Tan 1925, 42).[26]

"He probably has instructions to be merciful. But God help the victim of Chinese mercy!" (Rohmer 2008, 46; cf. 1922, 85)[27]

"Yes, I saw him; a squinting Cantonese he calls Kwee. I don't like him." (Rohmer 2008, 58; cf. 1922, 102)[29]

"It's possible that he was ordered to act mercifully." (Tan 1925, 112)[28]

"Yes, I saw him, somebody from Canton, who is named Kwee. I can't be comfortable seeing him." (Tan 1925, 135–6)[30]

The above passages again demonstrate how Tan Tjin Kang consciously de-racialised the source text. This is not to say that 1920s Malay lacked the resources to accurately translate such racialised descriptions. A relatively small number of sentences in which racism was directed to non-Chinese people were left intact in the target text, including "Something born in a plague-spot of Burma—the home of much that is unclean and much that is inexplicable" (Rohmer 1922, 147; Tan 1925, 194)[31] and "He rang the bell beside the door. Almost immediately it was opened by a negro woman—gross, hideously ugly" (Rohmer 1922, 182; Tan 1925, 241–2).[32] Rohmer's much-quoted description of Fu-Manchu, too, was translated into Malay with relative accuracy. This famous passage occurred early on in the novel, when Nayland Smith first alerted Dr Petrie to his existence, after they had witnessed the antagonist's most recent murder victim. As with such epithets as "sibilant" (Dutch: *sissend*), "squinting" (Dutch: *loensch*), "guttural" (Dutch: *keelachtig*), and "wolfish" (Dutch: *wolfachtig*) elsewhere in the book, adjectives employed to dehumanise the story's Asian characters—such as "feline" (Dutch: *katachtig*) and "awful being" (Dutch: *verschrikkelijk wezen*) in the passage below—never made it into the Malay translation. At the same time, the descriptions of Fu-Manchu's power, genius, and potential danger to the white establishment remained intact:

"Imagine a person, tall, lean and feline, high-shouldered, with a brow like Shakespeare and a face like Satan, a close-shaven skull, and long, magnetic eyes of the true cat-green. Invest him with all the cruel cunning of an entire Eastern race, accumulated in one giant intellect, with all the resources of science past and present, with all the resources, if you will, of a wealthy government—which, however, already has denied all knowledge of his existence. Imagine that awful being, and you have a mental picture of Dr. Fu-Manchu, the yellow peril incarnate in one man." (Rohmer 2008, 13; cf. 1922, 27–8)[33]

"Picture before your eyes: a person, tall but lean, high-shouldered, with a brow like Shakespeare and a face like Satan, his head shaved bald, and long eyes shining green like the eyes of a cat. Give him the evil cunningness of an Eastern race, accumulated in one body with much intelligence, which constitutes the source of old and new knowledge, with the resources of a rich country—which, however, has denied knowing that such a person exists. Picture this portrait before your eyes, and you know the personality of Dr. Fu-Manchu, the "Yellow peril" gathered together in one body." (Tan 1925, 32)[34]

Thus far, all the above passages were directly relevant to the storyline. At numerous points, however, the original book wanders into lengthy digressions describing the otherness of the Orient, not unlike the work of Ritter. For Rohmer, these include exoticised descriptions of Karamaneh's beauty, the evil genius of Fu-Manchu, and the implied superiority of the West. Possibly the most notorious example in the latter category is the following passage, describing a murder scene caused by Fu-Manchu's henchmen, where suddenly an "exotic perfume" could be smelled:

> It was a breath of the East—that stretched out a yellow hand to the West. It was symbolic of the subtle, intangible power manifested in Dr. Fu-Manchu, as Nayland Smith—lean, agile, bronzed with the suns of Burma, was symbolic of the clean British efficiency which sought to combat the insidious enemy.
> (Rohmer 2008, 64; cf. 1922, 111)[35]

Almost all such passages were left intact in the Dutch translation, but omitted in the Malay one, making a connection with the growing anti-colonial sentiments among Indonesia's Malay-literate readership nearly inescapable. Not only would few people have purchased a book that depicted their race as inferior to Europeans, the uncritical translation of such passages into the Malay vernacular would have probably sparked outrage by the 1920s.

Tan's methods of deracialising *The Mystery of Dr. Fu-Manchu* are comparable to those applied by Kommer, although the former stuck closer to the original text. The intended effects, however, were probably different. Kommer omitted anything that may have deterred (potential) readers from buying this book, seemingly driven by desire for profit maximisation combined with a genuine affinity with Indonesia's non-European populations. It is tempting to read Tan Tjin Kang's translation within the context of its social milieu and time—which was characterised by growing anti-colonial sentiments and pan-Chinese chauvinism. Why would a Chinese-owned printing press facilitate the translation of a story in which a Chinese arch-villain plots to overthrow the Western world? As has been speculated in passing, "[i]n the colonial context and seen from the perspective of the colonized, this creation might have appeared as the hero of decolonization, or at least as the fulfiller of vengeful fantasies" (Jedamski 2014, 234). Such a theory becomes considerably more attractive upon considering that most of Fu-Manchu's negative characteristics were left out in the Malay translation. Whereas Rohmer's original as well as Roldanus's Dutch translation systematically link the antagonist's bad habits to his race, authors of Malay literature had for decades circumvented racialised descriptions in their translated works. What was gained, as a result, in translating the novel into Malay was a more compelling, possibly even heroic portrayal of the fictional character Fu-Manchu—and by extension of an increasingly self-confident anti-colonial China—in the eyes of readers with no knowledge of (or interest in) the source text. Along similar lines, a number of Malay short stories in 1935 featured the courageous "Dr. Führman Chu," whose name was clearly inspired by that of Fu-Manchu (Chandra 2016, 46–7; Salmon 1981, 165). The image of Fu-Manchu wreaking havoc on the Western world, then, must be seen as part of a "retaliatory discourse" (cf. Torres-Saillant 2003, 281) that taps into contemporaneous notions of pan-Chinese pride, chauvinism, and—indeed—a reproach of white supremacy.

The Malay translations of both *De Dubbele Moord* and *The Mystery of Dr. Fu-Manchu* demonstrate how racially charged passages were deliberately reworked or circumvented to render Western stories palatable to local audiences. It remains unclear, however, whether race *specifically* served as a criterion for omission, or formed part of a larger set of phenomena deemed undesirable for Asian preferences, including religious moralistic digressions and Eurocentric descriptions that would have been obvious if not irrelevant for Indies-bred readers. It is crucial, therefore, to also investigate the translational politics of Western stories dealing with race without overtly expressing or subliminally hinting at Western superiority. The most prominent example I have found in this category is the Malay translation of *My Chinese Marriage*. What happened with stories that addressed race without constantly resorting to stereotypes of Asians or implying their inferiority?

Talking about race, the good way?

My Chinese Marriage is the autobiographical story of Mae Munro Watkins (c.1890–1926), a white student from Ann Arbor, who defied the expectations of family, friends, in-laws, and meddlesome strangers by marrying her Chinese college friend Tiam Hock Franking (Huang Tianfu) in 1912. The book has received considerable attention in the fields of Chinese-American Studies and Mixed-Race Studies (Bieler 2015; Teng 2013; Ye 2001). It recounts how the couple met at the University of Michigan, how they moved to Shanghai in the wake of their controversy-riddled marriage in the US, how they raised their children in China, and how they eventually reconciled with Tiam Hock's parents, who had stopped paying for their son's tuition after finding out he was seeing an American girl (M.T.F. and Porter 1991). Sadly, this remarkable interracial marriage was not destined for a long life. Tiam Hock passed away in 1919, at the young age of twenty-nine, upon returning to the US to accept a prestigious position in San Francisco. Mae Watkins died in Ann Arbor in 1926, leaving three children (Bieler 2015, 140).

Two years after Tiam Hock's untimely passing, *My Chinese Marriage* came out in print. Mae Watkins's saccharine and heart-warming account had been ghost-written by Katherine Anne Porter (1890–1980), who would later become a famous journalist. It was published in four parts in the magazine *Asia: The American Magazine on the Orient*, and in book form one year later in 1922. Given the extreme controversy surrounding interracial marriages in the US and this specific one in particular, the story was published under the pseudonym M.T.F., whereas Tiam Hock's name was changed to Chan-King (M.T.F. and Porter 1991). His precise regional origins (Amoy) were likewise left unspecified, as was anything remotely to do with sexuality. In contrast to the anger and controversy *My Chinese Marriage* generated in white American circles, the book was extremely popular among Chinese-American students (Teng 2013, 73–4). A Chinese translation by Han Song and the well-known journalist Zou Taofen appeared in 1932 (Han Song and Zou 1932; cf. Teng 2013, 276 n. 77). Interestingly, and not to my knowledge pointed out in the wider literature, an anonymously authored translation in Malay existed ten years earlier. It appeared in 1922, the very year that *My Chinese Marriage* came out in book form in the US.

This Malay version—*Akoe poenja Pernikahan dengen Saorang Tionghoa* (My Marriage with a Chinese)—was anonymously published in Batavia by the printing house *Sin Po*, which was also known for its aforementioned pro-Chinese newspaper under the same name. The type of Malay used in the target text, and the political orientation of its publisher, would suggest that the anonymous author-translator was of Chinese origins. Like *The Mystery of Dr. Fu-Manchu*, but unlike *De Dubbele Moord*, this story was translated in a relatively literal way. The book's three-page introduction first clarifies that it tells the true story of a female author only known as "M.T.F." This short clarification is followed by a translation into Malay of a very positive review of the source text originally published in *The Chinese Students' Monthly* (Tow 1921), to which the Batavia-based author apparently had access. The quoted reviewer of the English original can be identified as Julius Su Tow, then working as a secretary of the Chinese Consulate-General in New York (cf. Moon 2004, 165). The introduction of *Akoe poenja Pernikahan* was concluded by a succinct editorial note: "We feel that further praise and discussions are unnecessary. We simply hope that this story will become a topic of conversation for all its readers" (1922, 5).[36] This goal seems to have been achieved; even a decade later, the Malay translation was still being sold. It was advertised in the newspaper *Sin Po* with the following words: "A beautiful and interesting story. How love shapes destiny, causing an American girl to marry a Chinese and live happily ever after, etc., etc. The entire book can be bought for 1.75 guilders in Batavia's well-known shops" (Figure 6.4).

As *My Chinese Marriage* was not punctuated by lengthy, Eurocentric digressions contrasting the East to the West, *Akoe poenja Pernikahan* was an almost word-for-word translation into Malay with no deliberate omissions. The original work consists of 169 pages, the translation of 140. The book's translator[37] was generally well-equipped to find Malay equivalents for the Asianised English of those days, including *baboe* (maid-servant) for "amah" (nursemaid), *koetsir* (coachman) for "mafoo" (stable boy), *gang* (street of residential houses) for "li" (lane between buildings), and *perdjamoean* (banquet) for "tiffin" (light meal). Even more so than the previous two translated stories, Hokkien loanwords were richly drawn from. This was especially the

120 Tom G. Hoogervorst

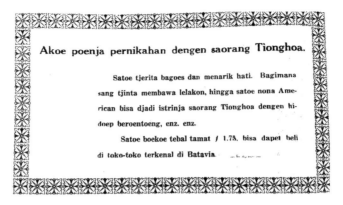

Figure 6.4 1932 advertisement of Akoe poenja Pernikahan.
Source: KITLV Collection, Leiden University Library.

case in the second part of the story set in China, which contains numerous specialised loanwords such as *hengdjin* (almonds), *kayloa* (mustard), *kwatji* (melon seeds), *langtjia* (rickshaw), *taotjioh* (catsup), *tesi* (spoon), *tjap tjaij* (chop suey), and *tjimtjeh* (courtyard) (see Table 1 in Appendix). The Malay translation also features the Mandarin word *San Chiao*, where the source text has "Three Religions" (Buddhism, Confucianism, and Daoism). In contrast to Kommer's occasional use of Hokkien loanwords to maintain authenticity while still ensuring accessibility for non-Chinese readers, the Malay translation of *My Chinese Marriage* was so evidently aimed at Chinese-Indonesian audiences that its usage of Hokkienisms—presumably incomprehensible to non-Chinese readers—would have augmented rather than hindered its success.

A number of Dutch loanwords likewise served to translate concepts in the source text for which no Malay words existed, including *avontuur* (adventure), *conservatief* (conservative), *Internationaal Concessie* (International Settlement), *liberaal* (liberal), and *zenuwachtig* (nervous). In other instances, short Malay descriptions replaced unfamiliar English terms: *melanggar prikawarasan* (violating healthiness) for "unhygienic," *penjakit jang bakerdja di paroe* (a disease that affects the lungs) for "phthisis," and *tersepoeh Timoer* (tempered by the East) for "thoroughly orientalised." As in *The Mystery of Dr. Fu-Manchu*, we also find examples of semantic broadening to circumvent over-specific and therefore hard-to-translate concepts, e.g., *andjing item* (black dogs) for "chow-dogs" and *itoe masa* (that time) for "that fall." In a small number of instances, the translator appears to have misread the English original, causing—one would imagine—confused looks among the readers. So, in the Malay version, Chan-King was said to have quickly made friends with the protagonist's father and mother "with true Chinese difference" (*perbedahan Tionghoa jang toelen*) instead of "true Chinese deference," whereas China was curiously likened to "a wise, wide old woman" (*nene-nene jang tjerdik dan loeas*) instead of "a wise, wise old woman." In other instances, the English was translated in so literal a fashion that it may not have made much sense to readers with limited access to European languages, as in *form dari logic* (a form of logic), *sanget mystic* (the most mystic), and *zonder prejudices* (without prejudices).

Pidgin English also features in *Akoe poenja Pernikahan*, but its function is completely different from what has been discussed in the previous section. Whereas the faulty English of Fu-Manchu's henchmen served to highlight their otherness and fault of character, in *My Chinese Marriage* it was used affectionately by the couple's household personnel, with whom the protagonist grew increasingly intimate. The Pidgin English phrases were left intact in the Malay translation, but unlike in the original, they were followed by a translation into grammatically correct Malay: "He all time go to see—all time come to see ('People may visit each other at any time—and receive visits at any time')" (*Akoe poenja Pernikahan* 1922, 56)[38] and "Missee sabe master have got one mother? ('Madam, does the master still have a mother?')" (*Akoe poenja Pernikahan* 1922, 73).[39] As one would suspect, authors and journalists working for *Sin Po* were well aware of the language hierarchies in British colonies and the low status of Pidgin English. For example, the newspaper once published a well-known anecdote in which the Chinese statesman Dr Wellington Koo (1888–1985) was patronisingly addressed in Pidgin English by a European lady, after which he astonished and embarrassed her with his spotless Oxford English ("De 'Chineesch' die geen Engelsch sprak" 1938). By translating the Pidgin English of *My Chinese Marriage* into grammatical Malay, while also leaving the original phrases intact, *Akoe poenja Pernikahan* reassured its readers that proficiency in European languages was not to be seen as a yardstick of civilisation, nor Chinese-affected English as something worthy of derision. Doing so marked a clear contrast with contemporaneous (and subsequent) European fiction and its insistent portrayal of Chinese and other Asians as linguistically inadequate.

My Chinese Marriage was overall positive towards Chinese people, so that its translator did not feel the need to "clean up" its racially charged passages. In the same way that the Pidgin English phrases were left intact, the protagonist's self-reflexive commentary on her initial prejudices against Chinese people—as well as those of others in her environment—were translated without the strategic omissions seen in the previous two stories. As the original manuscript of Watkins's story is now lost, it is unclear whether the following extracts reflect Mae Watkins's own thoughts on Chan-King or the interpolations of her ghost writer Katherine Anne Porter:

The progress of my interest in him was gradual and founded on a sense of his complete remoteness, an utter failure to regard him as a human being like the rest of us. He was the first of his race I had ever seen. (M.T.F. 1922, 5)	I grew fond of him in a very gradual way, and my fondness was founded on my feeling of being completely isolated from him. I was absolutely incapable of seeing him as a human being like the rest of us. He was the first of the Chinese race I had ever seen. (*Akoe poenja Pernikahan* 1922, 10)[40]

I remember being uneasy for fear of wounding him by some thoughtless remark that would reveal my true state of mind about China. I lost sight of the race in the individual. (M.T.F. 1922, 6)	I remember feeling uneasy out of fear that I had made him uncomfortable with my thoughtless remarks revealing the state of my sentiments on China. Because of one person, race became invisible to my eyes. (*Akoe poenja Pernikahan* 1922, 11)[41]
An American woman asked me, when he was about six weeks old, if I did not feel a sense of alienation at the sight of the wee, oriental face at my breast. Quite simply and truthfully I answered, no. My husband was not in any way alien to me. How then, could our child be so? (M.T.F. 1922, 99)	When the baby was about six weeks old, an American woman asked me if I didn't feel alien at the sight of the baby's oriental face at my breast. Simply and truthfully, I answered, no. Not even my husband I experienced as alien; so how could I feel that way about our own child? (*Akoe poenja Pernikahan* 1922, 84)[42]

The almost literal Malay translation of *My Chinese Marriage* demonstrates that the omission of racially charged passages in Western literature was a conscious choice rather than a rigidly applied convention. The Malay language lacked neither the vocabulary nor the linguistic resources to accurately translate Dutch or English parlance about race and ethnicity. Malay-language translators simply omitted what they deemed would upset or annoy their targeted readership, yet whenever Asians were described in positive or neutral terms, they felt no need to make "improvements" to the source text. The sharp (and redundant) racialised edges, in other words, were trimmed off, and when these were absent in the first place, Malay translations stuck increasingly close to the original. It furthermore speaks volumes that a Western story depicting Chinese people in a positive light was translated into Malay in less than a year after its original publication. To the best of my knowledge, the English original was never translated into Dutch or any other European language. Its Malay translation, *Akoe poenja Pernikahan dengen Saorang Tionghoa*, clearly served to endorse China (and its people)—in this instance through the eyes of a highly educated American—as a nation that deserves to be respected and admired. It is equally revealing that a novel titled *Nona Olanda sebagi Istri Tionghoa* (A Dutch Woman as a Chinese Wife) appeared three years afterwards. Written by Njoo Cheong Seng (1925), this work of fiction centres on the relationship between a Chinese man and a Dutch woman in Surabaya (Maier 2004, 197–200; Siegel 1997, 269) and may have been inspired by *Akoe poenja Pernikahan*. Both texts are best regarded as conscious expressions of pan-Chinese nationalism and self-redefinition, which by then had become a global trend (Karl 2002).

Concluding remarks

One frequently hears, typically from the upper echelons of today's power hierarchies, that racism in Western literature should be assessed by the standards of its time. This study has demonstrated that, even in colonial times, racially charged formulations in Western novels were actively rejected by their Asian consumers. A disproportionate number of Malay author-translators were of Chinese or Eurasian origins. Leveraging between and having access to multiple cultures, they had the power and responsibility to filter knowledge across ethnolinguistic boundaries. They consciously de-racialised Western stories in order to ensure a satisfied clientele, yet such strategic reworkings led to more than just financial gain. The three translated stories discussed here demonstrate that translation was also politically motivated. It served to subvert the colony's hierarchies of epistemic authority through deliberate attempts to "de-Europeanise" the narratives. As a consequence, translation into Malay rendered mass literature more palatable to a forward-looking, ethnically heterogeneous readership with access to vernacular but not necessarily European discourses. As time went by, translations became increasingly "respectful" to their source texts, yet hardly less critical to their contents. Author-translators felt little compulsion to faithfully translate anything deemed undesirable by their targeted readers, and notions of copyright remained somewhat fluid throughout the colonial period. Their selectively diminished fidelity to the source text, then, reflected the priorities of profit maximisation and ideological zeal.

The author-translators—one Eurasian, one Chinese, and one anonymous but presumably also Chinese—of three vastly different literary works, set in different continents, and featuring characters of different regional and racial origins, shared the same facility to use language creatively in order to make the source texts locally acceptable. The most productive linguistic strategies to do so were strategic omission and semantic broadening. In doing so, none of them became particularly rich or widely known; they simply responded to society's demands. The hybrid Malay idiom of late-colonial Indonesia, with its inherent tendency to adopt vocabulary from Dutch and Chinese, proved sufficient for them to translate even the most peculiar Dutch and English word arrangements, despite a small number of mistranslations and other errors. It is interesting to repeat that even the Eurasian writer Herman Kommer used a number of Chinese loanwords in his Malay. While the author clearly aimed to set his story in a Chinese milieu, this choice also illustrates the linguistic competencies of his multi-ethnic readers, who would have appreciated his eye for authenticity. But even without borrowing from Dutch or Chinese, the early twentieth-century Malay language could facilitate a discourse on race and ethnicity without resorting to constructions and formulations deemed artificial by its readers. Whenever phrases were selectively abridged or passages were omitted, extra-linguistic considerations were at play. Gratuitous expressions of racism and other ways of invalidating Asian people—including under the guise of humour, poetry, defective language skills, and verbal abuse—rarely found entry in their Malay translations unless they were absolutely crucial to the storyline. The use of Malay, hence, proved a powerful act of defiance, challenging the colonial hegemony over literary discourses and "received" wisdom.

This invites a more nuanced understanding of translational politics in colonial contexts. How colonial were the activities of author-translators from liminal groups, who could claim to be fully part of neither the colonising elites nor the colonised masses? Herman Kommer's European ancestry granted him employment for the colonial administration, during which he was able to hone the literary skills that would later become his livelihood. And yet, this particular career path alienated him—a Eurasian who preferred the company of non-Europeans—from the Dutch elites in ways that people further removed from the centres of power could not have experienced. He died in poverty and in voluntary isolation from Surabaya's European community, yet he did not "go native"; Indonesia had always been a part of him, regardless of the advantages conferred upon him by his racial make-up. The lives of the two Chinese-descended author-translators were considerably less documented. It is significant that they both worked for *Sin Po*, which would have situated them ideologically in the anti-colonial, pro-Chinese movement. This is clear from the books they chose to translate, as well as the way they translated them. Cumulatively, none of the authors discussed in this paper were specifically preoccupied with the political project of Indonesia's independence from the Netherlands, nor did they state anywhere that colonialism as a system was reprehensible. What they did was more subtle, and only possible through the plurilingual competencies that came with their in-betweeness. They expropriated Western literature, offering its authors neither credit nor apology, and transformed these texts to suffice the demand of the masses: to enjoy popular stories *on* their own terms and *in* their own terms. Such translations encoded a different set of possibilities, in which the Asian was appreciated rather than underestimated, and respected rather than ridiculed. Therein rested their true power.

Appendix
Chinese words and names used in this study

Table 1 Chinese words

Attestation	Characters	Meaning
Djingge	二［曰雅女］	Second-ranked concubine
Entjim	阿嬸	Mother
Hengdjin	杏仁	Almonds
Kayloa	芥辣	Mustard
Kwatji	瓜子	Melon seeds
Langtjia	人車	Rickshaw
Li	里	Lane between buildings
Mafoo	馬伕	Coachman
Pak Koen Thauw	打拳道	Boxer
San Chiao	三教	The three religions
Sinké	新客	China-born immigrant
Taotjioh	豆醬	Catsup
Tesi	茶匙	Spoon
Thauwtjang	頭鬃	Queue
Tjap tjaij	雜菜	Chop suey
Tjimtjeh	深井	Courtyard

Table 2 Chinese names

Ang Sioe Tjing	翁秀清
Gouw Peng Liang	吳炳亮
Han Song	寒松
Huang Tianfu	黃添福
Kwee Kek Beng	郭克明
Kwee Tek Hoay	郭德懷
Lie Kim Hok	李金福
Njoo Cheong Seng	楊章生
Sin Po	新報
Tan Tjin Kang	陳秦江
Tio Ie Soei	趙雨水
Zou Taofen	鄒韜奮

Notes

1 *Satoe tjerita iang amat loetjoe, indah dan ramei dan iang betoel soedah kadjadian kira kira saratoes taon laloeh di tanah Djawa Koelon.* All translations in this chapter are mine.
2 *[. . .] een dier, in uitgestrektheid menig Duitsch vorstendom evenarende, landerijen [. . .].*
3 *[. . .] omstuwd van eene reeks Chinesche beeldjes, die wel onder de gedrogtelijksten gerangschikt konden worden.*
4 *[. . .] hoezeer hare schoonheid niet in den smaak van Europeanen kon vallen en dat stijve, koude en uitdrukkingslooze op het gelaat vertoonde.*
5 *[. . .] wie nagaat, hoe koud, koel en onverschillig, ten minste uiterlijk, een inlander is zelfs in de belangrijkste zaken en omstandigheden, kan het niet verbazen, dat niet de minste trek op haar gelaat, haar moorddadig voornemen en hare wraakzuchtige plannen verried.*
6 *[Tan Happon] was een Sinké en scheen met zijn goede vijftig jaren, grooten knijpbril op den neus, tranende oogen, vuile aangestokene tanden en vergrijsden staart [. . .] juist geen aanlokkende partij voor onze zestienjarige, bloeijende maagd te zijn, doch zoo veel te meer voor hare ouders, enkel om den wille van den bruidschat.*
7 *Kerna begitoe ia inilah iang di trima lamarannja, maskipoen sinsang Tan Hap Pon oemoernja soedah ampir anem poeloeh taon. Tautjangnja iang pendek itoe soedah poetih dan giginja soedah banjak iang hilang, maka ia tiada sekali pantes aken djadi soeaminja Kong Hong Nio iang masi moeda dan amat elok serta tjahajanja poen gilang goemilang sebagei boelan poernama ampat belas hari.*
8 *Maar het was niettemin bepaald, misschien wel in den hemel der Chinezen, als zij er een hebben, dat zij nog eens Hijmens juk zou dragen.*
9 *Voor dat keeltoeknijpen is het volk niet bang, en een ferme krissteek of het hoofd afslaan zou meer vrees inboezemen, want zonder kop durft niemand in het paradijs voor den profeet te verschijnen.*
10 *"Ik houde te veel van u en heb te groote verpligting aan u, om niet opregt en hartelijk uw eeuwig heil te wenschen en uwe schoone ziel te behouden. Gij kent God niet en wat zijn uwe ellendige goden te vergelijken bij den Eenige, bij mijn God?—Wat uwe afgodenoffers bij onze gebeden tot Hem en onzen Profeet. Gij weet niet, Nonja!"*
11 *"Sajang sekali, njonja ada sa-orang iang amat baik boedi tiada mengenal pada Toehan Allah dan Nabi Mohamad. Njona tiada taoe. . ."*
12 *"Zwijg van en denk niet meer aan hem, maar zweer hier op dit graf, bij al wat u dierbaar is, bij uwen profeet – het zij zoo, daar gij Islams toch altijd op hem pocht – bij de schim uwer moeder—leeft zij nog?," "Neen, zij is dood, Baba!," "Zweer, zeg ik u, bij den geest uwer moeder, dat gij uw man vergeten en mij uw gansche leven lang liefhebben, volgen en immer trouw wezen zult—zweer!"*
13 *"Djangan angkau seboet lagi soeamimoe itoe, di sini di atas ini koeboer, angkau moesti soempah, iang angkau maoe loepa soeamimoe, dan aken toeroet dengen setia padakoe."*
14 *Wie op een schoone vrouw vertrouwt, heeft al zijn hoop op zand gebouwd.*
15 *Misschien heeft hij ze hier boven nu reeds afgedaan.*
16 *"Apabila betoel kau pertjaja ada noraka, maka di sanalah akoe nanti bajar padamoe itoe oewang!"*
17 *"En als u het goed vindt, zullen we na het diner die vreeselijke dingen verder bespreken."*
18 *"[. . .] djika kaoe soeka, sesoedahnja bersantap nanti kita bitjaraken itoe semoea."*
19 *"Sir Crichton ada djadi boedak cocaine, tapi ada tanda-tanda jang bertentangan dengen tanda dari ratjoen cocaine."*
20 *"Sir Crichton was verslaafd aan cocaïne, doch er zijn aanwijzingen, die in strijd zijn met cocaïnevergiftiging."*

21 *"Tjoema satoe sadja bisa melarang akoe pergi."*
22 *"Slechts Één kan mij beletten te gaan."*
23 *"Niet scheren—niet scheren,"* wauwelde hij, terwijl hij met zijn schitterende oogen schuin van den een naar den ander van ons beiden keek. *"Te laat! Sluiten winkel!" "Daarmee kom je met mij niet verder!"* brulde Smith met een verbazingwekkend grove stem en hij schudde een kunstmatig vuil gemaakte vuist onder den neus van den Chinees. *"Ga naar binnen en geef mij en mijn kameraad een pijp. Opium schuiven, gele vuilik – begrepen?"*
24 *"Tida bisa tjoekoer! Tida bisa tjoekoer. Soeda laat, toko bakal toetoep." "Dengen begitoe kaoe tida bisa oesir akoe,"* treak Smith dengen soeara kasar jang dibikin-bikin sedeng ia tondjolken ia poenja kepelan jang sengadja dibikin mesoem di bawah idoengnja itoe orang Tionghoa. *"Ajo masoek dan kasi akoe dan akoe poenja kawan satoe tjangklong. Isep tjandoe, mengarti?"*
25 *De dacoit slingerde zich met de behendigheid van een aap onder het raam, terwijl met een doffen plof iets op het karpet viel.*
26 *Itoe dacoit lempar apa-apa dengen pandei sekali, dan satoe barang djatoh ditempat aer.*
27 *Hij heeft waarschijnlijk instructies om genadig te zijn. Maar God moge het slachtoffer van Chineesche genade bijstaan!*
28 *"Boleh djadi ia dapet prentah boeat berlakoe moerah."*
29 *"Ja, ik heb hem gezien; een loenschen Cantonees, dien hij Kwee noemt. Ik mag hem niet."*
30 *"Ja, akoe soeda liat ia, satoe orang dari Canton, jang dinamaken Kwee. Akoe tida bisa seneng meliat ia."*
31 *"Iets, geboren in een peststreek van Burma – het tehuis van veel, dat onrein, en van veel, dat onverklaarbaar is"* (Rohmer 1922, 147); *"Satoe hal jang terlahir di sarang pest di Burma, tempat banjak kakotoran dan banjak tida bisa dibikin terang"* (Tan 1925, 194).
32 *Hij trok aan de bel naast de deur. Bijna onmiddellijk werd die geopend door een zware, afschuwelijk leelijke negerin* (Rohmer 1922, 182); *Ia tarik tali lontjeng dan lekas sekali pintoe diboeka oleh saorang prempoean neger jang djelek sekali* (Tan 1925, 241–2).
33 *"Stel je iemand voor, groot, slank en katachtig, hooggeschouderd, met een voorhoofd als Shakespeare en een gezicht als Satan, een bijna geheel kaal geschoren schedel en langwerpige magnetische oogen van het echte kattengroen. Geef hem al de wreede geslepenheid van een geheel Oostersch ras, samengebracht in een reusachtig intellect, al de hulpbronnen van vroegere en tegenwoordige wetenschap, al de hulpbronnen, als je wilt, van een rijke regeering—die echter reeds ontkend heeft iets van zijn bestaan af te weten. Stel je dat verschrikkelijk wezen voor en je hebt een geestelijk portret van dr. Fu-Manchu, het gele gevaar belichaamd in een man."*
34 *Bajangkenlah didepan mata: saorang jang tinggi tapi langsing, poendaknja tinggi, dengen djidat seperti Shakespeare dan moeka seperti setan, kepala jang ditjoekoer botak, dan matanja pandjang dan bersinar idjo seperti matanja koetjing. Kasilah katjerdikan jang djahat dari satoe bangsa Timoer, terkoempoel dalem satoe badan jang mempoenjai banjak kapinteran, jang djadi soember dari pengatahoean koeno dan baroe, soember pertoeloengan boeat satoe negri jang kaja, tapi jang sangkal ada taoe, tentang adanja saorang begitoe. Bajangkenlah itoe portret didepan mata, dan kaoe djadi taoe matjemnja Dr. Fu-Manchu, "bahaja Koening" tergenggam dalem satoe badan.*
35 *Het was een ademtocht van het Oosten, dat een gele hand uitstak naar het Westen. Het was een symbool van de subtiele, ontastbare kracht, zooals die zich manifesteerde in Dr. Fu-Manchu, evenals Nayland Smith—mager, behendig, gebruind door de zon van Burma—het symbool was der zuivere Britsche kracht, die den geniepigen vijand trachtte te bestrijden.*

36 *Poedjian dan pemandangan jang lebi djaoe kita rasa blon perloe. Kita harep sadja ini tjerita nanti bisa mendjadi bahan boeat omong-omong bagi sekalian pembatja.*
37 Unlike the previous two stories, the translation of *Akoe poenja Pernikahan* is done in so literal a fashion that "author-translator" would not be the right term here.
38 *"Sembarang waktoe orang pegi mengoendjoengin—sembarang waktoe orang dikoendjoengin."*
39 *"Njonja, apa toean masih ada poenja iboe?"* Perhaps a better translation of the last sentence would have been "Does madam know that the master still has a mother?".
40 *Dengen tjara jang lambat sekali akoe djadi ada poenja soeka padanja, bagitoe djoega akoe poenja kasoekahan berdasar atas perasahan jang akoe ada terpisah sanget djaoe dari ianja. Sama sekali akoe tida bisa pandang ia sebagi satoe menoesia jang sama dengan jang laen-laen antara kita. Ia ada bangsa Tionghoa jang pertama akoe dapet liat.*
41 *Akoe inget jang akoe pernah merasa tida enak kerna koeatir akoe soeda bikin ia tida senang dengen oetjap-oetjapan jang tida dipikir doeloe dan jang mengoendjoek sikepnja akoe poenja perasahan pada Tiongkok. Lantaran satoe orang kebangsahan djadi tida keliatan oleh matakoe.*
42 *Koetika itoe anak beroesia kira-kira anem minggoe, satoe prampoean Amerika menanja kaloe akoe tida merasa asing meliat itoe anak baji jang moekanja model Timoer di dadakoe. Dengen tjara saderhana dan dengen sadjoedjoernja, akoe djawab, tida. Sedeng soeamikoe akoe tida rasaken asing; tjara bagimana kita poenja anak sendiri akoe bisa rasaken demikian?*

References

Adam, Ahmat. 1987. "Golongan Peranakan (Indo dan Tionghoa) dan Perkembangan Bahasa Melayu Rendah di Indonesia menjelang 1900." In *Sastera Melayu dan Tradisi Kosmopolitan: Kertas Kerja Hari Sastera '85*, 32–50. Kuala Lumpur: Dewan Bahasa dan Pustaka.

———. 1995. *The Vernacular Press and the Emergence of Modern Indonesian Consciousness (1855–1913)*. Ithaca, NY: Cornell University Press.

Akoe poenja Pernikahan dengan Saorang Tionghoa. 1922. Batavia: Sin Po.

Arens, Koos. 1999. "Het Onverslijtbaar Kleed: Over de Verhalen van W.L. Ritter (1799–1862)." *Indische Letteren* 14, no. 1: 31–50.

Asad, Talal. 1992. "The Concept of Cultural Translation in British Social Anthropology." In *The Poetics and Politics of Ethnography*, edited by James Clifford and George E. Marcus, 141–64. Berkeley: University of California Press.

Bassnett, Susan, and Harish Trivedi. 1999. "Introduction: Of Colonies, Cannibals and Vernaculars." In *Post-Colonial Translation: Theory and Practice*, edited by Susan Bassnett and Harish Trivedi, 1–18. London and New York: Routledge.

Berens, Jill. 1991. "De Indische Nederlander H. Kommer en zijn Maleise Verhalen." *Jambatan* 9, no. 2: 76–86.

Bieler, Stacey. (2004) 2015. *"Patriots or Traitors": A History of American Educated Chinese students*. 2nd ed. London and New York: Routledge.

Bloom, Clive. 1996. *Cult Fiction: Popular Reading and Pulp Theory*. Houndmills: Palgrave Macmillan.

Chandra, Elizabeth. 2011. "Women and Modernity: Reading the Femme Fatale in Early Twentieth-Century Indies Novels." *Indonesia* 92: 157–82.

———. 2016. "The Chinese Holmes: Translating Detective Fiction in Colonial Indonesia." *Keio Communication Review* 38: 39–63.

Chin, Grace V.S., and Tom Hoogervorst. 2017. "From *Soetji* to *Soendel*: Negotiating Race, Class and Gender in a Netherlands Indies Newspaper." *Intersections: Gender and Sexuality in Asia and the Pacific* 41. http://intersections.anu.edu.au/issue41/chin_hoogervorst1.pdf.
Cogan, Thomas J. 2002. "Western Images of Asia: Fu Manchu and the Yellow Peril." *Waseda Studies in Social Sciences* 3, no. 2: 37–64.
Cohen, Matthew Isaac. 2016. *Inventing the Performing Arts: Modernity and Tradition in Colonial Indonesia*. Honolulu: University of Hawai`i Press.
Coppel, Charles Antony. 2002. "Mestizo Society as an Imagined Community." In *Studying Ethnic Chinese in Indonesia*, 124–35. Singapore: Singapore Society of Asian Studies.
"De 'Chineesch' die geen Engelsch sprak." 1938. *Sin Po* 817: 32.
Dornseiffer, Sylvia I., and Jan ten Kate. 1991. "W.L. Ritter, Een Haarlemmer in de Oost." *Indische Letteren* 6, no. 2: 79–91.
Frayling, Christopher. 2014. *The Yellow Peril: Dr Fu Manchu and the Rise of Chinaphobia*. London: Thames & Hudson.
Greene, Naomi. 2014. *From Fu Manchu to Kung Fu Panda: Images of China in American Film*. Honolulu: University of Hawai`i Press.
Gupta, Prasenjit. 1998. "Post- or Neo-Colonial Translation? Linguistic Inequality and Translator's Resistance." *Translation and Literature* 7, no. 2: 170–93.
Han Song, and Zou Taofen. 1932. *Shēnghuó zhōukān dúzhĕ xìnxiāng wài jí: Dì 1 jí* (生活周刊讀者信箱外集: 第一輯). Shanghai: Shenghuo Shudian.
Hellwig, Tineke. 2002. "Scandals, Homicide in Batavia and Indo Identity: Literary Representations of Indies Society." *Archipel* 63: 153–72.
Hoogervorst, Tom. 2016. "Manliness in Sino-Malay Publications in the Netherlands Indies." *South East Asia Research* 24, no. 2: 283–307.
Hoogervorst, Tom., and Henk Schulte Nordholt. 2017. "Urban Middle Classes in Colonial Java (1900–1942): Images and Language." *Bijdragen tot de Taal-, Land- en Volkenkunde* 173, no. 4: 442–74.
Jedamski, Doris. 2014. "Translation in the Malay World: Different Communities, Different Agendas." In *Asian Translation Traditions*, edited by Eva Hung and Judy Wakabayashi, 211–45. Manchester: St. Jerome Publishing.
Karl, Rebecca E. 2002. *Staging the World: Chinese Nationalism at the Turn of the Twentieth Century*. Durham, NC and London: Duke University Press.
Keppy, Peter. 2008. "Keroncong, Concours and Crooners: Home Grown Entertainment in Early Twentieth-Century Batavia." In *Linking Destinies: Trade, Towns and Kin in Asian History*, edited by Peter Boomgaard, Dick Kooiman, and Henk Schulte Nordholt, 141–57. Leiden: KITLV Press.
Kommer, H. 1900. *Tjerita Njonja Koog Hong Nio: Satoe Toean Tanah di Babakan Afdeeling Tangerang, Betawi*. Batavia: W.P. Vasques.
Liem, Maya H.T. 2012. "A Bridge to the Outside World: Literary Translation in Indonesia, 1950–1965." In *Heirs to World Culture: Being Indonesian, 1950–1965*, edited by Jennifer Lindsay and Maya H.T. Liem, 163–190. Leiden: Brill.
M.T.F. 1922. *My Chinese Marriage*. New York: Duffield.
M.T.F., and Katherine Anne Porter. 1991. *My Chinese Marriage: An Annotated Edition*. Austin: University of Texas Press.
Mahdi, Waruno. 2006. "The Beginnings and Reorganization of the *Commissie voor de Volkslectuur* (1908–1920)." In *Insular Southeast Asia: Linguistic and Cultural*

Studies in Honour of Bernd Nothofer, edited by Fritz Schulze and Holger Warnk, 85–110. Wiesbaden: Harrassowitz Verlag.
Maier, Henk. 2004. *We Are Playing Relatives: A Survey of Malay Writing.* Singapore: ISEAS.
———. 2006. "Explosions in Semarang: Reading Malay tales in 1895." *Bijdragen tot de Taal-, Land- en Volkenkunde* 162, no. 1: 1–34.
Moon, Krystyn R. 2004. *Yellowface: Creating the Chinese in American Popular Music and Performance, 1850s–1920s.* New Brunswick, NJ: Rutgers University Press.
Niranjana, Tejaswini. 1992. *Siting Translation: History, Post-Structuralism, and the Colonial Context.* Berkeley: University of California Press.
Njoo, Cheong Seng. 1925. *Nona Olanda sebagi Istri Tionghoa.* Surabaya: Tan's Drukkery.
Pan, Lynn. 1990. *Sons of the Yellow Emperor: A History of the Chinese Diaspora.* Boston, MA: Little, Brown and Company.
Rafael, Vincente L. 1988. *Contracting Colonialism: Translation and Christian Conversion in Tagalog Society under Early Spanish Rule.* Ithaca, NY and London: Cornell University Press.
Ritter, W.L. 1855. "De dubbele moord." *Biäng-Lala* 4, no. 1: 162–235.
Rohmer, Sax. 1922. *Het Geheim van Dr. Fu-Manchu.* Meulenhoff: Amsterdam. Translated by W.J.A. Roldanus Jr.
———. (1913) 2008. *The Return of the Ultimate Villain Fu Manchu.* Sheffield: PJM Publishing. Collected by Phillip J. Morledge.
Sai, Siew-Min. 2016. "Mandarin Lessons: Modernity, Colonialism and Chinese Cultural Nationalism in the Dutch East Indies, c.1900s." *Inter-Asia Cultural Studies* 17, no. 3: 375–94. http://doi.org/10.1080/14649373.2016.1217635.
Salmon, Claudine. 1981. *Literature in Malay by the Chinese of Indonesia: A Provisional Annotated Bibliography.* Paris: Archipel.
Sengupta, Mahasweta. 1995. "Translation as Manipulation: The Power of Images and Images of Power." In *Between Languages and Cultures: Translation and Cross-Cultural Texts*, edited by Anuradha Dingwaney and Carol Maier, 159–74. Pittsburgh, PA and London: University of Pittsburgh Press.
Seshagiri, Urmila. 2006. "Modernity's (Yellow) Perils: Dr. Fu-Manchu and English Race Paranoia." *Cultural Critique* 62: 162–94.
Siegel, James T. 1997. *Fetish, Recognition, Revolution.* Princeton, NJ: Princeton University Press.
Shiraishi, Takashi. 1990. *An Age in Motion: Popular Radicalism in Java, 1912–1926.* Ithaca, NY and London: Cornell University Press.
Sol, Nicole. 1991. "Wilhelm Leonard Ritter (1799–1862): Een Europeaan in Nederlands-Indië." *Indische Letteren* 6, no. 1: 33–47.
Sutedja-Liem, Maya. 2007. *De Njai: Moeder van alle Volken. 'De roos uit Tjikembang' en Andere Verhalen.* Leiden: KITLV Press.
Tan, Tjin Kang. 1925. *Rasianja Dr. Fu-Manchu.* Surabaya: Ang Sioe Tjing.
Taylor, Antony. 2011. "'And I Am the God of Destruction!': Fu Manchu and the Construction of Asiatic Evil in the Novels of Arthur Sarsfield Ward, 1912–1939." In *Evil, Barbarism and Empire: Britain and Abroad, c.1830–2000*, edited by Tom Crook, Rebecca Gill, and Bertrand Taithe, 73–95. Houndmills: Palgrave Macmillan.

Teng, Emma Jinhua. 2013. *Eurasian: Mixed Identities in the United States, China, and Hong Kong, 1842–1943*. Berkeley: University of California Press.
Termorshuizen, Gerard. 2009. "De Slangengrot: Over Herman Kommer en Henri Carel Zentgraaff." *Indische Letteren* 24: 217–27.
Toer, Pramoedya Ananta. 1982. *Tempo Doeloe: Antologi Sastra Pra-Indonesia*. Jakarta: Hasta Mitra.
Torres-Saillant, Silvio. 2003. "Dominican Blackness and the Modern World." In *Perspectives on Las Americas: A Reader in Culture, History & Representation*, edited by Matthew C. Gutmann, Félix V. Matos Rodríguez, Lynn Stephen, and Patricia Zavella, 274–88. Malden: Blackwell.
Tow, J.S. 1921. "Book Review: My Chinese Marriage. By M.T.F. New York: Duffield & Co., 1921, $1.75." *The Chinese Students' Monthly* 17: 421–2.
Tymoczko, Maria. 1999. *Translation in a Postcolonial Context: Early Irish Literature in English Translation*. Manchester: St. Jerome Publishing.
Venuti, Lawrece. 2008. *The Translator's Invisibility: A History of Translation*, 2nd ed. London and New York: Routledge.
Yamashita, Shinji, James Siegel, and Noriaki Oshikawa. 1997. "Indonesian into Japanese: An Interview with Noriaki Oshikawa." *Indonesia* 64: 125–37.
Ye, Weili. 2001. *Seeking Modernity in China's Name: Chinese Students in the United States, 1900–1927*. Stanford, CA: Stanford University Press.

7 Translating Islam

Conversion and love in Bruneian fiction

Kathrina Mohd Daud

Introduction

The two Bruneian novels that this chapter will examine, Norsiah Gapar's *Pengabdian* (Submission 1987) and Aisha Malik's *Jewel* (2017), are strikingly similar in their depiction of cross-cultural romances in the context of Brunei Darussalam. Both novels feature romances in which one partner converts to Islam for the sake of the relationship, and an ideological commitment to the state-propagated national philosophy of *Melayu Islam Beraja* (Malay Islamic Monarchy), including prescriptive gender identities and roles. In particular, the nature of conversion and the version of Islam that the novels depict overlap in significant ways.

These similarities are striking for a number of reasons. First, the novels were written in two different languages, with *Pengabdian* in the national language of Malay and *Jewel* in the global lingua franca of English. As Kathrina Mohd Daud, G.V.S. Chin, and Maslin Jukim note in their history of the development of English- and Malay-language literature in Brunei, there is little evidence that the two literatures are "even aware of each other in any substantial way" (2016). On the contrary, in fact, it seems evident that the two literatures draw on different literary ancestries and influences. Second, the two novels were written thirty years apart within a literary landscape where there continues to be a paucity of production—to date, Bruneian writers have produced fewer than twenty novels in English, with the first published in 2009. While Malay-language literature has received more state support, its contemporary production continues to be minimal. However, while the literary landscape has not changed much, as a nation Brunei Darussalam has undergone significant infrastructural, social, and economic changes over the last thirty years since achieving independence in 1984, including weathering the Asian financial crisis of 1997, and the inevitable linguistic and social changes wrought by globalisation.

For all intents and purposes, these novels were written independently of each other. To arrive at the same point, therefore, one assumes that they had recourse to a shared literary genealogy. It is the contention of this chapter that this genealogy can be understood through Said Faiq's elucidation of the centripetal pressures of a global master discourse about Islam. Centripetal pressures, according to Norman Fairclough (1995), "follow from the need, in producing a text, to draw upon given conventions, of two main classes; a language, and an order of discourse—that is, a historically particular structuring of discursive (text-producing) practices" (7). Faiq (2004) uses this understanding of centripetal pressures on global literatures to contend that since "historically, the perception of the Arab and Islamic worlds has been regulated by *topos* (singular: *topoi*): primary stereotypes which constitute reservoirs of ideas and core images from which most representations [. . .] generate their specific discourse features" (39), translations of Arabic literature have been unable to escape the limiting and exoticising representational strategies of the West, thus creating a master discourse about Islam that reflects the West's dialectic of "attraction and repulsion" (Faiq 2004, 40) with the Arab/Islamic world, including Western-centric assumptions and knowledge productions about the Other that stand as signs of universalism and humanism (Faiq 2004, 41). Translations of Arabic literature, and knowledge about the Arab/Islamic world, are thus prevented from standing independently of this master discourse and must engage with these "familiar and established" (Faiq 2004, 42) strategies of stereotyping, signification, and power. Consequently, world and minor literatures also orbit around this master discourse, given the inevitable globalised processes of literary transmission and translation, and the historical and current dominance and centrism of Western knowledge production. In Southeast Asia where translation is a "foundational practice" (Ricci 2011, 14) of the Islamic literary networks in the region, particularly in producing the "Arabic cosmopolis" (Ricci 2011, 32), the relationship with the master discourse offers insight into how the two distinct Bruneian novels may have been mapped onto each other. Although the novels are not in conversation with each other within the context of Bruneian literature, they nonetheless draw on global ideas of Islam that have been mediated through regional Islamic literary networks.

These centripetal pressures have shaped, influenced, and dictated the evolution of the global Muslim novel, forcing a consistent return to the concerns of Orientalist and exotifying discourses, if only to reject, defy, and subvert them. This return, however, also creates commonalities of theme and trope that offer the reader a way of approaching and translating texts across cultures, as this chapter does in its examination of the "conversion for love" trope, a trope that is prevalent in global Muslim fiction as well as its local variant. Indeed, the relationship between conversion to Islam and translation is historically significant in Southeast Asia. Ronit Ricci notes that in Southeast Asia, "religious conversion gave rise to translation endeavors, and the products of these in turn encouraged further conversion" (2011, 188), and that

> conversion to Islam meant, in part, the translation of stories from Arabic or Persian into Tamil, Malay and Javanese [. . .] such translations

introduced those who became Muslim or who were potential converts to the terminology, beliefs, stories and rituals of a new religion, expressed in their own familiar idiom.

(2011, 214)

Indeed, the "absence of contemporary local Islamic sources for the earliest period of the spread of Islam" (Richard W. Bulliet in *Conversion to Islam in the Medieval Period*, 1979, quoted in Ricci 2011, 184) means that comparative study of fictional literary representations of conversion has become a familiar approach to understanding conversion to Islam.

Today, a recurrent conversion trope in global Muslim fiction is that of "conversion for love" in cross-cultural romance. Literary representations of cross-cultural romance are a natural nexus for considering issues of identity, a consistent concern as Muslim writers seek to carve out a space to resist the dominance of Islamophobic narratives that have historically been perpetuated by Western media (especially when many of these Muslim writers are from, or, of the West); or, as in the case of Brunei and Southeast Asia, subject to its dominance in the media. The negotiation of gendered cultural expectations as well as racial, ethnic, and national hierarchies (intra-Asian and Asian-Western) and religious sensibilities in fictional cross-cultural romances throws into relief the fault-lines and clash-points of identity. The translation of this global trope into local contexts not only highlights the distinctiveness of local Islamic practices and identities, but also legitimises national and cultural identities that are separate from the Arabic cosmopolis and the Western-produced Muslim "Other." Simultaneously, the use of this global trope signals how minor literatures are in conversation with global Muslim fiction and communities, allowing them to be a part of but not subsumed by or conflated with the global Muslim *ummah*, or community.

This struggle is particularly charged in small postcolonial Islamic nations such as Brunei, whose representations of Islam in the local context and imaginary have become important ways of representing and translating local perspectives in a landscape in which global Islamophobic narratives dominate. In the past, Brunei's "moderate" approach to Islam has been lauded by leaders in the region, and Brunei has been called on to head a "modern" Islamic civilisation. More recently, Brunei's announcement of its implementation of the Syariah Penal Code Order in 2013 was met with inflated international coverage, with Western media widely condemning the decision. In 2019, Hollywood celebrities such as George Clooney and Ellen DeGeneres called for the widespread boycott/sanctions on Bruneian businesses overseas to express their outrage over the implementation of the final stage of the Syariah Penal Code Order, which includes the death penalty for same-sex sexual relationships (see also the editor's Introduction). The tenor of this condemnation placed the local implementation of Syariah law within the context of global Islamophobic narratives, and was critiqued by regional journalists who pointed out that Western media outlets were not only reporting from outside the region, they also made little concerted effort to engage with local voices and perspectives.

Local representations of Islam (in Brunei, and elsewhere) cannot ignore this global context, and therefore have to self-consciously negotiate these perceptions of Islam in their own narratives. The inability to escape this discourse is an inevitable response to the aforementioned "centripetal pressures" perpetuated by a global "master discourse" (Faiq 2004, 36) about Islam. These centripetal pressures limit and shape the terms by which Muslim identity can be articulated and localised—it becomes even more important, then, for writers to represent the distinct and multiple ways that Islam is practised in order to push back against these flattening, homogenising narratives that hold real repercussions for Muslims in the world today. This chapter will examine one of these articulations by focussing on how the global trope of the cross-cultural romance is translated in two Bruneian romance novels, *Pengabdian* and *Jewel*. A key aspect of these romances is the conversion of one of the romantic partners to Islam for the sake of the relationship. By considering how these conversions and the romance that hinges on them are represented, and how Islam is represented in the convert figure, this chapter also examines how local Bruneian fiction translates and relates to global Islamic fiction.

Intersections of Bruneian identity

To understand the stakes of the two novels, it is necessary first to provide some context on Bruneian identity. The tripartite national ideology of oil-rich Brunei Darussalam is Malay Islamic Monarchy, *Melayu Islam Beraja* (MIB), in which the Malay culture, Islamic faith, and the monarchic system of governance are upheld in national rhetoric to be the "living foundation" upon which the success (implied: economic, worldly) of the nation rests (Muhammad Hadi 2018). Malays constitute 66 percent of the 400,000 strong population, Chinese 10 percent, and other races 24 percent. It is a Muslim-majority country, with Malayness officially and ideologically linked to Muslimness while Muslim subjects are governed by Syariah law, although civil law is also practised. It should be noted that Brunei is largely free of the political, religious, and racial unrest that have historically been witnessed in the neighbouring countries of Malaysia, Singapore, and Indonesia, and that this can be attributed in no small part to a stable economic climate comprised of generous government subsidies of education, healthcare, and other staples.

Nevertheless, as my reading of these two novels will show, the relatively peaceable relationships between different racial groups in Brunei Darussalam does not preclude pressure on non-Malays to assimilate and acculturate into Malay cultures and identities. Noor Azam Haji-Othman has previously noted that this move towards a single national "Bruneian identity" (2012, 175), or Bruneianisation, became a concern amidst a growing national consciousness in the lead-up to Brunei's independence in 1984, when the tripartite national ideology was officially articulated for the first time. This official articulation was the result of a number of socio-historical factors, including the development of formal education, technological and infrastructural developments, modernisation, and globalisation. Noor Azam shows that this distillation of diverse ethnic, linguistic, cultural, and racial identities into a single "common" (2012, 176) national identity that privileges the Malay culture has not simply occurred organically but is the result of national policy and priority: "the national philosophy was to be the medium through which this creation of a common identity was to be achieved" (2012, 176). Given the widespread propagation of the national philosophy of MIB, it is not surprising that Bruneian identity has become largely synonymous with a Malay Muslim hegemony. Consequently, D.E. Brown notes that it is "socially advantageous to identify with Brunei Malays" (in *Brunei: The Structure and History of a Bornean Malay Sultanate*, 1960, quoted in Noor Azam 2012, 184), something that has historically been easier for indigenous populations to do.

Additionally, Brunei, like Malaysia, does not legislatively accommodate interfaith marriage between Muslims and non-Muslims. As in Malaysia, non-Muslims in Brunei can marry Muslims only after conversion to Islam (Chee et al. 2009, 2). Given that Malayness in Brunei is officially conflated with Muslimness, Muslim-non-Muslim marriages are for all intents and purposes instances of interracial marriage between a Malay and a non-Malay partner. There are no empirical studies or significant records of conversion motives to situate or contextualise interracial relationships in Bruneian society, against which to understand their occurrences in local fiction. In this lack of record, conversion to Islam in Brunei echoes global trends. Anecdotally, of course, we know intermarriages have always been relatively common in Bruneian society, with intermarriage between Malays and the Chinese going back several centuries (Nur Shawatriqah and Hoon 2018, 7). More importantly, while it is common knowledge that "mixed-marriage couples often face challenges pertaining to reconciling differences in culture, religion, traditions and social class" (Nur Shawatriqah and Hoon 2018, 7), tracing out the precise nature of these differences as a way of understanding negotiations of identity more clearly remains a relevant and urgent endeavour. This is particularly true in the context of Brunei, in which constructions of identity bind religion and race together with nationality and national loyalty.

The two novels discussed in this chapter grapple with these hegemonic constructions, and consider how conversion to Islam interweaves with acculturation into Malay Muslim privilege. Written thirty years apart, the novels also offer a telling insight into how perspectives on race, religion, gender, and class have or have not evolved in the years since Brunei's independence. In doing so, they also explore the concept of "Bruneianisation" in action via conversion.

Converting for love in Brunei

Published in 1987 and the winner of an inaugural novel writing competition held by the National Language and Literature Bureau (*Dewan Bahasa dan Pustaka*, DBP), *Pengabdian* is a Malay-language novel that features an ostensibly nationalistic story about the importance of sacrifice for and dedication to the project of nation-building. The main protagonist is Siti Nur, a UK-trained medical doctor who specialises in paediatric care. The novel follows her everyday life as a doctor, which is characterised by filial obedience, Islamic values, and national service. Siti Nur is an exemplary daughter and sister, credited with providing financially for her immediate and extended family, and is a moral and spiritual role model for her siblings as well as a dedicated government doctor. *Pengabdian* is also a love story. Siti Nur is being courted simultaneously by her childhood sweetheart and fellow doctor Sam, and a new suitor, the police officer Shukri. While Siti Nur has always loved Sam, their relationship fractures in university because of the Chinese Sam's atheism and Siti Nur's increasing religiosity due to her friendship with pious Malaysians. Unbeknownst to Siti Nur, in the years since their separation, Sam has been learning about Islam and has plans to convert. After he does, Sam changes his name to the Malay "Faisal," and they marry despite Siti Nur's ovarian cancer and inability to consummate the marriage.

Written in English, *Jewel* revolves around the romance between the Eurasian Yasmin Colburn and the Muslim Malay ("fully Malay" in contrast to the mixed-race Yasmin and his mixed-race relatives) Prince Danial. Set in the fictional Malaysian state of Mekar, easily deciphered as a stand-in for Brunei (oil-rich, Malay Muslim-dominant, small population), the romance that develops between Yasmin and Danial is hindered dually by the newly religious Danial's desire to pursue a *halal*, or religiously permissible, courtship and Yasmin's status as a non-Muslim. After a life-threatening car accident, Yasmin converts to Islam and, through the lens of her new religious knowledge, understands the motivation, religious legalities, and operational logistics of a *halal* courtship, as performed by Danial. She accepts his marriage proposal and the novel ends with a "fairytale wedding" (Aisha 2017, 1199) between Danial and Yasmin.

As mentioned in the introduction, similarities in these two conversion experiences are striking. Despite the generic differences, different languages, and three decades between the two novels, there are many points of similarity between the two conversion experiences, including the motivation for conversion, the construction of the "happy" endings, and the cultural assimilations that must be experienced so that the societal status quo can be maintained by the end of both novels. In both novels too, the trigger for the new converts' desire to learn more about Islam is due to their romantic interest in their Muslim partners. The Muslim partners in both *Pengabdian* and *Jewel* are model, practising Muslims, and are considered pious by their communities. Both Siti Nur and Danial are also idealised as good citizens and role models of their gender: Siti Nur is repeatedly referred to as the beautiful, well-mannered, and soft-spoken young doctor with strong values, while her single status is the subject of much speculation, given her desirable status. Danial is likewise a model monarch-in-waiting. They are both leaders in their communities who represent local Malay values and concerns: Siti Nur is a respected doctor who stands up to the expatriate doctors in the national hospital, while Danial is the third in line to the throne of Mekar, with similarly philanthropic responsibilities. As the crown prince, Danial is expected to join the ministerial cabinet to help with state issues such as unemployment, crime, and poverty as soon as he finishes university (Aisha 2017, 1342).

After the conversions and subsequent marriages, however, the fates of these Muslim partners take very different turns. Siti Nur dies of ovarian cancer on the day Brunei gains independence—on her deathbed she urges Sam (now known as Faisal) to go to the official celebration, saying "I want you to attend the event. I want you to know what it feels like to be the citizen of a free country"[1] (Norsiah 1987, 157). Sam attends the event in full traditional Malay dress, and at the stroke of midnight, Siti Nur dies. The symbolic significance of Siti Nur's death has been explored more fully elsewhere (Kathrina 2018, 51–2), but, for the purposes of this chapter, it should be noted that Sam's symbolic birth as a Malay Muslim citizen of a newly independent Brunei is at the cost of Siti Nur's life. Her utility as a Bruneian female par exemplar has expired with Sam's final assimilation into the Malay Muslim culture.

In contrast, the royal wedding that closes *Jewel* is a more traditional happily-ever-after. What it does have in common with *Pengabdian*, however, is that the ceremony heralds the assimilation of Yasmin and her family into the Malay Muslim monarchy. At the ceremony, Yasmin's parents wear the traditional Malay dress and Yasmin herself is dressed traditionally by Danial's mother, the *Permaisuri* (Queen), and her sisters. As a new "Muslim princess" (Aisha 2017, 1221), Yasmin has, like Faisal before her, become reborn as a Malay Muslim citizen, as indicated by her clothing. It must be noted that Yasmin's parents' inclusion in this cultural conversion is an echo of the events of *Pengabdian*, in which Sam's Chinese parents also convert to Islam by the end of the novel. In both cases, the conversions of not just the central protagonists but of their families indicates that these conversions are not just individual events, but symbolically communal. This is significant because in both novels, both Sam's Chinese parents and Yasmin's Sabah-born Kadazan mother are, in legal terms, already citizens of the state. However, the religious conversions and cultural assimilations that are key to the harmonious happy-ever-after concept in the novels also imply that legal citizenship does not indicate full acceptance by or inclusion into the state—that is the privilege and domain of Malay Muslims and those who assimilate into that identity.

Furthermore, the use of Siti Nur and Danial as triggers for the conversions of Sam and Yasmin indicates that one of the roles of a good citizen is to propagate the faith by any means necessary. The fact that these marriages are love marriages, however, must also be considered; the marriages are presented not as sacrifices or acts of martyrdom for a greater good, but as happy endings. The ideological work of these novels can be further understood by examining the characterisation of the converts, and how they are translated within local and global contexts.

Desirable converts

One of the reasons that the Muslim partners are able to be happy as a result of their marriages is due to the desirability of their convert partners. Prior to their conversions, the converts are presented as exemplary individuals, with their only flaw being their non-Muslim status. Sam is a well-respected and wealthy doctor in the hospital, pursued romantically by nurses, and approved of by his local and non-local peers; he is also a loving and filial son. Yasmin is a brilliant and beautiful university student, whose self-professed "social awkwardness" (Aisha 2017, 527) is more of a narrative gambit to introduce empathy with an otherwise idealised character than a plausible flaw. Even prior to Yasmin's conversion, she dresses modestly and behaves in a conservative way; she is furthermore "family-oriented, serious, and didn't seem to have any male friends as far as [Prince Danial] could see" (571)—a description that preserves her pre-conversion innocence, compliant femininity, and chastity, although the novel is also quick to note that she has many admirers to cement her objective desirability. The need for the converts to be excellent characters even prior to their conversions suggests narratively that it is the best and brightest who are attracted to Islam, and also that Islam is able to attract the best and brightest. In these cases, it is not the poor or the needy who embrace the call to Islam; it is those who are already at the top of the social hierarchy. The conversion of those who are already high in the social hierarchy due to their personal qualities in turn elevates the status of Islam as desirable. At the same time, Sam's and Yasmin's non-Malay and non-Muslim status renders their personal qualities null and void in the context of Bruneian society. It is only once they convert that these qualities can be appreciated and utilised for national development via their marriages.

After their conversions, both converts are portrayed as pious and devout Muslims. Crucially, the actions that characterise these exemplars are interesting. In Sam's case, his first act as a Muslim is to stop eating pork, while Yasmin's is to put on the headscarf. Both actions are enjoined by Islam for both genders, but they also signal what actions are perceived as most significant in signalling a gendered piety. Sam's attraction to the "disciplined lives" (*hidup mereka teratur dan berdisiplin*; Norsiah 1987, 49) of the devout Malaysians he lives with in London is echoed eerily by Yasmin's reflections on and admiration of Danial's "disciplined life" (Aisha 2017, 945). The primary quality prized in Muslim men, it seems, is discipline in adherence to the daily religious practices of prayer and chastity. In Muslim women, piety is signalled by the willingness to subject their feminine bodies to, at the very minimum, policing, as in Yasmin's case; and in the extreme variant of Siti Nur's case, erasure and destruction. This is foreshadowed prior to Yasmin's conversion, when Danial is "relieved to know she wasn't Muslim. Because if she were, he would have some reservations about her current dress code," despite that dress code being relatively modest and consisting of "long sleeved sweaters and long pants" (Aisha 2017, 561). This is notable, given the global and persistent widespread media attention paid to the issue of Muslim women's dress, thereby placing the issues that Yasmin faces within the wider context of global Islam.

Importantly too, romantic foils are set up in both novels to highlight exactly which characteristics are most and least desirable in a romantic partner, and to signal the presence of the most prized qualities in Sam and Yasmin. In the case of Siti Nur and Sam, the romantic foil is Shukri, whom Siti Nur admits to herself is "the ideal candidate for a husband" (*calon seorang suami yang ideal*; Norsiah 1987, 39). Shukri is "a police officer with a bright future, just as handsome as Sam. Good-hearted. Most importantly, they shared the same faith. [. . .] But Siti Nur did not love him"[2] (39). In *Pengabdian*, Siti Nur's only consideration is that Shukri is a Muslim and Sam is not. Here, it is apparent that the masculine traits that are prized are a stable and steady job, income, and prospects. However, when they exist outside of a Malay Muslim package, these traits, while valued, are rendered null and void. In *Jewel*, Yasmin's romantic rivals are, like Shukri, laid out as ideal candidates as spouses:

> There was Puteri Asiah, the daughter of Sultan Shah, a pretty, well-educated fashionista, currently running her father's businesses in the UK. And Laila, the independent, headstrong daughter of Salim Khan, the media mogul, also finishing graduate studies like him. And his second cousin from his mother's side, Meena, a petite, graceful young girl, perhaps not even twenty.
>
> (Aisha 2017, 670)

The three women whom Danial has previously been considering for marriage are assessed on their professional capabilities, looks, and social statuses (wealth and relationship with the royal family).

Most crucially in both conversions, while the trigger for more religious knowledge is romantic, both converts are adamant that the motivation itself is internal, spiritual, and voluntary, rather than external. In deciding to convert, Sam affirms that "he submitted his heart to Islam with full gladness and sincerity. Not for Siti Nur's sake. But because he truly believed that Islam was the truest, best way"[3] (Norsiah 1987, 49). Prior to his conversion,

Sam has long intellectual conversations with Siti Nur about religion in general and Islam in particular, but in the end his conversion is a result of his experiences in the UK, where he compares his upper-class, "white, godless friends" (*kawan-kawan Mat Salleh yang tidak beragama*) with "Muslim, Malaysian youths who were active in propagation" (*pemuda-pemudi Islam dari Malaysia yang giat berdakwah*; 48). He is most impressed by their sober, disciplined lifestyles, especially in "a country filled with temptation. A country where every street corner was littered with shops selling pornography and pictures of naked women"[4] (49). Sam is taken by the pious youths' ability to live "true Islamic" (*Islam yang tulen*) lives in the midst of this decadence:

> Their lives were disciplined and orderly. They prayed five times a day. In the winter, they got up in the freezing cold to fulfill the dawn prayer. They went hungry during the fasting month. While doing this, they carried out their daily responsibilities faithfully.[5]
>
> (Norsiah 1987, 49)

It is the lived reality of the Islamic faith and its daily rituals that convince Sam of the rightness of Islam. It is worth noting that this may be an inadvertent commentary on the (in)ability of men to be converted and convinced by women; it may also be an implicit social critique of the extent to which Bruneian Muslims live Islamically devoted lives, given that it is with Malaysian Muslims that Sam's heart is opened to Islam despite having grown up with Bruneian Muslims. However, the pivot that I want to focus on is the fact that the novel makes it clear that Sam's conversion is the result of true intellectual and emotional acceptance of Islam, rather than one motivated by his love for Siti Nur.

Likewise in *Jewel*, Yasmin, after her near-death experience, begins questioning the meaning of life, determinedly avoiding the prince and reading the Qur'an. Her abrupt decision to embrace Islam is based on "logic, reasoning and intellect" (Aisha 2017, 1135) and not "blind faith" or "whatever emotions the prince could conjure in me" (1117). She reads blogs written by converts, but the words that truly convince her are to do with answering the questions of "why was I there, and where was I headed?" It is the Quranic verse—"Allah made this life in order to test man so that every person may be recompensed after death for what he has earned. . . " (1125)—that is pivotal to Yasmin's decision to convert to Islam, as she asks what is the point of doing good deeds or being good. The verse thus gives meaning and reason to Yasmin's instinctive philanthropic inclinations. In both novels then, there is a decided emphasis on Islam itself convincing the converts. The fact that the conversion here is couched in the rhetoric of faith rather than national or social rhetoric is significant. In translating Islam, both novels deliberately divorce the notion of personal persuasiveness from the convert's decision. At the same time, it is also important to note that both also pay quite scant attention to the theological underpinnings of Islam as a faith and religion: Yasmin's actual conversion happens behind the scenes—the reader learns of her conversion and decision to wear the *hijab* at the same time as Danial—while Sam's Islamic education seems limited to ritualised behaviour.

And yet both conversion experiences are tellingly situated in global, cosmopolitan settings of cultural and religious translation and interchange. London is a key setting in both novels, being the place where both Sam and Yasmin spend time studying. Sam's experiences with devout Malaysian youths are more influential than his time with Siti Nur or growing up in Brunei. This influence is an implicit critique of Bruneian practices of Islam (or lack of), which are exposed by offering a global perspective of Islam as a point of comparison. Similarly, Yasmin is surprised to learn about Islam's transnational Arab roots in the region, and that Islam is not just a local but a global religion. Again, it is not clear why this revelation is significant to her choice to convert, but certainly Yasmin's initial forays into learning about Islam come from the internet, in particular English-language blogs written by converts rather than interactions with fellow Mekar citizens. In both cases, Sam's and Yasmin's (as well as Siti Nur's and Danial's) attraction is to a religion that is translationally rhetoricised to transcend nationality; it is in this manner that both novels are situated firmly within a global discourse.

Implicitly then, local practices of the religion are revealed as lacking; alternatively, this narrative tactic might be seen as a critical commentary on the notion of division between local and global Islam. At the same time, the translation of Islam within the global context legitimises it as a faith beyond the local parochial context—in fact, it endows all the faithful characters in the two novels with a cosmopolitan quality. This is significant for two reasons. First, the postcolonial legacy. The desire to be legitimised by the former colonial power is present in this insistence that Islam is not a backwards, barbaric faith but a modern and cosmopolitan religion. While Brunei was never officially colonised by the British, it was a British protectorate from 1906 to 1984. Brunei never lost her sovereignty, but the influence, power, and presence of the British in Brunei was extensive enough that historians and politicians have argued over whether Brunei was a de facto colony of Great Britain due to the ambivalent nature of this protectorate agreement (Hussainmiya 2006, 1). Thus, the protectorate legacy can functionally be considered a postcolonial legacy. Second, the insistence that the local practice of Islam has its roots in global practices appeases the desire of a small nation such as Brunei to be included in the global discourse.

The rewards of conversion

The romantic interests are portrayed as the worldly reward for conversion, that is to say the converts are rewarded with both happiness in this life and the promise of happiness in the divine hereafter. Yasmin becomes a "Muslim princess with a fairytale wedding," who falls in love with both

"Islam and my prince" (Aisha 2017, 1224). Sam achieves assimilation into the Malay cultural context as well as marriage to the love of his life, Siti Nur. Without these conversions, happy endings are not possible for the converts. The novels' translational praxis thus asks readers to associate conversion with both divine and worldly success. The specific nature of worldly success is not just the romantic union, but a symbolic inclusion into the national identity of Malay Muslim monarchy. Happy endings are for Malay Muslim citizens—and Malay Muslim citizenship is the desired happy ending.

This is particularly interesting in light of the converts' racial heritage. Sam, as a Chinese man, is part of a community that *Pengabdian* portrays as stingy and individualistic via the characterisation of Sam's father, Peter. Peter is wealth-obsessed and concerned about the increasing competitiveness of the Malays in the business sector. Sam berates his father for his obsession with individual legacy, and reminds him of how Peter immigrated to Brunei with nothing but the clothes on his back and was able to create a good life for himself. The perceived ingratitude of the Chinese community and the refusal to integrate into the Bruneian (Malay) community is "corrected" by Sam's conversion. Sam's subsequent adoption of a Malay name and dress works to effectively erase his Chinese heritage. By the end of the novel, his colleagues at the hospital have forgotten his Chinese heritage so quickly that it causes confusion when a call comes for Dr Samuel instead of Dr Faisal. Sam's immediate integration into the Malay community is so effective that he is able to call upon them for a blood transfusion when his father needs it, a plea that the non-Malay community ignores. Thus the "solution" for the problem of the non-Malay community in Brunei is presented in the novel as conversion and assimilation.

In *Jewel,* Yasmin's Eurasian heritage is a double-edged sword of privilege and adverse social and gendered stereotypes. Tellingly, Danial is obsessed with Yasmin's Eurasian looks, a postcolonial legacy of veneration of whiteness. Yasmin's appeal is that she possesses what are, in the novel, perceived as "Asian" values of modesty, chastity, and family orientation, coupled with what is perceived as the "superior" looks of a Caucasian. Danial sighs that "she was a rare old-fashioned creature, inside the body of a sensational runway model" (Aisha 2017, 588). When she eventually puts on the headscarf, Danial blushes at how it accentuates her Eurasian qualities. However, Yasmin herself notes the "preconceived" negative stereotypes that she encounters as a Eurasian woman; for example, she is expected to be "outgoing" and "audacious" (181)—coded language for promiscuity. In fact, at one point Yasmin wonders if the prince and his friends just want to euphemistically *"have fun* with the half-Caucasian girl" (180). In contrast, the Eurasian males in *Jewel,* including Yasmin's brother, Jeff, and Danial's friend, Adam, thoroughly exploit the advantage of "mixed-blood" "good looks" (212). It becomes clear that as a Eurasian woman, Yasmin shoulders the policing of both the white and Asian communities, whereas the Eurasian men enjoy the privileges afforded them in both.

In *Jewel*, whiteness does not have the same subject positionality as Chineseness due to Brunei's history as a former British protectorate. Whiteness is associated with the decadent immorality of the West, as exemplified by Sam's encounters with godless British youths in *Pengabdian*, and Yasmin's being perceived as promiscuous due to her Eurasian heritage. At the same time, whiteness is also venerated, as shown by the respect accorded Siti Nur and Sam's medical training in the UK, and the recurrent admiration of Yasmin's mixed-blood beauty (even by the royal family) as well as her education in London. Thus, as a result of the complicated relationship that the local community has with whiteness, Yasmin's conversion to Islam and subsequent assimilation into Malay Muslim identity is translated differently compared to Sam's conversion in *Pengabdian*. In *Jewel*, whiteness is not a problem to be solved for national harmony (as Sam's Chineseness is), as Yasmin's whiteness is seen as foreign to the local landscape rather than a part of it. However, Danial and his family's eagerness to acquire and possess Yasmin's beauty suggests that the incorporation of this specific racial make-up into the royal family elevates the status of Malayness and Islam. I contend that this is because whiteness, as symbolised by Yasmin, affirms the superiority of the Malay Muslim identity through her conversion and willing inculcation of Malay culture. Her willingness to adopt a Malay identity is given extra weight because of the historically elevated value of whiteness in a postcolonial landscape.

The two novels—in which conversion is rewarded by love and the bequeathing of Malay Muslim identity—not only situate global Islam as a local practice, but also have more in common than they have differences. Where the conversions differ, they do so in the gendered expectations of piety and responses to racial/cultural diversity albeit within the same social and cultural contexts. Encouraging conversion and the duty of a good Bruneian citizen becomes a way of both removing ethnic diversity from the population and legitimising the superiority of the Malay culture. Islam itself, translated as cosmopolitan and transcendent, arrives to the two converts via lived practices and international links.

Global Muslim romance

To what extent are the stories of Sam and Yasmin echoes and transmutations of global Muslim literature? To what extent does the global literary network of Muslim fiction and the centripetal pressures of the global master discourse about Islam shape and constrict the possibilities of the cross-cultural romances in these Bruneian texts? I want to provide in this section a very brief comparison with Western Muslim literature, specifically female-authored American Muslim romance, with a comment in the conclusion on other world literatures to underline the specificities of how both *Pengabdian* and *Jewel* have translated global Muslim literature.

While the earliest spread of Islam yields little by way of conversion narratives, Western conversion narratives have a specific history in the Muslim world. Martha Hermansen identified the basic genres of Western Muslim conversion narratives as the short testimonial, the pilgrimage account, the Sufi-oriented narrative, the esoteric quest motif, the explanation, and the narratives that tackle issues faced by Western Muslims living in their native societies (1999, 86). The evolution of these conversion narratives in the twentieth century is characterised by the changing perspective on the cultural contact between the West and the Muslim world during this period. Hermansen notes that "over this period there is a gradual decolonisation in perspective and an increasing domestication and internalisation of embracing Islam for Europeans and Americans" (1999, 88). The convert trope in contemporary American Muslim literature thus contends with a long history of conflict between Islam and the West that has been racialised and gendered.

I wish to point out here two main characteristics of the American Muslim romance genre through which one can approach the question of translating the convert trope in *Pengabdian* and *Jewel*. The first characteristic is that of the role of cross-cultural romance in upholding or resisting the status quo—seen in the "happily-ever-after" endings in the two Bruneian novels, which work to uphold the national ideology by having the two converts assimilate into the dominant Malay Muslim national identity. Cross-cultural romance is a frequent feature of American Muslim romances. However, because Muslims are a minority in the US and the UK, the dynamics of privilege operate differently in these texts when compared to the Bruneian texts in which the Malay Muslim identity is dominant, while conversion to Islam confers access to this identity upon the convert. In contrast, Islam has been so demonised and racialised (and conflated with Arabness/Otherness) in American media that conversion to Islam actually removes the convert from a privileged position in the status quo.

In her romance conversion memoir chronicling her conversion to Islam, *The Butterfly Mosque: A Young American Woman's Journey to Love and Islam* (henceforth *The Butterfly Mosque*, 2010), American Muslim writer G. Willow Wilson is frank about how converting to Islam, and marrying an Egyptian man, shifted her status in the American social hierarchy.

> I liked being a non-Muslim so much that I kept my new religion a secret and prayed alone behind a locked door. [. . .] To the rest of the world, I was an upper-middle-class American white girl with bland politics and polite beliefs and in this coveted social stratum I was happy. The status quo had been good to me. I was reluctant to abandon it—even for love, even for God.
>
> (Wilson 2010, 43)

This status, conferred by the intersecting privileges of race, class, and gender, is erased by conversion to Islam because of the way that Islam and Muslims are perceived across global discourse. In both Bruneian and American narratives, conversion shifts the convert on the social hierarchy; the direction of the shift is dependent on the position Islam occupies within the society. This position is also influenced by the fact that in both Bruneian and American texts, Islam is closely tied with racial/ethnic identity, and therefore the dominant discourses about race with which it is most closely associated. These intersecting considerations of gender, race, and class are a perpetual concern across the genre in articulating the convert's position, thereby showing that the master discourse about Islam influences how the convert is received and translated, and under what terms they are able to discursively position themselves and be positioned in society.

Like *Pengabdian* and *Jewel*, Wilson's work is thus part of and in conversation with the conversion for love trope in global Muslim writing. This trope engages heavily with the "love jihad" concept, which is the alleged practice of Muslim men feigning love in order to convert non-Muslim women into the faith. The actual truth of this alleged practice is dubious at best, and reports about conversion and conversion motives in the US and Europe are conflicting and patchy. It has been estimated that 66 to 80 percent of Western converts to Islam are female (which is estimated to be over 10 percent more than the Bruneian case, but with a considerably higher margin of error) and the most frequent route into Islam is marriage (Allievi 2006); furthermore, Tom Rosentiel reports that only 58 percent of conversions are for religious reasons while 18 percent are for family and marriage reasons (2007, 22). What can be surmised, however, is that the extent to which this trope has been internalised into Islamic conversion narratives has much to do with, in particular, dominant Orientalist stereotypes that invoke the fear of and fetishise Arab men and other men of colour, especially in the context of romantic relationships with white women.

This gendered Orientalist lens concerns the second characteristic I want to highlight, which is that of the convert's motivation for conversion. In *Pengabdian* and *Jewel*, the converts are firm in their conviction that while the romantic interest may have sparked their learning about Islam, the decision to convert arises from a genuine love for Islam itself. This suggests that there may exist some stereotypes about converting for the sake of marriage in the Bruneian context that question the sincerity of converts. This stereotype is persistent globally, and tends to be gendered because of the "love jihad" trope above, while also complicated by nationalist narratives surrounding religion and gender. For example, in American Muslim romance memoirs, there is likewise a persistent, repeated resistance to the idea that conversion is in any way influenced by a romantic interest. This resistance occurs pre-emptively and repeatedly in female-authored conversion narratives; it does not appear in male-authored narratives. Examples of this resistance are below:

> First, let me make something clear: I did not get into all "this" by dating a Muslim man. Many people assume that any white woman who stumbles into Islam does so through a man. . .
> ("Even Muslim Girls Get the Blues," by Sayed 2012, 56)

I didn't convert to Islam for my husband, nor did I do it in an attempt to save my marriage. I did it for Allah, and for me. My husband never insisted I convert...

("From Shalom to Salaam," by Levine 2012, 67)

"You converted for him?"
"No, I converted before we ever said anything to each other. . . ."

(*The Butterfly Mosque*, by Wilson 2010, 57)

This repeated insistence is understandable given the stereotypes about male domination in Islam in popular American discourse. Yasir Suleiman has noted that any admission of conversion linked with marriage is viewed with suspicion, "as though it detracted from her own worth as a convert" (2013, 40). This gives us some insight into Sam's and Yasmin's refusal to attribute their conversions to their romantic interests. Their sincerity must come from Islam's superior truth and not from nationalistic or social interests, especially if Islam is to legitimise and be legitimised in tandem with the ideology of Malay Islamic Monarchy. In American Muslim romances, the defensive narrative reactions that reject the idea of conversions motivated by love or (pre) spousal pressure are situated within a sense of contemporary American feminine identity and linked to feminist and nationalist loyalties:

> The truth is, if it weren't for Ahmed, I might never have found Islam. But I couldn't admit it, even to myself. I was a feminist, and I wasn't changing religions for any man. I wasn't changing anything for any man.
> He never asked me to convert.
> ("Love at Third Sight" by Dunn 2012, 108)

In both the Bruneian and American cases, religious motivation must be read in light of the social repercussions for the converts. In the American case, cross-cultural romance does not mean erasure of the culture of origin and consequent assimilation into the dominant culture as it does for Sam and Yasmin; instead, it means giving up the privileges of belonging to the dominant white culture. Conversion to Islam means assuming the racialised profile of Muslims in the US—it is not a desired choice on the part of the American converts. It is a downwardly mobile move, rather than an upwardly mobile one. At the same time, love is not considered an appropriate motivation for conversion in both Bruneian and American texts. The cross-cultural romances are pursued almost tangentially to conversions, although this can be read—as in the excerpt from the short story "Love at Third Sight" above—as a narrative feint. The tropes of conversion persist, but the subversions and permutations of the power dynamics contained within the converts' choices in the Bruneian and American texts show powerfully how religion is embedded along the axes of the converts' cultural, class, gendered, racial, and national identities, inevitably affecting their places in their respective social hierarchies. More than that, these permutations show how central is the concern of multiple identities in Muslim fiction, and how these identities are negotiated and translated in the context of global narratives that demonise Islam and Muslims. This brief comparison serves to demonstrate the influence of the "master discourse" about Arabs and Islam in world and minor literatures, and across languages. The persistence of this master discourse must be fully examined and understood if Muslim fiction and narratives about Islam are ever to escape its flattening, generalising effects.

Conclusion

I have focussed on showing how cross-cultural conversion romance in Bruneian novels are in conversation with global forms of the genre through the case study of American Muslim romances. Both the American and Bruneian texts attempt to translate Islam as transcending national and social concerns, with the Bruneian converts finding Islam in the global, cosmopolitan sphere rather than the local setting, and the American converts needing to resist the prevalent local discourse about a demonised Islam in order to find the truth of Islam for themselves. This is made possible in both cases through the material and human interchanges made possible by globalisation and transnational mobility flows. In fact, the way that Bruneian texts are in translational conversation with global Muslim texts, as evidenced by the handling of the convert trope, is in itself a commentary on this interchange. However, the tensions and identities at stake in the Bruneian novels are less gendered than their American Muslim counterparts, while the nuances of race are also deeper and broader. The Bruneian novels struggle to negotiate a way to transcend racial barriers via conversion and cross-cultural romance, but these have ended in the erasure of cultural heritage and assimilation into the dominant Malay Muslim hegemony. The ideological consistency in the two Bruneian novels, despite the gap of thirty years between the two publications, shows exactly how successful the push for a single national identity has been since Brunei gained independence in 1984.

This chapter has necessarily been limited in scope, but there is much room for further study. Future studies may wish to consider Southeast Asian cross-cultural romances, in particular the Indonesian blockbuster *Ayat-ayat Cinta* (Verses of Love), which had a phenomenal impact on Islamic romance in the region and considerable influence. British Muslim romances are also gaining a lot of traction in a genre that scholar Layla Abdullah-Poulos refers to as still "sui generis" (2018, 2). Another rapidly growing genre is American Young Adult Muslim fiction, part of a larger movement towards diversity in publishing and which also features cross-cultural romances. While there has been significant work done on mapping the circulation, transmission, and translation of Islamic texts, ideas, and literary forms within South Asia and Southeast Asia (Ricci 2011, 1), this chapter shows that this mapping can be performed across global Muslim fiction, using the premise that certain tropes, which persist in response to a global master discourse about Islam, also offer sites of commonality for interrogation and critique as they are translated into distinctive local contexts.

Notes

1 *Siti mahu abang hadir di upacara itu. Siti mahu abang merasakan uniknya perasaan menjadi anak pribumi sebuah Negara yang merdeka.* All translations are author's own.
2 *Shukri seorang pegawai polis yang mempunyai masa depan yang cerah. Yang tidak kurang tampannya. Baik hati. Yang pentingnya seagama [. . .] Tapi Siti Nur tidak menyintainnya.*
3 *Ia telah merelakan hatinya dengan ikhlas. Bukan untuk memujuk Siti Nur. Tapi atas dasar kepercayaan bahawa agama Islam itulah anutan yang paling mulia.*
4 *Negara yang penuh godaan itu. Negara yang berselerak dengan kedai-kedai hatta di kaki lima menjual barang-barang porno; gambar-gambar perempuan berbogel.*
5 *Hidup mereka teratur dan berdisiplin. Mereka mengerjakan sembahyang lima waktu. Dan di musim salji sanggup bangun di pagi yang menggigil untuk menunaikan sembahyang subuh. Berlapar dahaga di bulan puasa. Di samping itu mereka mengendalikan tugas mereka seharian dengan baik.*

References

Abdullah-Poulos, Layla. 2018. "The Stable Muslim Love Triangle—Triangular Desire in African American Muslim Romance Fiction." *Journal of Popular Romance Studies* 7: 1–20. http://jprstudies.org/2018/11/the-stable-muslim-love-triangle-triangular-desire-in-african-american-muslim-romance-fictionby-layla-abdullah-poulos/.
Aisha Malik. 2017. *Jewel*. Self-published. Kindle.
Allievi, Stefano. 2006. "The Shifting Significance of the Halal/Haram Frontier: Narratives on the *Hijab* and Other Issues." In *Women Embracing Islam: Gender and Conversion in the West*, edited by Karin Van Nieuwkerk, 120–49. Austin: University of Texas Press.
Chee, Heng Leng, Gavin W. Jones, and Maznah Mohamad. 2009. "Muslim-Non-Muslim Marriage, Rights and the State in Southeast Asia." In *Muslim-Non-Muslim Marriage: Political and Cultural Contestations in Southeast Asia,* edited by Gavin W. Jones, Chee Heng Leng, and Maznah Mohamad, 1–32. Singapore: Institute of Southeast Asian Studies.
Dunn, Patricia M.G. 2012. "Love at Third Sight." In *Love Inshallah,* edited by Ayesha Mattu and Nura Maznavi, 28–38. Berkeley, CA: Soft Skull Press.
Faiq, Said. 2004. "The Discourse of Intercultural Translation." *Intercultural Communication Studies* XIII, no. 3: 35–46. https://web.uri.edu/iaics/files/04-Said-Faiq.pdf.
Fairclough, Norman. 1995. *Critical Discourse Analysis*. London and New York: Longman.
Hermansen, Martha. 1999. "Roads to Mecca: Conversion Narratives of European and Euro-American Muslims." *The Muslim World* LXXXIX, no. 1: 56–89. https://doi.org/10.1111/j.1478-1913.1999.tb03669.x.

Hussainmiya, B. A. 2006. *Brunei Revival of 1906: A Popular History.* Bandar Seri Begawan: Brunei Press Sdn Bhd.
Kathrina Mohd Daud, Chin, G.V.S., & Maslin Jukim. 2016. "Contemporary English and Malay literature in Brunei: A comparison." In Noor Azam Haji-Othman, J. McLellan & D. Deterding (Eds.), *The use and status of language in Brunei Darussalam: A kingdom of unexpected linguistic diversity* (pp. 241–51). Singapore: Springer
Kathrina Mohd Daud. 2018. "Articulating Female Citizenship in Norsiah Gapar's *Pengabdian.*" In *The Southeast Asian Woman Writes Back: Gender, Identity and Nation in the Literatures of Brunei Darussalam, Malaysia, Singapore, Indonesia and the Philippines*, edited by Grace V.S. Chin and Kathrina Mohd Daud, 41–54. Singapore: Springer.
Levine, S.E. Jihad. 2012. "From Shalom to Salaam." In *Love Inshallah*, edited by Ayesha Mattu and Nura Maznavi, 217–30. Berkeley, CA: Soft Skull Press.
Muhammad Hadi bin Muhammad Melayong. 2018. "MIB: Our Soul, Identity." *Borneo Bulletin*, February 12. https://borneobulletin.com.bn/mib-our-soul-identity/.
Noor Azam Haji-Othman. 2012. "It's Not Always English: 'Duelling Aunties' in Brunei Darussalam." In *English Language as Hydra: Its Impacts on Non-English Language Cultures,* edited by Vaughan Rapatahana and Pauline Bunce, 175–90. Bristol: Multilingual Matters.
Norsiah Haji Abd Gapar. 1987. *Pengabdian.* Bandar Seri Begawan: Dewan Bahasa dan Pustaka.
Nur Shawatriqah Binti Hj Md Sahrifulhafiz and Chang-Yau Hoon. 2018. "The Cultural Identity of the Chinese-Malays in Brunei: Acculturation and Hybridity." Working Paper no. 42, Institute of Asian Studies, Universiti Brunei Darussalam, 1–29. http://ias.ubd.edu.bn/wp-content/uploads/2018/11/Chinese-Malay-Cultural-Identity-Brunei-IAS-Working-Paper-42.pdf.
Ricci, Ronit. 2011. *Islam Translated: Literature, Conversion, and the Arabic Cosmopolis of South and Southeast Asia.* Chicago, IL and London: The University of Chicago Press.
Rosentiel, Tom. 2007. "Muslim Americans: Middle Class and Mostly Mainstream." *Pew Research Center*, May 22. https://www.pewresearch.org/2007/05/22/muslim-americans-middle-class-and-mostly-mainstream/.
Sayed, Deonna Kelli. "Even Muslim Girls Get the Blues." In *Love Inshallah*, edited by Ayesha Mattu and Nura Maznavi, 152–61. Berkeley, CA: Soft Skull Press.
Suleiman, Yasir. 2013. *Narratives of Conversion to Islam in Britain: Female Perspectives.* Cambridge: University of Cambridge.
Wilson, G. Willow. 2010. *The Butterfly Mosque: A Young American Woman's Journey to Love and Islam.* Seattle, WA: Grove Press.

8 Cinematic erasure

Translating Southeast/Asia in *Crazy Rich Asians*

Kelly Yin Nga Tse

Introduction

Based on Singaporean American author Kevin Kwan's best-selling novel and directed by Asian American director Jon M. Chu, the film *Crazy Rich Asians* has rapidly turned into a cultural phenomenon that generates heated debates since its release in August 2018.[1] The film swiftly became a major box office hit, which has been uncommon for the genre of romantic comedy in Western cinema (Rodriguez 2018). For many of its fervent supporters, Chu's cinematic project has made history in terms of confronting the deleterious politics of representation in Hollywood, the key cultural apparatus of the US. For its detractors, however, the very same notion of representation is itself the problem at stake in the film's own rendition of "Asia" that empties out Southeast Asia. This polarisation in the reception of Chu's film, as I will show, illustrates the politics of cultural translation that transpire in a trans-Pacific context.

Situating the film within the discourse of the economic rise of Asia, this chapter reads *Crazy Rich Asians* as a cinematic instance of cultural translation that embodies the contradictions of mediating cultures in a global context. Far from an ignorant and naïve process, Chu's filmic translation of Singapore hews to the narrative of Asia' spectacular rise in order to empower Asian Americans in white America. Ironically, this is a grand narrative that postcolonial Singapore partakes in as part of its national self-branding. The appropriative mode of translation that Chu's film undertakes is, however, not unproblematic, as it is predicated upon the convenient erasure of Southeast Asia in a capitalist narrative that pivots around a China-dominant Asia. Yet simultaneously, I argue that the film's poetics of excess also operates as a visual rejoinder to its parodic potential and, thus, self-critique. This formal feature allows the spectator to read otherwise: that the film's affirmation of global Chinese capital is premised upon an amnesia of Singapore and Southeast Asia at large, where capitalism has engendered profound inequalities along racial and class lines.

With its 102 minutes of cinematic runtime, *Crazy Rich Asians* charts the Cinderella-esque love story of Rachel Chu, a Chinese-American economics professor at New York University who teaches game theory, and her unassuming Singaporean Chinese boyfriend Nick Young, heir to the wealthiest dynasty in Singapore. Rachel only belatedly discovers Nick's familial status and financial power when attending the luxurious wedding of Nick's best friend, which is known to be the paramount event of the year in the Southeast Asian city state. To her amazement, the economics professor is then exposed to a glittering world of gold, wealth, lavishness, and extravagance in Singaporean high society, a "crazy rich" world in postcolonial Singapore amidst a rising Asia. Rachel soon finds herself alienated due to both the jealousy of other young bachelorettes and her perceived otherness in Singapore: her American identity and her single mother's working-class immigrant background. Apart from the envious girls on the island, Rachel confronts Nick's mother, Eleanor Young, the domineering matriarch of the house, who represents a recalcitrant force of opposition to her partnership with Nick. The tension between American individualism and Asian collectivity then becomes the focal point of dramatic conflict in the film. Eventually, Rachel and Nick manage to win over the matriarch who agrees to their marital union. As befits the generic conventions of a romcom, Chu's film concludes predictably in a Cinderella moment of the happily ever after.

In what follows, I read *Crazy Rich Asians* as a Hollywood cinematic project of translating "Asia." I begin by outlining the reception history of Chu's film. In particular, I focus on its radically disparate reception from across the globe. The discussion then turns to the nebulous process of cultural translation that the film enacts in relation to Asian American advocacy and Southeast Asian politics. Thereafter, I explore the satiric potential of the film through its stylistic excess, showing how this formal design covertly creates space for the film's self-critique. This chapter ends by reflecting upon the ethics of cultural translation within the trans-Pacific context.

Mixed reception history

Since its appearance on the silver screen, *Crazy Rich Asians* has had a rather mixed reception across the Pacific Ocean. Film critics have been polarised in their assessments of the Asian American production. On the one hand, Chu's film has been widely lauded as a momentous work in recognising ethnic Asian actors and actresses and the representation of Asians in general on Hollywood screens. Apart from the fact that director Chu is an American of Chinese and Taiwanese heritages, the film's main cast includes Constance Wu (Taiwanese American), Henry Golding (Malaysian British), Michelle Yeoh (Malaysian), Gemma Chan (Chinese British), Awkwafina (Chinese/South Korean American), Lisa Lu (Chinese-born American), and other artists and performers who are of Asian descent. In a review in *The Guardian*, Gretchen Smail remarks that Chu's film represents "a watershed moment, for both Hollywood and everyone involved in the project" (2018). This is augmented by the fact that it has been twenty-five years since a Hollywood studio film "features an entirely Asian, Asian American and diaspora Asian cast" (Smail 2018). The last one was of course *The Joy Luck Club* in 1993, which was based on Amy Tan's novel of 1989 and directed by another Asian American director, Wayne Wang. Wang's *The Joy Luck Club* was itself preceded by *Flower Drum Song* in 1961, a majority Asian-cast film based on the Broadway musical of 1958 and directed by German American director, Henry Koster. In a similar vein, Peter Bradshaw writes in *The Guardian* that the "mostly all-Asian cast" of Chu's film represents "a corrective to the Hollywood racism that decrees Asian characters can only be shown fleetingly, if at all, and then mostly in subservient roles" (2018). At its positive end, critical opinion has affirmed the cultural work that the Asian American film performs in enhancing the visibility of a largely under-represented racial and ethnic constituency of America on Hollywood screens.

For its devotees, *Crazy Rich Asians* allows for a new pan-Asian imaginary in which Asianness, even if essentialised and reified, is celebrated in a white-dominant global film industry. According to Chu, the Asian American director himself, making the film is part of his attempt at shifting the dynamics of representation in Hollywood. Although the film could have been a Netflix show, Chu is reportedly aware that a Netflix release "wouldn't have been right in proving Asians can carry a movie" (*South China Morning Post* 2018). This sentiment is shared by the actress, Constance Wu, who has been an advocate for the "better representation of people of colour in Hollywood" (*Financial Times* 2018). Wu attributes the popular embrace of Chu's film to the fact that "an underserved, under-represented population hasn't had a cultural touchstone in a very long time" (*Financial Times* 2018). The lead male actor Henry Golding also notes the political significance of Chu's film. That is why the film crew worked hard to prove that "people of colour can tell amazing stories" (Rahman-Jones 2018). Similarly, the actress Gemma Chan emphasises the symbolic status that the film has assumed among Asian ethnic minorities outside of Asia. The actress brought her parents to the London premiere for the film and recalled how "it was a really emotional experience" for them to watch "a film made in Hollywood where people looked like [them]" (Chung 2019). Understandably, the visibility of Asianness on Hollywood screens in which whiteness has long been the norm is a powerful sight for many spectators of Asian heritage.

On the other hand, however, Chu's film has not been particularly well-received outside of America and has been subjected to different degrees of criticism in various parts of Asia. Much discontent stems from the film's lack of authentic racial and ethnic representation of Singapore and, in general, Southeast Asia. In China, for instance, "cinemagoers are not crazy over the movie" like many of their Asian American counterparts are (*The Straits Times*, 2018). This is because they see it as a "banana film," catering to Asian Americans in America rather than Asians in Asia. In Singapore, responses to the film have not been favourable. Some argue that while the film ostensibly helps "promote racial diversity in Hollywood," it largely "ignores the racial diversity in Singapore and Asia" (Jiang 2018). This is not unfathomable given the film's focalisation of ethnic Chinese characters, the dominant ethnic group in Singapore, and its negligence of racial minorities such as the Malay and Indian Singaporeans (Jiang 2018). Indeed, despite the practice of multiracialism in the Southeast Asian island state, Chu's film only features a few presumably Malays and/ or Indians fleetingly on the screen: a man in the hawker centre and two turbaned security guards with bayonets outside the mansion of Nick's paternal grandmother.

Another main criticism of Chu's film comes from its almost exclusive focus on the class of the "crazy rich" in postcolonial Singapore. The display of extreme wealth means that the film does not pay much attention to the class, or rather underclass, of the crazy poor in Southeast Asia. It is perhaps no wonder then that for many Malaysian movie-goers, while the film breaks "the stereotype of Asian actors playing *kung fu* or action roles," it is deemed inauthentic in its portrayal of Southeast Asia (Jiang 2018). Yonden Lhatoo, while recognising the importance of the film in affirming people of Asian ancestry, finds the celebratory rhetoric around it problematic. Drawing attention to the disparity in the rich-poor gap in ostensibly affluent Asian locales such as Hong Kong, Lhatoo calls for "empathy and compassion for crazy poor Hongkongers" instead (2018). Of course, notwithstanding its national prosperity, Singapore has its own crazy poor too: apart from the local Singaporean poor, there are also the economically disadvantaged immigrant labourers and domestic helpers from other Southeast Asian countries. Jeva Lange is right when she argues that Chu's film has a "money problem" (2018). It is particularly dismaying when the audience is ultimately "left with a story about wealth for the sake of being about wealth," despite the film's investment in the diversity of representation (Lange 2018).

Here, one is compelled to raise several interrelated questions about the controversial status that Chu's Asian American film inhabits: Why has *Crazy Rich Asians* drawn such discrepant responses from audiences across the globe? What might such divergences in reception speak about the film's project of translating "Asia"? Given the entrenched negligence of Southeast Asia in global media representation, what kind of "Asia" is translated on Hollywood's silver screen? Indeed, whose Asia and for whom? To what extent might Southeast Asia be said to be mistranslated? In what ways does the film initiate critical reflection on the ethics of cross-cultural translation, if it does?

Translating "Asia" into America

As I demonstrate, the controversy of *Crazy Rich Asians* stems from the cultural translation of Asia that the film enacts. Deployed in the context of this chapter, cultural translation names a strategy that approaches translation as a creative re-packaging of source material that performs new critical functions in contexts that are different from the original ones. As a cultural practice, translation not only entails interlingual transaction, which engages the source language and the target language, but also entails the broader phenomenon of translating a specific culture into another culture. It is crucial to note here that, as a cultural phenomenon, translation may entail both positive outcomes and negative implications. Bella Brodzki captures this duality when defining translation as a process that includes "all cultural transactions, from the most benign to the most venal" (2007, 2).

To unpack the complex translational politics of Chu's film, it is crucial to analyse cultural translation through a postcolonial frame. As Susan Bassnett argues, cultural translation inhabits a prominent status in postcolonial scholarship (2013, 340–58). After all, Homi K. Bhabha discusses "culture as translation" with respect to postcolonial migrant culture (2004). In many ways, a postcolonial perspective helps underscore the politics of difference in translational encounters. Bassnett and Lefevere are right when they maintain that there is "always a context in which the translation takes place, always a history from which a text emerges and into which a text is transposed" (1990, 12). This postcolonial attention to contextualisation reminds us that acts of cultural transmission are socially embedded and politically contingent. It also reminds us that translational traffics are not independent of racial and class politics. Relatedly, placing translation under the purview of postcolonialism can alert us to the power dynamics that inform cultural mediations. According to Tejaswini Niranjana, translation is not a neutral process but one that can consolidate power inequalities between languages and cultures. Historically, translation has worked to naturalise "hegemonic versions of the colonized, helping them to acquire the status of what Edward Said calls representation of objects without history" (Niranjana 1992, 176). What Niranjana highlights is that translation does not necessarily empower but may disempower a particular people and culture. This is echoed by Mahasweta Sengupta who sees translation as a form of manipulation. The translator, according to Sengupta, can easily choose "only those texts that conform to the target culture's 'image' of the source culture," thus confirming the hegemony of the dominant culture (1995, 160).

Applied to my reading of *Crazy Rich Asians*, cultural translation refers to how Chu's film as an Asian American production translates Asia (the source culture) in such a way that serves Asian American politics in America (the target culture), but displaces the complexity of Singapore and the broader Southeast Asia. To understand the film's logic of appropriative translation, it is important to note that as a cinematic production by and from Asian America, Chu's film is *not* concerned with translating a complex and nuanced picture of Singapore, or for that matter, Southeast Asia. Instead, Chu's film is primarily interested in translating an idea of "Asia" that is "helpful" for Asian American politics in a largely white America, rather than for Asians in Asia. The opening scene of racial encounter, in which Eleanor and her children are asked by a white concierge in a London hotel to try their luck in "Chinatown," establishes the film's narrative investment in racial politics, which often haunts Asian America. As will be evident, Chu's cinematic project is concerned with translating Asia *into* America, thereby serving an Asian American agenda. This act of appropriative translation, as I have implied, entails offering a particular image of Asia that is highly selective, incomplete, and even contested. This particular image of Asia being appropriated and translated into America is one that is economically rising, financially confident, with its people physically attractive and culturally assertive.

In the context of white America, wherein Asian Americans are the ethnic minority, the powerful and appealing image of an advancing postcolonial Asia can be empowering for the historically marginalised racial subjects. Instead of invoking the racial wounds that attended the overtly debilitating labels of "yellow peril" or the "red scare" (targeting mainly ethnic Chinese) of the Cold War era, or even the prescriptive label of "model minority" (targeting Asian Americans) in contemporary US (Ono and Pham 2008), Chu's cinematic narrative now construes ethnic Chinese in Singapore as "crazy rich" and "crazy beautiful" people on Hollywood screens in the postmillennial present. "Asianness" is re-packaged as a sign of success and prosperity rather than one of threat, impoverishment, and backwardness. For Asian Americans, Chu's filmic account might be seen as a counter-narrative that resonates with what Bill Ashcroft et al. have designated as a tactic of "writing back," in which postcolonial subjects contest the assumptions of the imperial centre through writing (1989). The new mark of postcolonial "Asianness" operates as a form of symbolic racial retaliation against a white America that has denigrated and rejected its racial others. It is liberating and reassuring to watch Chu's affirmative film precisely because it helps alleviate the racial injury that endures in the Asian American psyche. The exhilaration that the film promises to the wounded minority subject is attended by a renewed confidence in postcolonial "Asianness," as translated from Asia into America.

The appropriative translation that *Crazy Rich Asians* conducts, as I venture, is a result of its prioritisation of Asian American politics over representational complexity in relation to Southeast Asia. Right from the outset, Chu's film makes explicit the national locality of its enunciation (Asian America) to the audience. The aerial scene which shows Rachel and Nick on their way to the Singapore wedding already points to the fact that the film is narrated from an Asian American perspective, rather than from a resident Singaporean or Southeast Asian perspective. This outsider's point of view of Singapore is sustained through the American-ness that Rachel embodies or is seen to embody throughout the film. Indeed, one might argue that the film indicates its Asian American lens by highlighting Rachel's perceived lack of authentic Asianness by Singaporeans in Singapore. The cinematic staging of a foreign viewpoint culminates in another aerial scene in which Nick proposes to Rachel in an airplane near the end of the film. The aerial motif, which operates as a visual cue for the film's trans-Pacific border-crossing, insistently inscribes its Asian American cinematic gaze. By making transparent the process of its cinematic translation of "Asia," the film enunciates the embeddedness of its camera angle.

What the film's camera then zooms in on is a glamorous and glamorised Asia as illustrated through the specific case of postcolonial Singapore. Through its visual mediation, the film explicitly tells the audience that Asia has risen. Rachel, the Asian American visitor, is introduced to the lavish lifestyle of Singaporean high society: Nick's cousin, Astrid, is a fashionista who easily spends millions on jewellery in Shanghai; Nick's grandmother owns a grandiose mansion at the fictional Tyersall Park; jet-setting shopping trips are also common, as are getaways to secluded Southeast Asian islands for Singaporean socialites. This particular image of "Asia" as a site of capitalist triumph is a narrative of Asian success that can appeal to Asian Americans on the other side of the Pacific Ocean. This is particularly so when one situates Chu's film in the fraught history of white racism against early Asian immigrants, who were what Lisa Lowe calls the "foreigner within" in America (1996, 8). That "the yellow race" of Asia can be better at the capitalist game than white America offers the possibility of affirming the dignity of Asian Americans as racial and ethnic other in the US. This is salient when Peik Lin's father, in encouraging his children to finish their bowls, throws in a rather casual remark at the dining table: "Think of all the starving children in America." Chu's film thus translates a particular image of Asia into America, one that underscores the former's postcolonial triumph over the latter in the capitalist game. Indeed, Rachel's eventual marital union with Nick registers an endorsement of the rags to riches narrative: a capitalist narrative of the daughter of a single Asian American immigrant woman marrying up with Nick, the "crazy rich" Asian Prince Charming. Symbolically, this marital union reflects the strategic alliance of Asian America and "Asia," and the resultant capital gain of the former from the latter. Borrowing the enhanced financial status of Asia, Chu's cinematic counter-narrative thus works to recognise and assert Asian American subjectivity in white America.

In reclaiming postcolonial "Asianness" for Asian America through purposive mediation, however, there is no guarantee that Chu's film does not at the same time engender new forms of representational violence against Asians in Asia. Indeed, the very designation of "crazy rich Asians" can itself be read as the latest incarnation in a long list of fraught Orientalist tropes applied to Asian people. The sensational label conveniently performs the reductive operation of equating "Asianness" with "crazy richness." Equally troubling, perhaps, is the film's apparent celebration of capitalist achievements as it reflects an underlying American standard regarding the measure of success. These intricate dynamics complicate the issue of agency in the film's appropriative act. One might legitimately ask here: Does Chu's film animate the agency of Southeast Asia or does it subject the region to a preconceived set of ideologies? Is the image of crazy richness reflective of Singaporean agency or its lack thereof?

Erasure of Southeast Asia under "Asia"

Perhaps the most glaring act of erasure that the film's cultural translation enacts is the erasure of Singapore and Southeast Asia in general under the larger continental sign of "Asia." Here, it is important to note that the condition of possibility for the appropriative translation of "Asia" that Chu's film performs is the broader narrative of the economic rise of Asia, which has increasingly conferred Asian subjects legitimacy, visibility, and power in a global geo-political context. Notably, this grand narrative of Asia's advent in the reconfigured global economic order primarily revolves around the resurgence of China as an economic powerhouse. The centrality of China in the discourse of Asia's rise perhaps explains why the film begins with the legendary French Emperor Napoleon's quote about the economic giant: "Let China sleep, for when she wakes, she will wake the world." This opening reference indeed sets the tone for the film's appropriative mode of cultural translation that refigures Asia as a continent populated by ethnic Chinese populations. Despite its Singaporean setting, the film's random act of mistranslation (Singapore as China) suggests that it takes liberty in conflating Southeast Asia with East Asia. Or, more appropriately, the film absorbs Southeast Asia into a China-dominant conception of Asia. This lack of internal differentiation with regard to Asia as a continental entity reinstates the Asian American gaze of Chu's cinematic project, which is inevitably limited, and limiting.

Lost in Chu's filmic translation is the history of plurality in postcolonial Singapore in terms of its races, cultures, and languages. Notwithstanding the constitutional multiracialism of the city state, Chu's film centres largely on ethnic Chinese characters, the dominant ethnic group that comprises 76.2 percent of its citizen population, thereby neglecting most of the other racial groups such as the Malays, Indians, and Eurasians. This ethnic bias in the representation of postcolonial Singapore is of course a bias that is registered in the ethnic make-up of the film cast. It is also narratologically registered in the pan-Chinese imaginary that the film creates through financial circuits: Nick's cousin, Eddie, is based in Hong Kong; his another cousin, Alistair, is based in Taiwan; well-off Singaporean Chinese such as Astrid can go for a shopping trip easily in Shanghai. This citation of various affluent Chinese-dominant communities dovetails with Aihwa Ong's analysis of the increased accumulation of capital by transnational Chinese business elites across Asia, which has afforded them a form of flexible citizenship (1999). Critical of the racial politics of the film, Singaporean critic Nazry Bahrawi draws attention to how Chu's narrative "relegates Singapore's brown Asians to the periphery (2018)." That the Malays and Indians only figure in the film as "servants" to the ethnic Chinese masters in Singapore is, for Bahrawi, a sign of the film's "Sinofication," or what he defines as "the Asian equivalent of 'whitewashing'" (2018).

Remarkably, Chu's largely anglophone film incorporates acts of interlingual translation in its narrative space, which are part and parcel of its broader process of cultural translation. Yet again, its linguistic translation privileges sinophone languages in an otherwise multilingual Singapore. The film is peppered both with Mandarin dialogues in scenes of family feasts and popular Mandarin and Cantonese tunes, such as "Waiting for Your Return"; "I Want Your Love"; "Give Me a Kiss"; "Material Girl"; and even a Mandarin rendition of "Yellow," a popular song by the British rock band Coldplay. These pan-Chinese sonic devices, while significant in exposing the hegemony of English as a global lingua franca, also evidence the linguistic limits of the Asian American film as a "born translated" narrative, to borrow Rebecca Walkowitz's words (Walkowitz 2015). That is to say, though the film registers multilingual awareness (sinophone in addition to anglophone), that awareness is mostly restricted to the languages of the ethnic Chinese population in the island nation. Malay and Tamil, the other two official languages of multilingual Singapore, are effectively screened out. This linguistic politics of translation corroborates the film's larger cultural politics of translating the Asian other for the Asian American self, and its negligence of Singaporean social reality.

In some ways, Chu's film may be said to have unwittingly conflated Singapore with Malaysia. Various vignettes that presumably take place in Singapore are in reality shot in Malaysia, yet such regional differences are elided in the film. The luxury hotel Carcosa Seri Negara in Kuala Lumpur, for instance, is the basis of Nick's ancestral home in Singapore (Leong 2018). The scene where Eleanor the matriarch reads the Bible in front of her guests is filmed in the Be-landa House in Kuala Lumpur (Leong 2018). When Astrid is first introduced in a jewellery boutique, she in fact appears in the Astor Bar at St. Regis in Kuala Lumpur (Leong 2018). Araminta's bachelorette party is filmed at the Four Seasons Resort in Langkawi (Leong 2018). The scene of the "mahjong face-off" between Rachel and Eleanor happens in the Cheong Fatt Tze Mansion, an old Peranakan-style home converted into a boutique hotel in the Georgetown UNESCO Heritage site of Penang (Leong 2018). Despite the disparate postcolonial trajectories of Singapore and Malaysia, Chu's film seems to have capitalised on their shared history and cultural similarities in order to forward its Asian American politics. To some extent, the film's cultural translation here plays on American and global ignorance of the two countries' difference. Embedded within Chu's film then are layers of unspoken cultural biases and representational violence.

Apart from the mistranslation of postcolonial Singapore, *Crazy Rich Asians* also simplifies and reifies Southeast Asia at large. Though some Southeast Asian countries are evoked in the film, they function mostly to support the capitalist narrative of a Chinese-centric crazy rich "Asia." Myanmar, for instance, is mentioned briefly when Astrid purchases invaluable Burmese pearl drop earrings early in the film. Cambodia makes its appearance in a passing remark on "a rare Cambodian gong" that only the crazy rich can afford. A private island resort in Sumatra in Indonesia is featured in order to spotlight the jet-setting class to which the Singaporean Chinese bride-to-be belongs. Similarly, the "fictional" Rawa Island in Malaysia, where Colin's bachelor party is held, again bespeaks the island-hopping lifestyle of the rich.[2] This conversion of Southeast Asia into a capitalist playground for ethnic Chinese, which constitutes another form of translational violence, is predicated on multiple acts of social, political, and environmental amnesia: the forgetting of the Rohingya refugees of Myanmar, the forgetting of poverty in Cambodia, the forgetting of ecological crises such as deforestation and sulphur mining in Indonesia, and the forgetting of Malaysia's conflict with the indigenous Orang Asli over land development, among others. What goes amiss then is the opportunity to translate the sociopolitical diversity of Southeast Asia, which could have corroborated Chu's filmic campaign for diversity in America. In this seamless cinematic narrative of Chinese capital, Southeast Asia effectively vanishes the moment it emerges.

The cinematic accentuation of a China-centric "Asia" is particularly problematic when we take into account the ongoing lack of representation of Southeast Asia in the global cultural sphere. This speaks to the much-touted Hollywood productions of the "Vietnam War" such as *Apocalypse Now* (1979) and *Platoon* (1986), where the Vietnamese have been made largely invisible (Nguyen 2016). As Grace V.S. Chin eloquently illustrates in the Introduction to this volume, an "exclusionary" logic is at work when it comes to the literary cultures of Southeast Asia, which have been overshadowed by India in South Asia and China and Japan in East Asia:

> The same exclusionary practice can be seen in the study of Southeast Asian literatures, which have still not been given the kind of attention that has been showered on the literatures of their bigger, and more popular, Asian neighbours, notably India, a veritable "giant" in the construction and production of postcolonial studies, not to mention China and Japan, both of which are favourite locations for the study of world literature.
>
> (2)

In light of this history of exclusion in the cultural domain, *Crazy Rich Asians* as a visual translation of "Asia" is complicit with the economic narrative of Asia's ascendance that pivots around China and obscures Southeast Asia.

It bears reiterating that while *Crazy Rich Asians* is self-reflexive about what it does in terms of racial politics in America, the film is not ethically innocuous in its visual translation of Southeast Asia. A film that seeks to promote plurality in representation in the US cannot at the same time justify its own narrative suppression of difference in Singapore and Southeast Asia at large. That it reproduces the same logic of violence in its critique of the politics of racial representation in Hollywood is something that must be resisted. To be sure, the diversity of the (American) self that comes at the expense of the diversity of the (Asian) other offers no real social transformation. As mentioned earlier, the film's narrow visual focus on the "crazy rich" of Asia conveniently forgets the inequality that global capital creates along the axes of race, class, and other vectors. As it carries out its purposive translation, Chu's film imagines a singular and monolithic capitalist Asia that obliterates Southeast Asia.

The film's translational problems are further amplified by its generic entrenchment in the global commercial economy of the film industry. As Kevin Kwan reveals in an interview, Anna Wintour, the editor in chief of *Vogue*, was amongst "the first people to champion the book, excerpting and publishing part of it in an issue of the magazine" (quoted in Chiu 2018). The marketability and, hence, profitability of the book were already indexed by the anticipated readership of *Vogue*. The inceptive moment of the book's intimate connection to the commercial industry also applies to Chu's filmic rendition. As a popular romantic comedy, the film's box office success means that it undeniably benefits from the capitalist market that it supposedly seeks to satirise. This resonates with Vietnamese American writer and critic Viet Thanh Nguyen's critique of Asian America. As Nguyen argues, there has been an idealisation of Asian America such that its intellectuals and cultural producers sometimes fail to recognise their complicity with the global capital (2002). The complicity here includes the selling of ethnic and racial identity. Nguyen's critique rings true for *Crazy Rich Asians*, which is inextricably entangled with the activities of translating and marketing Chinese Asianness as a racial and ethnic commodity.

Visual politics of excess

Yet, despite the violence of its cultural translation of "Asia" into a site of crazy richness that empties out Southeast Asia, Chu's cinematic narrative is not without parodic potential. As I will argue in this section, the narrative elision of Southeast Asia as analysed above is potentially contested if not necessarily countered by the film's visual politics of excess, which reflects the stylistic excess of Chinese capital. Herein though lies the rub: as a successful tiger economy, has postcolonial Singapore not been complicit with the grand narrative of the ascendance of Chinese capital in Asia? If so, how exactly does Chu's film exhibit its satiric tendency through its visual form?

As I demonstrate, it is precisely through its excessive mode of representation in relation to Singaporean Chinese capital that Chu's film formally articulates its parodic critique. This assertion might seem counter-intuitive, but it need not be. The author, Kwan, has insisted that the novel is "meant to be deeply satirical" of the world it portrays (quoted in Chiu 2018). This satiric intent, I argue, inflects Chu's film adaptation, if in a less detectable way. What I propose here is that the Asian American film, through its excessive display of the material wealth of the ultra-rich Chinese in Singapore, formally forces the audience to see "Asia" and see *through* it as a staged spectacle, indeed a work of cinematic art designed to entertain and sell. Read in this way, the various scenes of feasts—from the sumptuous street food in the hawker centre to the exquisite gourmet food in Peik Lin's house and in Nick's grandmother's mansion—are self-reflexive scenes of literal food consumption that parallel the audience's visual consumption of the film. The culinary idiom of the film thus speaks to both the material abundance of a Chinese-focussed "Asia" and the audience's relationship with the film's exhibition of Chinese affluence in postcolonial Singapore. Stylistically exuberant, the film's rhetoric of excess does not simply invite the audience to indulge in the pleasure of cinematic consumption but also potentially makes them aware of, reflect on, even question the film's Chinese capitalistic excess and, indeed, the plausibility of such material excess in Singapore and the rest of Southeast Asia.

Admittedly, one can argue that such visual imagery of Chinese wealth easily plays into the self-translated image of postcolonial Singapore in the global theatre. As an Asian tiger, Singapore is the only country in Southeast Asia to inhabit the status of a "first world" economy, which makes it the richest state in the region. Singapore's transition from a backwater village to a global financial centre, as Chua Beng Huat notes, has made the authoritarian state a "model" for development by various developing nations (2017, 2). A "model" because, notwithstanding its authoritarian rule, Singapore is "an overwhelming middle-class society" (Chua 2017, 4). This economic miracle can readily translate into national self-pride that consciously or unconsciously makes the country complicit in the symbolic erasure of its poorer Southeast Asian neighbours.

More than the Southeast Asian states next door, postcolonial Singapore readily partakes in the grand narrative of the rise of a Chinese-dominant Asia. In his memoirs, the late Lee Kuan Yew described Singapore as "a Chinese land in a Malay Sea" that prospered due to its industrious Chinese population (1998, 23). Here, Lee's postcolonial reading of race relations in Singapore that prioritises *Nanyang* Chinese immigrants in fact reinscribes the regime of racial configuration in the British colonial era. As Daniel P.S. Goh and Philip Holden remind us, colonial racial governmentality placed Chinese as "commercial middlemen aliens," Malays and Indonesians as "indigenous peasant smallholders," and Indian as "municipal and plantation labourers" (2009, 5). This racial logic of colonial pluralism is replicated in state multiracialism in the postcolonial era. Angelia Poon notes how state multiracial ideology works to safeguard Chinese interests, "all the while without seeming to privilege any one particular racial group" (2009, 72). In the neoliberal present, the discrete racial grid allows Singapore to further profit from the economic opportunities afforded by the rise of China. Tapping into ethnic affinity in the face of new market realities, the promotion of Mandarin and Chinese culture is seen as a strategic means to help a Chinese-majority state to "forge stronger business ties with China" (Poon 2009, 79). To some extent, the racial inequality inherent in state multiracial policies also finds expression in the cultural domain. Kenneth Paul Tan identifies the reproduction of racial hierarchies in commercial films in

Singapore, arguing that the espousal of state neoliberal multiracialism entails the "complete absence, under-representation, simplistic representation, or negative representation of racial minorities" (2009, 127).

It is perhaps no surprise then that the Singapore state seizes the chance to promote itself through the global visibility of *Crazy Rich Asians*, given the film's focalisation of Chinese Singaporean capital. This state initiative happened despite the fact that the author Kwan is wanted by the Singapore government for shunning national service (Cain 2018).[3] In its efforts at national self-branding, the postcolonial island state has been complicit with cultivating the image of a "crazy rich" Singapore. In fact, after the film's world premiere in Hollywood, the Singapore Tourism Board and TAO Group—a restaurant and nightlife company—co-organised the "Crazy Rich Singapore Week" in Los Angeles. The event brought the Singapore contingent of the film crew to Hollywood, showcasing the island state's national talents abroad. As Kershing Goh, regional director of the Singapore Tourism Board Americas, remarks: "We hope that the film will inspire more visitors to discover the multitude of experiences in Singapore and ignite their passions for culture, food, entertainment and nightlife" (quoted in Loh 2018). What this confirms is the ease with which Chu's film can be co-opted by Singapore's national self-engineering. This national branding is ironic given the lack of recognition of the "use" of Malaysia as a significant place for the shooting of the film, and the lack of attention to other poor Southeast Asian neighbours, as seen earlier. With the complicity of Singapore in the reification of a crazy rich self-image, how does the film's formal excess enact satiric criticism of race and class politics?

Here a theoretical explication of the concept "excess" is necessary. By excess, I mean the film's stylistic investment in wealth display tends towards the superfluous and the redundant in a narrative of Chinese capital in postcolonial Singapore. It goes beyond the necessary and the "proper." In her famous formulation, film theorist Kristin Thompson defines "cinematic excess" as "aspects of the work which are not contained by its unifying forces" (1977, 54). In particular, cinematic excess is that which exceeds narrative content and enriches the spectator's perceptual field (Thompson 1977, 59). Thomson's theorisation recognises films as heterogeneous signifying systems that boast competing and conflicting forces. The repetition of certain visual codes, which lies outside narrative necessity, amounts to a stylistic overstatement. Devoid of a narrative imperative, such a stylistic overemphasis operates as a force of disunity that undermines the unity of the cinematic story. For Thompson, cinematic excess compels the audience to "linger over devices longer than their structured function would seem to warrant" (1977, 56). Implicating the spectator in its formal apparatus, cinematic excess then offers a form of reading otherwise: that which is other than its manifest narrative meaning.

In *Crazy Rich Asians*, Singaporean Chinese capital, which is racially marked and class dependent, speaks through the cinematic language of excess. The superfluous, for instance, expresses itself in the colour of gold that decorates the mansion of the upper-class Chinese. Peik Lin's house is inordinately golden, which functions as a visual exaggeration of opulence. Recall the golden fountain, golden statues, the golden door, gold-plated cutlery, gold-coloured wardrobes, gold-rimmed mirrors, and so on and so forth in the mansion. The formal indulgence in the colour gold is redundant insofar as the size of the mansion already conveys the narrative content of the rise of Chinese capital in Singapore. The inessential also manifests in the stylistic obsession with Chinese Singaporeans' fancy attire, the materiality of which surpasses narrative motivation. As with a fashion show, the audience is constantly presented with high-end apparel. This is conspicuous when the pyjama-clad Peik Lin helps Rachel find the right party dress from her wardrobe. The recurrent emphasis on luxury apparel is reiterated in the fashionista figure of Astrid and the pre-paid shopping spree during the bachelorette party. Such a cinematic fashion parade continues in the wedding scene which spotlights the bride's wedding gown, and culminates in the rooftop party scene crowded with well-dressed party-goers in the finale. Similarly, the film's many visual references to Chinese women's extravagant jewellery are unwarranted. These ornamental presences include Ah Ma's orchid-shaped Carnet brooch, Eleanor's diamond earrings and emerald ring, Astrid's Bulgari bracelet and diamond chandelier earrings, Rachel's hairpiece and diamond pendant, and the Swarovski crystals on Araminta's wedding veil, to name some prominent decorative pieces (Chouinard 2018). As the recurrence of these excessive details adds nothing to the capitalist story, they direct the spectators to contemplate their recalcitrant and tenacious nature. Through its excessive stylisation, Chu's film creates a critical distance between the spectators and the film itself, and by extension, between reality and fiction. The visual politics of excess in Chu's film thus serves as a potential rejoinder to the gap between the film (aesthetic construct) and the world of Singapore or Southeast Asia (lived reality).

That cinematic excess in *Crazy Rich Asians* can produce the opposite function as a satiric critique of its racial and class-based displacement of Southeast Asia requires some unpacking here. I take my cue from cultural critic Rey Chow's exegesis of Chinese visual culture in a global context. Analysing the mixed reception of the cinema of Fifth Generation Chinese directors in China and the West, Chow argues that Zhang Yimou's visually appealing cinematic work performs "a kind of postmodern *self*-writing or *auto*ethnography" which is "a form of *intercultural* translation in the postcolonial age" (emphasis original) (1995, xi). Chow's complex critique of orientalism in Zhang's films as itself performing a form of critique is instructive:

> For if orientalism, understood in the sense Said uses it, is in part a form of voyeuristic aggression, then what Zhang is producing is rather an exhibitionist self-display that contains, in its very excessive modes, a critique of the voyeurism of orientalism itself. [. . .] this ethnography

accepts the historical fact of orientalism and performs a critique (i.e., evaluation) of it by staging and parodying orientalism's politics of visuality.

(1995, 171)

Chow's argument here provocatively suggests that Zhang's cinematic excess is *not* merely an enactment of orientalism, but also a parody of orientalism in a cross-cultural global milieu.

While embedded in a different sociopolitical context, Chow's nuanced treatment of Zhang's cinematic aesthetics is useful for proffering an alternative reading of the visual excess and the project of translating "Asia" in Chu's *Crazy Rich Asians*. Following Chow's logic, Chu's cinematic excess can be perceived *not* necessarily just as an exhibition of Singaporean Chinese capital, but also potentially a critique of its elision of Southeast Asia based on the vectors of race and class. For the (well-trained) spectators, the spectacle of excessive Chinese opulence as staged in the film simultaneously reminds them of the possibility that this excessiveness signifies exclusiveness, and that the "Southeast Asia" that is translated on the screen is but an *image* of Southeast Asia, amongst multifarious possible images of Southeast Asia. Such scenes may even alert them to the possibility that the film perhaps only parrots the master narrative of the ascension of a China-oriented Asia in the global economic theatre. For the American audience, Chu's cinematic excess may be a reminder that the film is possibly only offering the audience the opportunity to see what they want to see, a mode of seeing that may continue to make them Orientalist voyeurs of the so-called "crazy rich Asians" who dislodge the poor and non-Chinese Asians in Singapore and the rest of Southeast Asia.

In this sense, the film's visual politics of excess serves as a stylistic commentary on the art of reading otherwise. As Chu's film ostensibly invites the audience to bask in the glossy surface afforded by Chinese capital, it also offers via the cinematic language of excess the opportunity for them to think *about* and perhaps *beyond* the material surface of the screen as a frame and a medium: what gets translated and included in its supposedly "Asian" frame? What lies outside the frame and the zone of translatability? To be sure, this possibility of reading otherwise is contingent on cinematic readers as close readers who are attentive to stylistic details. Without idealising cinema spectators, I nevertheless contend that through its poetics of excess, Chu's film allows for the possibility, even if somewhat circumscribed, of its own self-critique.

Conclusion

As my critical exegesis illustrates, *Crazy Rich Asians* concretises the complex politics of translating across cultures in the trans-Pacific space. There are multiple levels of appropriation at work in cultural mediation, which speak to local, regional, and global politics of (visual) difference. On the one hand, appropriative translation enables Asian Americans to lobby for racial recognition in America. Here, one may again borrow from Nguyen, who speaks in favour of Chu's cinematic project despite its various inadequacies. As an ethnic minority cultural producer in the US, Nguyen asks a pressing question regarding the audience's expectation of the film: if it is acceptable for white American directors to produce mediocre films in Hollywood and keep on producing them, why aren't Asian Americans entitled to it? (2018). Resisting the "Model Minority" narrative, Nguyen's question highlights the burden placed on ethnic minority cultural producers in America: that they must be the best and produce the best in order to persist as American cultural producers. This social burden suggests that Asian Americans must always be model minorities and produce exemplary works in order to secure their cultural place in America. Nguyen's observation about how racial inequality operates even in the critical assessment of cultural productions is perceptive. In Kwan's authorial verdict, "[t]his movie cannot be everything for everyone" (quoted in Chiu 2018). The film is not meant to translate the "entire entirety of the Asian experience"; instead, it is a "very specific movie about a very specific world" (quoted in Chiu 2018).

While the defence of racial parity remains a crucial battle in white America, it does not automatically give minority cultural workers immunity from suppressing *other* others. What Chu's film does not adequately address is the power differentials between Asian America and Southeast Asia that inhere in its filmic translation. Placing the politics of translation in the global arena, Asian Americans certainly have more cultural capital and visibility compared to Southeast Asians. Audiences located in Southeast Asia confront a double marginalisation vis-à-vis Hollywood representations. The long history of Hollywood's engagement or, rather, lack thereof with Southeast Asia is salient in that Southeast Asians in Asia are not just being represented by white America but are also now represented by Asian America. Southeast Asia, the object of the cinematic mistranslation is here doubly deprived of its representational agency. In resisting the historic representations of the racial other in America, Chu's film ironically ends up further marginalising the Southeast Asian other. It seems to convey the message that a Chinese-dominant Asia is a force to reckon with. This is a grand narrative that Singapore complies with, given its own Chinese-majority population and dominant economic status in Southeast Asia. Yet, as I suggest throughout, despite its desirability as a tactic of postcolonial recuperation for Asian America, the film's translational practice is detrimental to the global image of Southeast Asia, in particular, what Chin calls "the disenfranchised and 'brown-skinned' Southeast Asians."[4]

The lesson that must be learned here pertains to the cultivation of an ethics of translation that respects cultural alterity beyond the national horizon. This ethical mode of translation is not one-way, but multidirectional. Given what Sengupta sees as a highly manipulative process, translators ought to pay heed to the uneven global space that marks the production, circulation, and reception of cultural texts (1995, 159–80). They should avoid locking themselves into the tunnel vision of national politics that neglects the transnational repercussions of translated narratives. That Chu's film is predicated on its transnational borrowing from Southeast Asia means that it needs to go beyond the narrow national framework (America) that it works with to engage with *other* others. This resonates with what Emily Apter conceptualises as the translation zone: "a zone of critical engagement that connects the 'l' and 'n' of transLation and transNation" (2006, 5). An ethically robust form of transnational translation will only facilitate cross-border coalition and cross-class solidarity.

Irrespective of the film's problematic translation of Asia, its cinematic excess nonetheless indexes a certain self-reflexivity about its representational limits. Though by no means a straightforward interpretive trajectory, the film proffers the possibility of a different reading through its cinematic stylistics. Its formal excess invites us to visualise a potentially different Southeast Asia. As Gayatri Chakravorty Spivak eloquently reminds us in *Other Asias*, "Asia" must be pluralised as a continental category in order to accommodate its diverse histories and lived realities. For Spivak, Asia is "a position without identity" (2008, 239). The non-identitarian view is instructive here inasmuch as it contests Asia or, for that matter, Southeast Asia, as a totalising category that forbids other possibilities of imagining or translating it. Perhaps one need not be pessimistic about the work of appropriative translation by minority groups. Perhaps one can take some solace in the power of creative works whose formal excess makes possible multiple interpretive possibilities.

Notes

1 Kevin Kwan is a Singaporean American writer. Born in Singapore, he currently resides in America. Kwan earned his BA in Media Studies from the University of Houston–Clear Lake and a BFA in Photography from Parsons School of Design. Kwan is best known for his literary trilogy consisting of *Crazy Rich Asians* (2013), *China Rich Girlfriend* (2015), and *Rich People Problems* (2017). This chapter focusses on the film adaptation of Kwan's *Crazy Rich Asians* rather than the novel itself, as it is predominantly interested in the visual politics of translation in the cinematic medium and the ambiguity afforded by its formal language.
2 I say "fictional" because while Rawa Island exists in Malaysia and is named in the film, the actual shooting of the scene took place on another Malaysian island, Langkawi (Tan 2018).
3 Singapore adopts the policy of mandatory national service which demands that male citizens and permanent residents undertake two years of uniformed services. In 2018, the Singapore defence ministry faulted Kwan for evading military service by not registering in 1990, "despite notices and letters sent to his overseas address" (Cain 2018). Singapore also rejected both "Kwan's 1994 application to renounce his Singapore citizenship and a subsequent appeal" (Cain 2018).
4 I am very grateful to Grace V.S. Chin, editor of this volume, for her incisive and meticulous comments on the drafts of this chapter, which helped me flesh out the politics of Southeast Asia's erasure in the film.

References

Apter, Emily. 2006. *The Translation Zone: A New Comparative Literature*. Princeton, NJ: Princeton University Press.

Ashcroft, Bill, Gareth Griffiths, and Helen Tiffins. 1989. *The Empire Writes Back: Theory and Practice in Postcolonial Literatures*. London and New York: Routledge.

Bahrawi, Nazry. 2018. "Crazy Rich Asians: The Return of Sham-East Asia?" *Aljazeera*, September 2. https://www.aljazeera.com/indepth/opinion/crazy-rich-asians-return-sham-east-asia-180829064300724.html.

Bassnett, Susan. 2013. "Postcolonialism and/ as Translation." In *The Oxford Handbook of Postcolonial Studies*, edited by Graham Huggan, 340–58. Oxford: Oxford University Press.

Bassnett, Susan, and André Lefevere. 1990. *Translation, History and Culture*. London: Cassell.

Bhabha, Homi K. 2004. *The Location of Culture*. 2nd ed. London and New York: Routledge.

Bradshaw, Peter. 2018. "Crazy Rich Asians Review—Cinderella Does Singapore in a Riotous Romance." *The Guardian*, September 13. https://www.theguardian.com/film/2018/sep/13/crazy-rich-asians-review-jon-m-chu-constance-wu.

Brodzki, Bella. 2007. *Can These Bones Live? Translation, Survival, and Cultural Memory*. Stanford, CA: Stanford University Press.

Cain, Sian. 2018. "Crazy Rich Asians Author Wanted for Dodging Singapore Military Service." *The Guardian*, August 23. https://www.theguardian.com/books/2018/aug/23/crazy-rich-asians-author-wanted-for-dodging-singapore-military-service-kevin-kwan.

Chiu, Allyson. 2018. "Is 'Crazy Rich Asians' historic? 'That's Just Way Too Much Pressure,' Says Kevin Kwan, Who Wrote the Book." *The Washington Post*, August 13. https://www.washingtonpost.com/news/morning-mix/wp/2018/08/13/is-crazy-rich-asians-historic-thats-just-way-too-much-pressure-says-kevin-kwan-who-wrote-the-book/.

Chouinard, Haley. 2018. "Take a Look at the Opulent, and Real, High-End Jewelry of Crazy Rich Asians." *Galerie*, August 22. https://www.galeriemagazine.com/jewelry-crazy-rich-asians/.

Chow, Rey. 1995. *Primitive Passions: Visuality, Sexuality, Ethnography, and Contemporary Chinese Cinema*. New York: Columbia University Press.

Chua, Beng Huat. 2017. *Liberalism Disavowed: Communitarianism and State Capitalism in Singapore*. Singapore: NUS Press.

Chung, Winnie. 2019. "Gemma Chan Wants to Tell Stories for Asians Everywhere." *Inkstone News*, June 19. https://www.inkstonenews.com/arts/crazy-rich-asians-gemma-chan-wants-tell-more-asian-stories/article/3015186.

Financial Times. 2018. "Crazy Rich Asians Star Constance Wu on How the Movie Became a Movement." December 6. https://www.ft.com/content/60e45522-f752-11e8-af46-2022a0b02a6c.

Goh, Daniel P. S., and Philip Holden. 2009. "Introduction: Postcoloniality, Race and Multiculturalism." In *Race and Multiculturalism in Malaysia and Singapore*, edited by Daniel P. S. Goh, Matilda Gabrielpillai, Philip Holden, and Gaik Cheng Khoo, 1–16. London and New York: Routledge.

Jiang, Ada. 2018. "How do Asians React to 'Crazy Rich Asians'? We Take a Look at Audience Responses from China, Singapore, Malaysia and the Philippines."

South China Morning Post, September 17. https://www.scmp.com/magazines/style/news-trends/article/2164260/how-do-asians-react-crazy-rich-asians-we-take-look.
Lange, Jeva. 2018. "*Crazy Rich Asians* Has a Money Problem." *The Week*, August 16. https://theweek.com/articles/790381/crazy-rich-asians-money-problem.
Lee, Kuan Yew. 1998. *The Singapore Story: Memoirs of Lee Kuan Yew*. Singapore: Prentice-Hall.
Leong, Michelle. 2018. "7 Malaysia Locations Filmed in Crazy Rich Asians." *Culture Trip*, September 18. https://theculturetrip.com/asia/malaysia/articles/7-malaysia-locations-filmed-in-crazy-rich-asians/.
Lhatoo, Yonden. 2018. "Enough of Crazy Rich Asians, Think of Crazy Poor Hongkongers." *South China Morning Post*, August 25. https://www.scmp.com/news/hong-kong/community/article/2161325/enough-crazy-rich-asians-think-crazy-poor-hongkongers.
Loh, Genevieve Sarah. 2018. "Singapore Takes Over Hollywood as Crazy Rich Asians Premieres." *Channel News Asia*, August 13. https://www.channelnewsasia.com/news/lifestyle/crazy-rich-asians-premiere-singapore-actors-talent-party-10607358.
Lowe, Lisa. 1996. *Immigrant Acts: On Asian American Cultural Politics*. Durham, NC: Duke University Press.
Nguyen, Viet Thanh. 2002. *Race and Resistance: Literature and Politics in Asian America*. Oxford and New York: Oxford University Press.
———. 2016. *Nothing Ever Dies: Vietnam and the Memory of War*. Cambridge, MA: Harvard University Press.
———. 2018. "Asian-Americans Need More Movies, Even Mediocre Ones." *The New York Times*, August 21. https://www.nytimes.com/2018/08/21/opinion/crazy-rich-asians-movie.html.
Niranjana, Tejaswini. 1992. *Siting Translation: History, Post-Structuralism and the Colonial Context*. Berkeley: University of California Press.
Ong, Aihwa. 1999. *Flexible Citizenship: The Cultural Logics of Transnationality*. Durham, NC: Duke University Press.
Ono, Kent A., and Vincent N. Pham. 2008. *Asian Americans and the Media: Media and Minorities*. Cambridge: Polity Press.
Poon, Angelia. 2009. "Pick and Mix for a Global City: Race and Cosmopolitanism in Singapore." In *Race and Multiculturalism in Malaysia and Singapore*, edited by Daniel P.S. Goh, Matilda Gabrielpillai, Philip Holden, and Gaik Cheng Khoo, 70–85. London and New York: Routledge.
Rahman-Jones, Imran. 2018. "Crazy Rich Asians: Henry Golding on Becoming a Leading Man in His First Film." *BBC News*, September 14. https://www.bbc.co.uk/news/newsbeat-45498674.
Rodriguez, Ashley. 2018. "'Crazy Rich Asians' Is the Top-Grossing Romantic Comedy in 10 Years." *Quartz*, October 1. https://qz.com/1408252/crazy-rich-asians-is-now-the-top-grossing-rom-com-in-10-years/.
Sengupta, Mahasweta. 1995. "Translation as Manipulation: The Power of Images and Images of Power." In *Between Languages and Cultures: Translation and Cross-Cultural Texts*, edited by Anuradha Dingwaney and Carol Maier, 159–80. Pittsburgh, PA and London: University of Pittsburgh Press.
Smail, Gretchen. 2018. "Crazy Rich Asians Review—Glossy Romcom is a Vital Crowd-pleaser." *The Guardian*, August 13. https://www.theguardian.com/film/2018/aug/13/crazy-rich-asians-review-kevin-kwan.
South China Morning Post. 2018. "How Whitewashing in Hollywood Nudged Director Jon M. Chu into Making 'Crazy Rich Asians.'" August 19. https://

www.scmp.com/magazines/style/news-trends/article/2160201/how-whitewashing-hollywood-nudged-director-jon-m-chu.

Spivak, Gayatri Chakravorty. 2008. *Other Asias*. Malden, MA: Blackwell Publishing.

Tan, Kenneth Paul. 2009. "Racial Stereotypes in Singapore Films: Commercial Value and Critical Possibilities." In *Race and Multiculturalism in Malaysia and Singapore*, edited by Daniel P.S. Goh, Matilda Gabrielpillai, Philip Holden, and Gaik Cheng Khoo, 124–40. London and New York: Routledge.

Tan, Mei Zi. 2018. "Here Are Malaysian Locations Featured in 'Crazy Rich Asians.'" *Malay Mail*, August 15. https://www.malaymail.com/news/showbiz/2018/08/15/here-are-malaysian-locations-featured-in-crazy-rich-asians/1662727.

The Straits Times. 2018. "Chinese Cinemagoers Not Crazy over Crazy Rich Asians." December 2. https://www.straitstimes.com/lifestyle/entertainment/chinese-cinemagoers-not-crazy-over-crazy-rich-asians/.

Thompson, Kristin. 1977. "The Concept of Cinematic Excess." *Ciné-Tracts* 1, no. 2: 54–63.

Walkowitz, Rebecca L. 2015. *Born Translated: The Contemporary Novel in an Age of World Literature*. New York: Columbia University Press.

9 Translation and LGBT studies in the Philippines[1]

J. Neil C. Garcia

Introduction

I've been "doing" gay theory and writing about Philippine gay culture for a quarter of a century now, my primary research topic having been, almost from the very beginning, about these fields of inquiry.[2] What's important about this chronological reckoning isn't only the realisation of all the important passages that gay (and more recently, LGBT) life in the Philippines has undergone in the last two and a half decades—but also the fact that, as this chapter will seek to productively unpack, I've pretty much written everything about these allied subjects not in my first language of Tagalog, but rather in my second language which, as with most Filipinos, is English.

What does it mean when we render opaque the specificity of the language in which we have been inquiring and theorising, especially when the location in which they occur and to which they pertain is not "simple"—which is to say, monolingual or monocultural—but rather, culturally hybrid, syncretic, and helplessly mixed?

In other words, I'm interested in the question of *interlinguality* or translation, and how it may prove critically generative to frame our inquiries into the specificities of LGBT critical and theoretical work in our and perhaps other global locations from the perspective of how *translational it all is*. This is especially the case to the degree that in many different places around the world, LGBT discourse is being conducted in the anglophonic register, which of course merely reflects trends in technological and cultural globalisation as a whole.

I'm going to try to accomplish several tasks in this chapter. First, I will attempt to describe the linguistic situation in the Philippines as translational, by which I mean that it is constitutively and interlingually mixed or hybrid. In pursuit of this idea, I will recur to my previous studies of the two texts: first, of what may well be the earliest Filipino anglophone novel about the "homosexual" experience, Severino Montano's unpublished novel, *The Lion and the Faun* (c. 1960–1970); and, second, of a quizzical contemporaneous poem, "A Parable" ([1964]2002), by Rolando Tinio. Both authors were dramatists and posthumously declared National Artists, although it is the latter who actually reflected on the cultural implications of his bilingualism. I will attempt in my reading to identify these texts' translational moments, if only to show the persistence of local—indeed, quite possibly, untranslatable—meanings despite, or precisely because, of the textual uniformity of their anglophone surface.

Translation, as an interpretive procedure, will be the frame within which I will attempt to resituate and rethink the conceptual issues and debates that I've been grappling with in the area of Gender and Sexuality Studies across the past decades. I intend to argue that what I've repeatedly called out—and relatively endorsed—as the "moderately nativist" position in the study of gender and sexuality in the postcolonial context (Garcia 2013) is nothing if not another register of the critical position that recognises the translational dynamic between local and translocal—between "oral" and "textual," "traditional" and "modern," "Western" and "postcolonial"—conceptual histories. Finally, I will complicate the question of the critical difference that the idea of translation makes by briefly examining recent published attempts to do local gay and lesbian criticism in the Filipino language.

Central to these tasks is my contention—not exactly controversial, inasmuch as it's almost an academic commonplace by now—that critical interventions, unlike literary or creative writing, are by definition supposed to be more self-reflexive, particularly in regard to their presuppositions. Thus, while anglophone creative writers are not expected to be all that conscious that they are performing cultural translations when they write, this very same "indulgence" may not be so readily granted the critic or theorist, one of whose primary tasks is to examine his or her own logical premises when he or she composes his or her critiques.

It's in view of this imperative that I take to task recent attempts to produce Filipino-language scholarship in "Bakla and Tomboy (or Lesbyana) Studies,"[3] which do self-consciously translate essentialist precepts and arguments from international (mostly American) LGBT or Queer studies, and yet do so without mediating or translating them critically or self-reflexively enough. Hence, while seemingly local and/or "home-grown," this form of local theorising, because it does not question its own epistemological (in this case, necessarily socially constructed) assumptions, ironically merely replicates the sexological universalisms that the "nationalist" and *nativising* gesture—of writing resolutely and admirably in Filipino—supposedly avoids. It's indeed ironic that such avowedly "localist" attempts have not been as theoretically supple and self-reflexive as the critical work done by Filipino anglophone scholars, and instead have unwittingly channelled essentialist (really, Western) concepts of gender and sexuality.

Hybrid gender/sexuality

In the Philippines, one of Americanisation's most enduring effects is the socialisation of Filipinos into modern modes of gender and sexual identity formation. This process was "naturalised" and enforced through a variety of biomedical anglophone discourses, and has resulted in the entrenchment of the "homo/hetero" logic in the increasingly *sexually freighted* lives of educated Filipinos (see Suarez 2017).

As we know, it's to this dynamic that the Philippines owes the reality of local gay and lesbian cultures. There are many encouraging narratives that the urban-based sexualisation of Filipinos has engendered, and these are the narratives of cultural hybridity and translation, which may also be read as narratives of resistance. The perspective that inquires into the question of translation is different from cosmopolitanism, which I find tends to elide the issue of resistance, by and large. As postcolonial studies has productively elucidated across the last few decades, while nobody may be said to actively resist, as the poetics of postcoloniality itself demonstrates, something certainly may be said to be resistant to the degree that difference persists despite, or precisely because, of the illusion of equivalence that translation supposedly effects.

If we may recall, Homi K. Bhabha explains hybridity as the non-convergence between colonial power's intentions and the effects of those who receive them. In every new encounter, colonial authority repeats itself as different from the culture it seeks to subjugate. Each repetition of its differential and discriminatory discourse undermines the very claims of this discourse to a natural and singular originality: power repeats and imitates itself over and over, and is also diluted, compromised, and hybridised at every turn. As Bhabha eloquently puts it: "In the very practice of domination the language of the master becomes hybrid—neither the one thing nor the other" (1993, 33). Thus, all colonial norms, including those that pertain to gender and sexual identities and desires, become recontextualised and translated by the other culture, split between their claims and their performances, syncretised from the very moment of contact with the colonised. Colonial power isn't then a monolithic and absolute system, for it is necessarily fractured and transformed in its *relationality* with its subjects, over whom it exercises both a coercive and an empowering mystique.

For the simple reason that it illustrates the imperfect workings of a dominant discourse that transforms and is transformed in the very fact of its incumbency, Bhabha's theory exemplifies, for the colonial situation, Michel Foucault's notion of an internally incoherent, appropriable, and ambivalent power ([1984]1991, 62–3). Hence, as Bhabha explains it, hybridity is inevitable and constitutive of the colonial dynamic itself. This is because once situated, no colonial imposition, no imported concept, no foreign knowledge or cultural practice ever stays self-identical or absolute. And the curious thing is that none of this needs to be meant or schemed by anyone at all: given the transcultural quality of colonial life, hybridity just is. Consequently, postcolonial critique may be seen as an analytical procedure that seeks to surface not only the wilful resistances and dissidences, but also the "critical difference"—the irreducible specificity, which is a direct function of hybridity—that is implicit in postcolonial practices and texts. In light of the double-dealing "homogenising" project of imperialism, this difference or specificity may now be recognised not merely as evidence of cultural diversity in postcolonial societies, but as forms of dissidence and meaningful demurral, as instances of "performative subversion."

More specifically, we can say that some of these resistant and subversive narratives include LGBT activism itself, which—as Filipinos practise it, and despite appearances—is certainly not reducible to the same political "thing" that it arguably is, elsewhere. While it was the arrival of sexological thinking that pathologised Filipino LGBTs in the first place, as the example of increasingly politicised Filipino gays, lesbians, and transgenders illustrates, it was precisely this stigma that enabled the LGBT movement. This is especially so because like modern heteronormativity itself, this stigma needs to be translated to take effect.

To illuminate the workings of this intercultural process, I shall be performing a broadly postcolonial reading of Severino Montano's unpublished novel, *The Lion and the Faun*, paying attention to how, in this text, traditional understandings of gender have come to confront and dialogue with the homo/hetero distinction that the unfinished project of modernity continues to bequeath. It shall be my contention that this encounter has been a translational one, and as such it is characterised by slippages and creative transformations between the source and target texts.

The ironic and "resistant" dynamics of this translation are easily evident in early cosmopolitanising projects to normalise or masculinise the *bakla* (a Filipino word that all at once connotes ideas of intramale sexual attraction, male femininity, and male-to-female gender-crossing), whose effeminate identity remains "relevant" despite the wilful attempt to supplant it. In the case of Tinio's poem, the seemingly universal referents may on closer look be seen as poetic translations meant to at once generate ambiguity (a desirable poetic quality) and circumvent the conservative religious (Catholic) discourse that dominated the anglophone Philippine writing of his time.

The question of English

We need to begin by reminding ourselves that English is a language that continues to occupy an ironic place in the lives of many Filipinos. Hence, to the degree that Philippine literature in English is translational, it cannot be simply representational or realistic: realism is a signifying practice that presupposes a culturally homogeneous and linguistically uniform ground upon which the "consensus" of representational fidelity can happen. And yet, much of the criticism of this literature has generally failed to take note of this crucial precondition, enacting a category mistake with ruinous consequences. Because realism is a foundational compositional and critical concept, it only follows that the various literary practices encoded in Philippine anglophone writing still need to be *postcolonially specified*, and their translated or syncretic qualities critically recognised and unpacked.

The Philippines's anglophone tradition represents local realities by translating them, both in the technical and in the cultural senses of the word. If, within a monocultural context, realism is always already the translation from imitation to "creation," then in the linguistically plural situations of postcolonial societies this already fraught process (of verbal "mimesis") can only be even more complex and confounding. Comprised mostly of domesticised (rather than foreignised) cultural translations, Philippine literature in English negotiates the plurality of cultural and linguistic registers and ideas of local and non-English realities, and encodes them uniformly in/as English (Garcia 2014, 99–127). The critical task, then, is to *postcolonially interpret* its seemingly self-evident themes, images, and gestures by translating them back into the specific conditions and situations that generated them.

In the Philippines, the most popular local term for the male homosexual— the pejorative *bakla*—started out as an ungendered adjective to denote a state of confusion or fear. During the Spanish period, it slowly became synonymous with the local gender terms for womanish men, except that unlike the words that it eventually came to eclipse—words for gender-crossers, generally—it carried with it the force of macho insult (Garcia 2009, 420–56). With Americanisation, upon the arrival of the psychological style of reasoning—that, among things, implanted sexological categories—*bakla* was slowly but securely "homo/sexualised," so much so that it is now understood as a synonym for "male homosexual," although as it occurs in popular culture it still mostly connotes the earlier ideas of effeminacy and even "transgenderism."

The *bakla* is therefore, at best, a partially homosexualised identity— partial because only he and not his love object (the "real man") gets imputed with the orientation, despite their mutual indulgence in (and enjoyment of) what is technically homosexual sex. In this matrix, gender would appear to be partially yoked to a customary privileging of depth or core-ness (in Filipino psychology, *kalooban,* literally "insideness," which is gendered and heteronormatively defined); external, even genital, acts can be qualified, to an extent, by this interiority. In other words, residual indigenous valuations of gender have simply served to modify—that is to say, hybridise—the newly "implanted" sexual order.[4] A case in point: despite the popularly recognised fact that the *bakla* has sex with the *tunay na lalake,* or "real man," it is only the former—the effeminate *bakla*—who is perceived as the homosexual in Filipino culture; his masculine partner remains "heterosexual," which is equated with the "realness" of his masculinity and is the very reason he is considered desirable by the former.

Translating the *Bakla*: Montano's *The Lion and the Faun*

Severino Montano was the moving force in Philippine theatre before and after the Second World War. His work in Philippine anglophone theatre was extensive and, in terms of his staging innovations, undeniably significant (see Maniquis 1994). He wrote his novel well before his death in 1980 and it provides an interesting early example of how American-sponsored homosexualisation in the Philippines has ironically produced an abjected identity that may be seen to embrace its abjection, and to speak *of* and *for* itself.

The novel is a provocative and largely autobiographical roman-à-clef.[5] Comparing the known facts about Montano's life with those of his main character, Dr Diosdado Medalla, the reader is indeed encouraged to carry out a "biographical interpretation" of the text, which effectively parodies and satirises the shallow and hypocritical lives of Manila's *culturati,* and even makes broad hints at a possible romantic dalliance between Medalla (whose nickname is Dadong) and his famous dearest friend, the late Philippine President Ramon "Monching" Magsaysay.[6] Nonetheless, despite the gossipy subplots and rather crass intrigues, the main story is still Dadong's relationship with the younger Amihan, an Army major stationed at the ROTC (Reserve Officers' Training Corps) office of the university where Dadong teaches and has founded a theatre company. Despite the novel's numerous interesting distractions involving well-known socialites and celebrities, this is still, in the main, a love story.

Dadong's background is interesting. Like Montano, for whom he is a fictional stand-in, he has lived and studied in Washington DC for several years before returning to the Philippines to teach and do theatre as well as privately practise a kind of vulgar psychoanalysis. While in the US, he had a romantic relationship and cohabited with a German-born American, an economist for the State Department by the name of Leonard Blumenthal. Despite this candid revelation, however, the novel takes pains to paint a "masculine" and "bisexual" picture of Dadong as a suavely intelligent and eminently eligible bachelor, who is admittedly homosexually oriented but can swing the other way just as effectively. In the opening chapter we are told that he was raped by their mulatta maid one drunken evening, an incident which convinces him that he can bring himself to "like" (Montano 1960–1970, n.p.) women too, although it's important to note that they have to be extremely intelligent, sexy, talented, and menially devoted to him first, before they can ever hope to catch his fancy.

Upon returning to the Philippines, he is pursued by all manner of desperate, vicious, and big-breasted women, with whom he is hopelessly bored. After all, being a well-travelled Renaissance man, he aspires after loftier things. And so, to amuse himself, he quickly puts his mind to building his magnificent "mansion of love" (Montano 1960–1970, n.p.), Villa Bello, including a garden in which he plants bamboo in memory of his beloved friend, the charismatic Philippine president Magsaysay, whose life was unexpectedly cut short in a plane crash outside Cebu City. Still in mourning, Dadong meets Amihan at a play that he is directing for the university. They quickly hit it off, fall desperately in love, and wistfully call each other "faun" and "lion," respectively (Montano 1960–1970, n.p.). Dadong fancies himself both a shrink and a mentor to his beloved, whom he compares,

Pygmalion-like, to a rough slab of marble from which he intends to carve his own marvellous sculpture of David. Amihan is unhappily married to a scheming first cousin who had seduced him, and thus forced him to marry her. By the time Amihan and the theatre director meet, the former is practically buried under a mountain of pesky and malnourished children, and feeling utterly oppressed by his empty marriage—a dismal fate the latter, needless to say, is determined to redeem him from.

Over the course of psychoanalysing his lover, Dadong discovers all the perversions that occurred throughout the latter's astonishingly amoral youth, including his incestuous attachment to his mother's milk-giving breast, his regular homosexual encounters with a colonel in the Philippine army and countless other men in the anonymous darkness of movie houses, sexual escapades with a number of female cousins, etc. Towards the end of the 500-page half of the novel's typewritten copy that I currently have, Dadong succeeds in convincing Amihan's wife to share her husband with him, for this is the only way—as he seriously impresses upon her—they can save him from impending insanity or even, heaven forbid, suicide. To her mind, it's all quite fine so long as her husband stays in the mood when it's her turn. Liberated from the exclusivity of his marital obligation, the lion makes love to his faun in the elegantly appointed bedroom of the latter's magnificent mansion.

The novel is formally flawed, needless to say. The glaring problems of narrative inconsistency, shallow characterisation, crass sentimentalism, belaboured and clichéd poeticism, and disorienting shifts in point of view admittedly detract from the novel's overall fictive effect. Nonetheless, our interest in this novel is not really its formal excellence (or its paucity), but rather its representational content, especially as concerns the issue of how Montano translates the story of the *bakla* into the story of the homosexual.

Because it is likely that Montano had been writing this novel on and off three or more decades before his death,[7] he simply had no access to the more sophisticated, affirmative, and feminist-inspired gay liberationist literatures that wouldn't have mandated a misogynistic attitude towards women in the project of articulating gayness and militating for its emancipation. Montano's appalling anti-woman attitude is all too evident everywhere in the text, from the unflattering description of the "loose" and "smelly" (Montano 1960–1970, n.p.) genitalia of Amihan's grubby tubercular wife, to the unfair characterisation of women as grasping, pathetic, and sex-starved gold-diggers.

In all probability, Montano's misogyny emanated out of the kind of masculinist imperative he was labouring under. To Montano's mind, it must have proved necessary to put down women in general in order to destroy the feminised and feminising stereotype that afflicted the Philippine *bakla,* an identity strangely missing in the novel. However, precisely because Montano has exiled all traces of effeminacy and *kabaklaan* from his text, we are forced to read the *bakla* as being in fact a central "force" in his articulation, for in repudiating this identity he could only have made it all the more foundational in the end.

Indeed, despite its main characters' testosterone-powered, ambisexually potent machismo, the novel's casting aspersion on women and conceiving them as vicious "competition" for the attention and affection of men are, finally, very *bakla* things to do. To the degree that the *bakla* is a feminised identity whose object of desire, as with a woman, is a *lalake* or "man," it is only logical that he should function as a woman's rival every now and then, as indeed Dadong does in relation to his partner's uncultured and "wretched little wife" (Montano 1960–1970, n.p.). It's important to note, however, that the beloved man's sexual preference as represented in the novel admits to both male and female erotic objects, although it's also clear that the genitally male lover (Dadong) needs to put in extra work—as well as to help out financially—in order to compete viably with the woman who, by the sheer privilege of her anatomy, gets to become the man's sad and ignorant wife.

As Michael L. Tan has argued, the largely verbal discourse on male bisexuality in the Philippines itself weaves in and out of the discourse on and by the *bakla*, who are both its apparent subject and its object, and whose anxiously disavowed presence therefore haunts it in a constitutive way (see Tan 1998). Indeed, because of this decision to forego openly implicating the *bakla* in the world it attempts to fictionally capture, Montano's text ends up languishing in phony Graeco-Roman mythologising, a project that he must have known would necessitate the maligning and devaluation of women, who indeed were second-class citizens in these classical worlds. Also, if his plays are any indication, he would seem to have held highly dubious and conservative beliefs regarding women in general, who are depicted as happily immolating themselves in at least his two most popular plays, for the sake of their unrequited love for men.[8] Needless to say, precisely because this novel denies the empirical inarguability of the *bakla* within the local setting the *bakla* "naturally" belongs to, it ends up being fantastical in more senses than one. Fantastical and sentimentally overwrought, to be precise.

In sum, then, Montano's text is a sprawling melodramatic story about an urbane and globally travelled theatre director who practises psychotherapy, and his tempestuous love affair with a much younger bisexual officer of the Philippine Army. Written in English, the novel problematises the sexual definitions of its main characters and uses the narrative pretext that the director—also the narrator—is a psychoanalyst in order to achieve this otherwise dour "expository" project. Needless to say, this fictive endeavour results in the mooting of local understandings of gender—namely, that the *bakla* is homosexual while the "real man" he loves is not—and the novel adopts the Western "essentialist" perspective on the issue and basically declares them both as homosexuals.

Montano's attempt to displace prevailing categories and translate the gender-intransitive discourse of orientation into the local setting does not quite succeed. On the one hand, its misogynistic subplot specifies its sexual politics as agonistic and peculiarly gender-inflected; on the other hand, despite the novel's textual insistence on their comparably masculine comportments and the mutuality of their *same-sexual* desire, the material "inequality" between the genteel, well-off, and supremely cultured unmarried older man and the economically burdened and married younger one is tellingly familiar, for it calls to mind popular cultural representations of *bakla* love (for the "real man") as financially transactional and therefore ultimately "non-reciprocal." Indeed, it's easy to see that the good director invests more in this so-called love between equals. (This novel actually "self-deconstructs" here: the profession of this love comes in the form of spoken dialogues as far as the benefactor-lover is concerned, but is merely indirectly reported or narrated in the case of the beloved.)

Still and all, the novel's "forward-looking" and cosmopolitan project is gay-affirmative: the word "gay" is mentioned only once, but it's enough to give the reader an awareness of its political agenda. That Montano chooses to play down effeminacy and focus instead on the gender-intransitive aspect of male homosexuality can only be seen as a "naive reaction" on his part: indeed, how can a novel about "intra-male" affection set in the Philippines not implicate the discourse and reality of effeminate homosexuality, embodied most forcefully in the ubiquitous persona of the *bakla*? How could Montano have even believed he could create a novelistic portrait of the Filipino gay man as masculine and non-*bakla*, when he intended this very same portrait to be, at least, recognisably Filipino?

And yes, like all the other mother tongues in the Philippines, Tagalog, the language of the world that this novel is set in, is gender-neutral. While seemingly inconsequential to Philippine anglophone criticism, the fact is that realistically, these local characters wouldn't have been a "she" or a "he." Thus, gendering these characters' identities and lives—from the Tagalog "source" to the English "target"—is and can only be ironic, to the degree that what the latter takes to be fundamentally binary is to the former, to all intents and purposes, unitary. An immense slippage takes place when one translates the pronoun *siya* to either "he" or "she." Hence, although the anatomical dimorphism of modern biomedicine—on which the homo/hetero binary rests—is translated into the Philippine linguistic context, this binary is far from coherent and simplistically assured. Montano's ignorance of this translational dynamic causes him to mistakenly believe that erotic equality can only be achieved in the supersession of the *bakla* identity—which is to say, its "masculinist homosexualisation." As we know, this is a project that can only fail, even if in his text it did generate interesting, albeit mostly ruinous, effects.

By contrast, we must remember just how extraneous the "homo/hetero" distinction is in our case, for it belongs to the sexological discourse that was brought to but only partially "implanted" in the Philippines by Americanisation. This "sexual regime" accompanied and enabled the overall modernising project of this dispensation, which basically instated the categories of

Western biomedicine in the country at the same time that it endeavoured to educate the Philippine masses and turn them literate.

Local Philippine cultures had no native categories for sexual orientation—especially where it impertinently pertains to the gender of one's sexual object choice—although they did profess native gender terms, which did presuppose some kind of "male/female" norm. We need to realise, however, that inasmuch as our native cultures were not literate but rather oral, such a norm was not scripturally dogmatic or categorically absolute. Which is to say: it was not textualised and/or "legislated" as being synonymous with anatomical givenness (and as such, to be considered practically immutable). Indeed, this norm, being more customary than anything, could be qualified and/or "modified" by affective considerations and rituals of interiority: the semantic richness and gendered quality of native concepts like *loob* ("inside")—as can be gleaned, for example, in the idiom, *pusong-babae* or "woman-hearted"—harks back and attests to this negotiability (Garcia 2009, 77, 190). According to Spanish accounts there lived, in various parts of the archipelago, "gender-crossers": individuals (especially genitally male ones) who were practically granted the social status of the "other" sex (they were "married" to men, for example), and were even seen as spiritually potent, and therefore held the prestigious office of soothsayer, shaman, or "priest" (see Brewer 1999).

Suffice it to say that a century of literacy and sexologisation has not wiped out Philippine cultures' customary understandings of (gendered) identity, especially among the great masses of Filipinos, whose education has not been very thorough, profound, and/or anglophone. In other words, in the Philippines, the more intensely literate, educated, Western-trained, English-speaking, urbane, urban, cosmopolitan, rich, and sexologically self-aware you are, the more "homo/hetero" you consequently become (which is to say, the more "homo/hetero" you consider yourself to be). While "homo/hetero" (or "gay/straight" or even "bi") do circulate as terms that Filipinos identify with, we must remember that, in many cases, they understand these words *translationally*—which is to say, qualitatively different from their original denotations. In most cases, "homo" or "gay" is understood by Filipinos as being the same as *bakla* or binabae ("womanish"), while "hetero" is conflated with *tunay na lalake* ("real man").

The interesting but altogether commonplace thing is that the two do engage in sexual relations, but as in earlier times the primary distinction between their identities is gender, rather than sex (which is to say, desire and/or the act it impels): the *bakla* is feminine-hearted or effeminate, the *lalake* is masculine. Easily we notice that a dyadic "female/male" norm still informs and symbolically operates in this arrangement. Because of this, a "receptive/insertive" distinction invariably also attends the libidinal relationship between the two. In other words, the *bakla* has been having sex with the *tunay na lalake* in the Philippines for a very long time, although it was only relatively recently—with the introduction of Spanish machismo and the arrival of sexological consciousness, courtesy of the literacy campaigns of

American modernity—that a religious and medicalised hierarchy between these identities came to exist.

We may need to think, therefore, of not one but, rather, multiple "heteronormativities." Unlike the West's discursively defined heterosexual matrix (Butler 1990), in the Philippines the sex/gender system allows, to a certain extent, for "non-alignment" between genitality and identity, precisely because its male/female dualism—which isn't borne out by the pronominal systems of any of its 180 languages—remains residually oral and customary rather than textually (and therefore, categorically) absolute. Popular *bakla* narratives aver that a man can be inwardly feminine and as such—going by this form of premodern and, in many ways, orally "negotiable" heteronormativity—the *bakla*'s object of desire must properly be the "real man" (Tan 1998, 207–26). In the Philippines, gender transitivity is something that the linguistic system itself to a certain extent permits, insofar as it doesn't really mark gender, by and large. Hence, the implantation of the discourse of sexuality in the Philippines has not successfully superseded or displaced its native gender concepts; indeed, this discourse—like other modern importations—has suffered (or enjoyed) the fate of being mis/translated.

Cryptic homosexuality: Rolando Tinio's "A Parable"

As a second case in point, allow me now bring up another postcolonial text: this time a poem written by the Tagalog-identified National Artist, Rolando S. Tinio, that provides us an extended and even more interesting example of how Filipino anglophone writers have translated the homosexual theme (Garcia 2012, 9–38)—which is to say in the beginning, at least, *intensely metaphorically*. Fellow National Artists Nick Joaquin and even Jose Garcia Villa (Garcia 2008, 163–80) had arguably done the same thing in their poetic efforts earlier on, using comparable ambiguating strategies, but for the purposes of this chapter, I will take up Tinio's memorable and intriguingly titled poetic effort, because of its evidently "universal"—some might say, colonial-minded—features.

> A Parable
> *for B.*
> by Rolando S. Tinio
>
> Like most of us, you wish for death:
> Like the Sybil of Cumae caged in glass,
> Without desire for the past of things,
> Without power to hold them at a distance.
>
> We suffer from excess of knowledge:
> Each instant starts at a mythic crossroad.
> We stand to choose the particular way
> We wish our tragedy to take.

> So we stumble on public parks
> And stop at the feet of statues asking
> Cryptic questions about strange beasts.
> So we dash along the bend
>
> Where highways meet, and enter cities
> Unrolling streets for us to tread,
> And in the night perform ablutions
> To clear our hands of all our choices.
>
> And still, in sleep we make our rounds,
> Descending labyrinths all doors,
> Making entrances of exits.
> Hell is an endless promenade.
>
> As in a gothic garden live
> With statuary in marbled white:
> They loom above your head, those heads
> Drilled with holes, as if the eyes
>
> Fixed inward and gazed themselves to stone.
> Memory is full of Gorgons,
> The plague that cries deliverance.
> Theban Magus, teach us to pluck
>
> The inner eye: this trick of mirrors,
> Bright as the burst of pomegranates.
>
> (Tinio [1964]2002, 44)

Offhand, we can say that this is a highly allusive and textually elusive poem, which is nonetheless self-aware about its "cryptic" nature. We can surmise as much, going by the title—"A Parable"—that immediately cues and urges one towards a nuanced and "layered" interpretation, as well as by the lack of clear textual clues concerning the poetic speaker's particular cultural and historical location. Tinio wrote this poem in the early 1960s when he was completing his graduate studies in the US. This was well before he experienced a change of nativist heart and turned into an eloquent champion of Tagalog.

As with Montano's novel, Tinio's text can only be read from the perspective of its difference or "postcoloniality." This difference is not, however, always verbally marked. It can be said that pretty much all of Philippine poetry in English actually sounds pretty "universal" offhand, but a historical reading of it quickly particularises this register in the lived experiences and situations of its specifically located writers and readers. In other words, put in its context, even the most universal-sounding anglophone poem written by a Filipino reveals the specific situation that gave rise to it, and that called it forth, into postcolonial expression (Garcia 2007, 12–18). That it is a homosexual speaker (and, possibly, author) who expressed and translated himself through the language that pathologised—by sexologically naming—him only renders this instance of postcolonial difference particularly poignant and remarkable.

Tinio's poem, devoid of Philippine place names and proper nouns, and couched in the classical idioms—all those references to Greek mythology—certainly qualifies as one such text. And yet, the representational project it engages in cannot be remotely self-evident, precisely because it is a postcolonial poem. As such, we need to think of it as a translation (which makes it an inherently complex and problematic articulation), whose "situatedness" is constitutive of what it actually is. In a personal essay, Tinio reflects on the topic of translation (1990, 191), arguing that when Filipinos speak or write in English they are translating from their native languages, except that the process has become so efficient and automatic that they hardly notice its reality anymore.[9] In seeming anticipation of this form of inquiry, Tinio decides to give his poem a title that plainly gestures towards the intense interpretive labour its reader will need to carry out in order to begin to understand it. This is a labour that seeks out signs of homosexual "presence" in the text and is analogous to the labour of seeking and reading for signs of the gay city that co-exists within the heteronormative one—an aspect or "quality" of urban living that sexual minorities, deprived of institutional support for their manner of loving, must experience and personally "navigate" in distinct and allegorical ways.

The poem, dedicated to an anonymous "B.," is spoken in the first-person plural "we," which implies a shared identity between the "I" and the "you," who is presumably the "B." in the dedication. The shared identity is defined right away as a function of a mysterious death wish, and by invoking T.S. Eliot's reference to the Sybil of Cumae in his masterpiece "The Waste Land" ([1922]2005)—a once-beautiful seeress whose spurning of a powerful god reduced her to an ampulla-encased prophetic eye, the speaker attributes this wish to the helpless remembering of the past (which effectively persists in all its spitefulness in the present), as well as the endless envisioning of a future that the speaker, speaking for both himself and the "you," is helpless to change or prevent from happening.

The certainty of the inescapability of this self-repeating life amounts to nothing if not a tragedy, and the remembering of it is the burden of this "inner eye"—which is, by poem's end, practically indistinguishable from this form of torturous introspection. The entire poem is devoted to metaphorically "summarising" this tragic life, primarily through the use of images and tropes that are painted across the poem's text in rather broad and almost blurry strokes. Cursorily reading the text, we do get suggestions of gay urban existence: cruising in public parks, travelling to unfamiliar cities, meeting and encountering strangers (who are evidently dangerous, because they are "beasts"), as well as the inevitable sense of dirtiness that afflicts the speaker at the end of the day—a "contamination" that needs to be washed away but can't really, since, even in sleep, even in the speakers' dream-life, the tragedy plays itself out, over and over again. It is interestingly at this point that the poem's text provides us with that particularly riveting and altogether telling detail—the intriguing passage, "making entrances of exits," here merely half-heartedly acknowledged as a dream-image. This, of course, is a shockingly frank metaphorical shorthand for penetrative anal sex, and its unobtrusive presence in this poem's text spectacularly opens it up to an unashamedly gay reading.

And so, yes, Tinio's "A Parable" is a Filipino gay poem—possibly one of the earliest in the country's anglophone tradition, written in the 1960s by one of its best poets, who wrote it while taking graduate studies in the US, a place whose worldliness and cosmopolitanism doubtless emboldened him. And yes, its sensibility is pretty urbane, going by its easy recourse to classical imagery and allusions, its confident aspiration after "universalism," and its depiction of the gay city as coinciding with the traditional one—for, indeed, anywhere can be a cruising ground for anonymous homosexual encounters, if one could "read" the codes well enough.

The sensitive nature of its topic should explain not only its encoded and highly figurative language, but also its existential anguish, the harrowing guilt (a "Memory [. . .] full of Gorgons") its speaker recognises, owns up to, and ultimately wishes to escape from—by asking the mythological seer Tiresias, who had lived life both as a man and as a woman, to divest him (as well as the addressee with whom the speaker identifies) of this regretful and tormenting "inner eye, this trick of mirrors / Bright as the burst of pomegranates." This exotic mythical fruit is, of course, rather famous and memorable for the following reason: it was the oral ingestion of its seed that condemned the goddess Persephone to spend so many of her days in hell. The last image of a "burst of pomegranates" is thus especially telling: the pomegranate is a seed-filled fruit, which is associated with the idea of worldly sensuality (and so, we may take it as the opposite of immortality). As the famous myth suggests, it is by gorging on this fruit that one shuts oneself out from salvation (and is thrust into hell). And yes, the image of a solid pulpy fruit bursting into a fountain of seeds can possibly strike us as particularly kinky.

That there remains much in the Philippines's anglophone literature that needs to be unpacked in this allegorical and complex manner is easy enough to accept: the arrival of English into the country made it possible to verbalise, if only carefully, "inconvenient" and "difficult" realities that this language had itself at once instituted and undermined. In other words, while it was colonial modernisation that introduced a sexological form of consciousness that admittedly stigmatised Filipino homosexuals, in the same breath it also provided them a discourse and an identity around which they may rally, but only—initially, at least—subtly, translationally, and *dissimulatingly* (Garcia 2008, 170). Moreover, Tinio's poem is one example of how the cosmopolitan lyric utterances of Filipino poets in English—which can be either vividly mimetic or permeated with so much allegorical opacity—are not really as "universal" as they may initially sound. Read in light of the cultural situation (in this case, repressive and religiously conservative) that framed them, these texts' various expressions of cosmopolitan-sounding, "universal" insights are grounded firmly in the exigencies and particularities of Philippine history.

Upon closer examination, then, this poem's collective "we" isn't universal. Situated in its time and place, the poem's subject-position is, rather, that of the historically located Filipino homosexual, whose colonial shaming and abjection as psychosexually deviant and sinful this poetic articulation registers all too painfully, but by the same token embraces as a possible place from which to speak, from which to "be." Finally, we can say that the "postcolonial difference" to be intuited in this work derives from the Philippine locality of the experience that spurred it—a locality that transformed, that translated, the language and resignified the colonial homophobic values it carried, precisely because this language became the medium through which a postcolonial gay subjectivity could, paradoxically, come to exist (Garcia 2007, 35).

Translational desires

The representational project in anglophone writings, creative and critical, requires cross-cultural dialogue—a practice of "double translation" that involves both the representational movement across cultures and the transcultural movement across realities. As I have attempted to briefly rehearse here, the postcolonial reclaiming of referential anglophone literary texts by Filipinos requires tracing the trajectories of this double or hybrid movement, with the view of proposing various modes of "postcolonial resistance"—as made possible by the metonymic gap between *mimesis* and *poeisis*, which cleaves all translational acts—particularly as they involve the reading of seemingly simple and "universal" representations. The idea of "cultural translation" (Pym 2010, 139–42) bids us to recognise that English in the Philippines is, from the very beginning, a contact or hybrid form and thus a kind of "creole" language (Tupas and Sercombe 2014, 2). And this is the case even in the most subtly localised—which is to say, the most "universal-sounding"—of circumstances.

Grounded in our immemorial orality, and permeated by a layering of cultural differences, both our literature and our criticism in English are, in many ways, translational—transformed as they necessarily must be across oral and scriptural systems, as well as across speech varieties and forms. As such, they negotiate the plurality of cultural and linguistic registers (and ideas) of the Philippine reality, and transcode them in this globally plural and pluralising medium. Suffice it to say that acknowledging the translational character of Gender and Sexuality Studies in the Philippines will require the rejection of the universalist accounts of Western biomedicine. However, such accounts unfortunately persist even in the writings of contemporary feminist and LGBT thinkers in our country, some of whom have been couching their work in Filipino.

To my mind, this interlingual position primarily urges the adoption of a "moderate nativist" perspective on the issue, which bids us to critique essentialism and consider the persistence of residual indigenous valuations of gender that modify—that is to say, syncretise—the newly implanted sexual order. Indeed, we can say that in the Philippines today, *bakla* signifies a culturally hybrid or syncretic notion that incorporates both local and translocal conceptions of gender transitivity and *homo* or "same" sexuality (Baytan 2008, 186). Thus, despite the modernising ideologies of gender and sexuality, it continues to preserve, within itself, residues of its "prehomosexual" past (for instance, the notion that *kabaklaan* is simply a matter of "confusion" and "indecisiveness," which are, in the first place, the oldest and even strictly genderless denotations of the word *bakla*).

The sexualisation of the Philippines has, in other words, been far from unproblematic or complete, and local valuations of gender have simply served to hybridise the newly implanted sexual order. As stated earlier, it is the effeminate *bakla* who is legitimately homosexualised by the activity. In like manner, the category "bisexual"—as it is used in the Philippines—doesn't strictly imply a bisexual object choice, but rather merely denominates a masculine-identified gender presentation on the part of the fully fledged gay man. (On the other hand, "lesbian" also tends to be exclusively conflated with the mannish identity of the "tomboy.") What this stubborn *genderisation* of concepts of sexuality tells us is that the sexualisation of Filipinos, while increasing and expanding in its virulence, has thus far not been entirely uniform or complete. Examining this process more closely, we can see that it has, in fact, often been skewed towards the stigmatisation of the undesirable and minoritised (and minoritising) identity: for instance, that of the *bakla*.

By the same token, we may also say that our local articulations of the gay and/or transgender identity do not simply repeat the colonially inflicted stigma of homosexuality as an immorality and/or an illness, for they can only be vitally informed by and "mixed" with earlier and more local conceptions. In other words, they do not only signify exclusively private and sexual concerns; they may also be seen as instances of postcolonial difference, as translational sites. This form of resistance isn't volitional (Bhabha 1993, 45) but inheres in the structure of colonial domination itself, which is always already interlingual in its operationality. The "gay" and now "transgender" identities—as Filipinos have increasingly come to view, understand, live, and champion them—are as much the ascriptions of these histories of cross-gender behaviour and homosexuality as the expressions of the various syncretic freedoms and desires that these selfsame histories have paradoxically conferred.

And so, the arrival into the Philippines of LGBT discourse (and its attendant identity effects) will not amount to a complete supersession of its cultures' existing categories for gendered personhood, but will simply demonstrate the same kind of translation/hybridisation that any other Western concept necessarily undergoes the moment it finds currency thereabouts. What this means is that narratives of *kabaklaan* remain and will continue to remain as a "common ground" across the gay, bisexual, and male-to-female transgender identities that must now increasingly emerge from the new global discourse of LGBT politics. Despite its apparent globality, the LGBT signifier must always signify locally and in the anglophonic case of the Philippines, translationally, whereas in other Global South locations it appears to function as an aspirational label—one that signalises the desire to appeal to the imaginary of global modernity and to break away from the strictures of traditional gender identities (in the case of the Philippines, for example, the *bakla*). It's important to note, of course, that the LGBT signifier cannot actually be said or expected to completely supersede indigenous gender concepts; instead, as we have rehearsed in our postcolonial readings of the anglophone works of writers like Montano and Tinio, it can only generate hybrid and translational forms of subjectivity.

Transliterations of theory

By contrast, practically all the articles in the 2003 anthology *Tabi-Tabi sa Pagsasantabi: Kritikal na Tala ng mga Lesbiana at Bakla sa Singing, Kultura, at Wika* (A Protest against Marginalisation: Notes on Lesbian and Gay Studies in the Arts, Culture, and Language). Edited by Eugene Y. Evasco et al., the articles in this anthology, while written in Filipino, merely transliterate the essentialist claims about gender and sexuality—contained in key texts in Western feminist, gay, lesbian, and queer traditions—and presume them to be entirely applicable in the case of the Filipino tomboy and *bakla*. The key theoretical materials—now orthographically recast into their Filipino "equivalents" as *homosekswalidad, heteropatriarka, seksismo, homopobya,* and others—are sourced unproblematically from these traditions, and none of them bother to critically engage with the theoretical work of local anglophone "gay" or "lesbian" critics, who have painstakingly unpacked and articulated the cleavages between our orally situated concepts of gendered selfhood on the one hand, and on the other the recently implanted discourses of sexuality (such as those informing the activism-endorsed SOGIE (Sexual Orientation, Gender Identity, and Expression) framework that has been animating Filipino LGBT politics of late). In this anthology, *bakla* is taken to be performatively and semantically the same as the homosexual—a naïve rhetorical move that erroneously allows the critic to canvass the latter's history in order to make sense of the former's reality.

While the very act of translating does of course transform these concepts—as we have postcolonially rehearsed in the creative works of Montano and Tinio—we must remember that the critical articles in this anthology are not just representational but also analytical (which is to say, they are supposed to be full-blown critiques). As such, the anthology may be faulted for not being critical or reflexive (or perhaps, sadly, intelligent), where it counts the most. Other than their unnerving silence on the question of sexuality's constructedness and historical specificity, it's perhaps their guiltless use of French feminist biologisms, of falsely universal psychoanalytic psychologisms (especially where the study of mediatised texts are concerned), or even of cosmopolitan "queerisms" on the level of conceptual framework that confounds and delegitimates these texts most spectacularly. While translations of a sort, because they ironically did not emerge out of a careful engagement with the definitional crises that lie at the very root of sexuality and gender research, they indeed are not self-consciously translational, which is how postcolonial theorisings about gender and sexuality in our particular trans/locality should primarily be.

The "fault" goes both ways, of course. The recent recourse, in Philippine anglophone gay criticism, to difficult and deconstructive "hauntological" theory—in order to register the pertinacity of *bakla* locality in the face of gay globality—need not even be necessary, if only the question of translation (which always already recognises semantic excess and the impossibility of equivalence) were made central to the analysis. In other words, in the regime of the globalised Filipino gay, the *bakla* will of course ever "haunt" the scene, because it is nothing if not the ground of the former's possibility (Benedicto 2008, 317–38). This kind of oversight is unique to anglophone criticism, which by and large has also not been responsive enough to the translational dynamic that conditions it, thereby suggesting certain class-specific overdeterminations. Hence, at least to the credit of those doing theoretical work in Filipino, the category of *kabaklaan* may not need to be abandoned at all, seeing as how it cannot be entirely superseded on the one hand, and is a powerful discourse that is certain to persist and inform whatever else they can throw at it, on the other.

Just now I'm thinking of the acclaimed 2016 film by Jun Lana, *Die Beautiful*,[10] in which the category *bakla* completely eclipses the politically correct and practically non-operative category of "transgender," and is restored to its empirical and semantic capaciousness, embracing the Filipino urban folk spectrum of identities and affects (from gradations of the feminine-identified to the unremittingly and brutally macho). If nothing else, this film's depiction of the persistence of these oral and local valuations sets in relief the limits of a textual and increasingly anglophonic globality, especially where sexual and gendered trans- and inter-culturations are concerned.

While the translatedness of LGBT critical and political discursivities in the Philippines is something that Filipino LGBTs themselves may not be conscious about, it nonetheless makes sense to suggest that they should study this cultural transformation more self-consciously, if only to have some say in its possible directions and deployments.

Notes

1 This chapter elaborates on a presentation I gave on 18 August at a laboratory, "Contesting race, gender and sexuality in Southeast Asian literature: From colonial past to postcolonial present," which was held during the 2017 European

Association for Southeast Asian Studies (EuroSEAS) Conference in the UK. See this volume's Introduction for details.
2 My book, *Slip/pages: Essays in Philippine Gay Criticism*, collects these earliest attempts at theorising. See Garcia (1998).
3 This is the Filipino translation for "Gay and Lesbian Studies"; it's been operationalised in a number of scholarly articles in Filipino about the topic of non-heteronormative gender and sexuality in the Philippines. See Evasco et al. (2003) for the very first anthology of such articles.
4 We must remember that what facilitated the colonial *sexualisation* of the *bakla* is the presence, in the native culture, of a discourse of valourised interiority or "transcendent depth," to which the colonial notion of gendered psychosexuality came to readily append itself. Among the Tagalog, this is the discourse of *kalooban*. This conceptual process entails the discursive movement away from the genitally sexed "external body" (*labas*) towards the realm of the psyche and interior selfhood (*loob*), and what's important to remember is that it did not completely negate or eliminate the importance of the former but, rather, merely casts both in a reverse and mutually exclusive relationship. This binarism effectively *absolutises* their difference from one another, effectively recasting the *bakla*'s identity into a perversion (which is to say, a "self-contradiction"). Moreover, this binarism was premised on the dichotomising of the gendered body into anatomically immutable and mutually exclusive male and female normative "types." This dimorphism is arguably colonial, as there is archival evidence to suggest that a number of pre-Hispanic cultures in the Philippines recognised the existence of "mixed," "liminal," and/or "alternative" bodies. From all available accounts, it would appear that, even during early colonial times, the male/female dualism did not exhaust all the possible "somatisations" of the gendered self the various Philippine *indios* could assume. The sexological discourse of homosexuality (as a psychosexual inversion) proved easy enough to "graft" on to *kabaklaan,* because of the equivalency or comparability that exists between the Western concept of the gendered inner self and the capaciously generative concept of *loob*. This sexualisation of local modes of mentality, behaviour, and personality was the inevitable result of the implementation of an English-based education system and, presumably, the "psychosexual logic" it introduced has prospered and become more stubbornly entrenched since then. See Garcia (2009, 151–97).
5 Reading the existing biographical accounts of Montano's life—such as the short one above—and juxtaposing them against this novel, I must say the "roman-à-clef" angle does seem, rather intriguingly, to hold water.
6 Ramon Magsaysay (1907–1957) was the third president of the Philippine republic after the Second World War. The year he died in a plane crash somewhere on the Philippine island of Cebu, the trustees of the New York-based Rockefeller Brothers Fund, with the consent of the Philippine government, established the Ramon Magsaysay Award (RMA) in order "to commemorate the late president of the Philippines and to perpetuate his example of integrity in government, courageous service to the people, and pragmatic idealism within a democratic society." For more information on the RMA, see http://www.rmaf.org.ph/index.htm. On the other hand, no account other than Montano's exists—that I know of, anyway—that imputes homosexuality to this famous former Philippine president.
7 This was told to me sometime in the middle of 1993 by my professor in Comparative Literature, the late Angelito Santos, who introduced me to Montano's unpublished novel—which had apparently been turned down for publication by several local presses in the 1970s—and allowed me to photocopy it.
8 I am referring to the popular plays, "Sabina" and "The Love of Leonor Rivera"— centrepieces in Montano's theatrical oeuvre. In the former, after learning of her

American boyfriend's infidelity, the main character commits suicide by shooting herself; in the latter, Leonor Rivera dies after giving birth to her first and last child by her British husband, but not before she professes, in a poetic soliloquy, her deathless devotion to her one and only love, the ill-fated national hero, Jose Rizal.
9 On a related note, I should mention that Tinio's understanding of bilinguality is neither self-evident nor simple: he has declared that while it's possible to learn two languages, it's not possible to think equally in both of them. See Tinio (1990, 270).
10 *Die Beautiful* is a dramedy that was scripted by acclaimed playwright Rody Vera and directed by Jun Lana. Shown at the 2016 Metro Manila Film Festival, this film insists on using the *bakla* signifier in dramatising the lives of "transgender" morticians and impersonators. It does this for the sake of verisimilitude and in recognition of the fact that *bakla* remains the operative category in most *bakla* lives (thus flagging the limits of LGBT globality). It's also different from other indie films in that its treatment is, astonishingly, pretty "mainstream," even when its story—as well as certain "touchy" scenes—isn't.

References

Baytan, Ronald. 2008. "*Bading na Bading*: Evolving Identities in Philippine Cinema." In *AsiaPacifiQueer: Rethinking Genders and Sexualities*, edited by Fran Martin, Peter A. Jackson, Mark McLelland, and Audrey Yue, 181–96. Champaign: University of Illinois Press.
Benedicto, Bobby. 2008. "The Haunting of Gay Manila: Global Space-Time and the Specter of Kabaklaan." *glq: A Journal of Lesbian and Gay Studies* 14, no. 2–3: 317–38.
Bhabha, Homi K. 1993. *The Location of Culture*. London and New York: Routledge.
Brewer, Carolyn. 1999. "Baylan, Asog, Transvestism, and Sodomy: Gender, Sexuality and the Sacred in Early Colonial Philippines." *Intersections: Gender, History and Culture in the Asian Context* 2 (May): 1–15.
Butler, Judith. 1990. *Gender Trouble: Feminism and the Subversion of Identity*. London and New York: Routledge.
Eliot, T.S. (1922) 2005. "The Waste Land." In *The Norton Anthology of Poetry*, edited by Margaret Ferugson, Mary Jo Salter, and Jon Stallworthy, 1344–56. New York: W.W. Norton & Company, Inc.
Evasco, Eugene Y., Roselle V. Pineda, and Rommel B. Rodriguez, eds. 2003. *Tabi-tabi sa Pagsasantabi: Kritikal na mga Tala ng mga Lesbiana at Bakla sa Sining, Kultura, at Wika*. Quezon City: University of the Philippines Press.
Foucault, Michel. *The Foucault Reader*. (1984) 1991. Edited by Paul Rabinow. London: Penguin Books.
Garcia, J. Neil C. 1998. *Slip/pages: Essays in Philippine Gay Criticism*. Manila: De La Salle University Press.
———. 2007. *At Home in Unhomeliness: Rethinking the Universal in Philippine Postcolonial Poetry in English*. Philippines: Philippine PEN.
———. 2008. "Villa, Montano, Perez: Postcoloniality and Gay Liberation in the Philippines." In *AsiaPacifiQueer: Rethinking Genders and Sexualities*, edited by Fran Martin, Peter A. Jackson, Mark McLelland, and Audrey Yue, 163–80. Champaign: University of Illinois Press.
———. 2009. *Philippine Gay Culture: Binabae to Bakla, Silahis to MSM*, 2nd ed. Hong Kong: Hong Kong University Press.

———. 2012. "Reading Auras." In *Aura: The Gay Theme in Philippine Fiction in English*, edited by J. Neil C. Garcia, 9–38. Pasig City: Anvil Publishing Inc.
———. 2013. "Nativism or Universalism: Situating LGBT Discourse in the Philippines." *Kritika Kultura: A Journal of Literary/Cultural and Language Studies* 20 (March): 48–68.
———. 2014. "Translation and the Problem of Realism in Philippine Literature in English." *Kritika Kultura: A Journal of Literary/Cultural and Language Studies* 22 (August): 99–127.
Maniquis, M. L. 1994. "Severino Montano." In *The Cultural Center of the Philippines Encylopedia of Philippine Arts, Vol. 7: Theater*, edited by Nicanor Tiongson, 355–56. Manila: Cultural Center of the Philippines.
Montano, Severino. c. 1960–70. "The Lion and the Faun." Unpublished MS.
Pym, Anthony. 2010. *Exploring Translation Theories*. London and New York: Routledge.
Suarez, Kiel Ramos. 2017. "*Sakit o Sala*: The (Post)colonial Medicalization of the Filipino Homosexual, 1916–1976," Master's Thesis, Central European University.
Tan, Michael L. 1998. "*Silahis:* Looking for the Missing Filipino Bisexual Male." In *Bisexualities and AIDS*, edited by Peter Aggleton, 207–26. London: Taylor and Francis.
Tinio, Rolando S. 1990. *A Matter of Language: Where English Fails*. Quezon City: University of the Philippines Press.
———. (1964) 2002. "A Parable." In *The Likhaan Anthology of Philippine Literature in English, from 1900 to the Present*, edited by Gemino H. Abad, 44–45. Quezon City: University of the Philippines Press.
Tupas, Ruanni, and Peter Sercombe. 2014. "Language, Education and Nation-Building in Southeast Asia: An Introduction." In *Language, Education and Nation-Building: Assimilation and Shift in Southeast Asia*, edited by Peter Sercombe and Ruanni Tupas, 1–21. New York: Palgrave Macmillan.

Index

Note: **Bold** page numbers refer to tables and *italic* page numbers refer to figures and page numbers followed by "n" denote endnotes.

Abdullah-Poulos, Layla 148
acculturation 51, 63n9, 136
Adam, Ahmat 101, 102
agency 7, 14, 15, 37, 39, 52, 60, 61, 62, 63n11, 76, 79n1, 109, 111, 157, 166
Aisha Malik 132, 137–141, 143; *Jewel* 132, 135, 137, 138, 140, 141, 143–145, 146
Alatas, Syed Farid 67
Alfian Sa'at 58, 59
America *see* US
American 2, 11, 12, 14, 23, 25, 67, 70, 74, 118, 119, 122, 144–148, 151–161, 165, 166, 167, 172, 176, 181, 190n8
American Muslim 144–148
anglophone 2, 3, 9, 17n3, 17n6, 22, 26, 101, 110, 158, 159, 171–175, 179–182, 184, 185, 187, 188
anti-colonial(ism) 3, 10, 13, 14, 18n17, 100, 102, 109, 110, 117, 124
appropriation 7, 9, 11, 12, 42, 61, 70, 165
Apter, Emily 67, 167
Archetype 11, 13, 71, 83, 84, 85, 88, 90, 97, 98
Asia 1–8, 10, 15–18, 35, 38, 48, 59, 63n10, 66, 67, 68, 78, 79n3, 100, 111, 118, 133, 134, 148, 149, 151–167
Asian American 151–159, 161, 165, 166
Ashcroft, Bill 6, 156
assimilation 48, 53–55, 63n9, 137, 138, 143, 144, 147, 148
authoritarian/authoritarianism 6, 162
Aw, Tash 3, 23, 39n3; *The Harmony Silk Factory* 39n3

Bachmann-Medick, Doris 1, 4
Bahasa *see* Malay

bakla 16, 172, 174, 175–181, 186, 187, 188, 189n4, 190n10
Bangsawan 43, 51, 53, 62n2, 63n10
Barber, Karin 78, 115
barriers 1, 3, 10, 17n2, 50, 54, 148
Bassnett, Susan 4, 68, 69, 70, 100, 155
Belsey, Catherine 22
Benjamin, Walter 25, 67
Bhabha, Homi K. 4, 5, 62n5, 155, 173, 186
bi *see* bisexual
bilingual 3, 9, 57, 58, 172, 190n9
binary/binaries/binarism 5, 9, 16, 56, 68, 77, 84, 88, 179, 189n4
bisexual/bisexuality/ies 6, 176, 178, 186, 187
Boomgaard, Peter 72, 73
border/borders 5, 16, 71, 82, 92, 157, 167
boundary/boundaries 4, 5, 9, 14, 16, 54, 56, 61, 67, 102, 123
British 2, 17n8, 23, 29, 33, 35, 36, 39n6, 57, 66, 75, 110, 117, 121, 142, 144, 148, 152, 159, 162, 190n8
British Malaya *see* Malaya
Brodzki, Bella 155
Brown, C.C. 44, 45, 46, 136
Brunei/Brunei Darussalam 2, 3, 7, 8, 9, 14, 15, 17n6, 18n12, 71, 132–149
Buddhism/Buddhist/Buddha 36, 38, 66, 73, 82, 84, 120

Carstens, Sharon A. 47, 49, 53, 55
Cambodia 2, 3, 9, 82, 84, 85, 86, 88, 89, 91, 92, 93, 94, 95, 97, 98n4, 98n6, 159, 160
Caucasian 143
Chamberlain, Lori 67

Chambert-Loir, Henri 5
Chatterjee, Partha 13, 18n17
Chauvinism 117, 118
Chbap 13, 84, 88, 91
Chbap for Women 85, 88
Chandra, Elizabeth 100, 102, 118
Cheah Boon Kheng 46
Cheong, Fiona 23, 39n4; *The Scent of the Gods* 39n4; *Shadow Theatre* 39n4
Chhay, Bora 82, 91, 95, 96; *Lost Loves* 82, 91, 95–97
Chigas, George 17n9, 84
China 2, 27, 28, 29, 34, 43, 44, 45, 46, 49, 50, 52, 54, 79n3, 103, 104, 107, 108, 110, 117, 118, 120, 122, **125**, 151, 153, 158, 160, 162, 164, 165, 167n1
Chinese 1, 5, 8, 10, 11, 12, 14, 15, 17n3, 23, 26, 27, 29, 30, 33, 34, 35, 36, 38, 42–51, 53–62, 63n9, 71, 78, 101, 102–105, 107, 108, 110, 111, 114, 115–124, **125**, 135, 136, 137, 138, 143, 144, 151, 152, 154, 156, 158–166
Chinese Indonesian 101, 104, 107, 111, 120
Christianity/Christian 66, 67
Chow, Rey 27, 28, 29, 30, 31, 32, 164, 165
Chu, Jon M. 151; *Crazy Rich Asians* (film) 15, 151–167
Chua, Beng Huat 2, 162
cinema 12, 13, 35, 82–98, 151–167; *see also* film
cinematic excess 15, 163, 164, 165, 167
class politics 155, 163
collective/collectivity 70, 83, 110, 152, 185
colonial(ism) 2, 3, 6, 7, 8, 10, 11, 13, 14, 17n5, 23, 27, 28, 33, 38, 45, 47, 68, 69, 70, 74, 82, 83–86, 88, 89, 90, 91, 93, 95, 96, 97, 98n1, 100–124, 142, 162, 173, 181, 184, 185, 186, 189n4
comparative literature 2, 4, 17n9, 189n7
compartmentalisation 47, 51, 54, 59, 61
Confucianism 78, 120
convert 15, 104, 108, 132, 134, 135, 137, 138, 139–148, 159
conversion 5, 14, 15, 45, 132–149, 160
Coppel, Charles Antony 101
cross-cultural 1, 4, 7, 8, 14, 15, 132, 134, 135, 144, 145, 147, 148, 154, 165, 185
culture 1, 3, 4, 5–14, 16, 17, 18n17, 23, 36, 38, 42, 47, 49–51, 53–57, 60, 61, 63n9, 68, 69, 70, 78, 79, 83, 86, 92, 94, 97, 102, 110, 123, 133, 135, 136, 138, 144, 147, 151, 155, 158, 160, 162, 163, 164, 165, 171, 173, 175, 178, 179, 180, 185, 186, 187, 189n4
cultural translation 5, 12, 16, 66–79, 151, 152, 154, 155, 158, 159, 161, 172, 175, 185
Curaming, Rommel A. 67

decolonise/decolonisation/decolonial 1, 3, 7, 10, 12, 13, 67, 68, 117, 145
democracy/democratic 26, 29, 66, 94–97, 98n6, 189n6
democratising power 29
Democratic Kampuchea 94, 95–97, 98n6
diaspora/diasporic 1, 3, 4, 43, 48, 60, 61, 153
difference 1, 6, 8, 12, 18n17, 26, 35, 43, 49, 52, 53, 54, 55, 56, 57, 58, 61, 66, 75, 78, 88, 91, 96, 120, 136, 137, 144, 155, 159, 160, 165, 172, 173, 174, 182, 183, 185, 186, 189n4
discourse 3, 5–8, 10, 12, 13, 15, 16, 26, 43, 44, 46, 48, 50, 53, 54–58, 60–62, 100, 101, 102, 118, 123, 133, 135, 142, 144, 145, 146, 147, 148, 149, 151, 158, 171, 173, 174, 178, 179, 181, 184, 186, 187, 188, 189n4
discursive/discursivities 7, 8, 9, 25, 53, 133, 146, 181, 188, 189n4
displacement 17n8, 55, 164
dominant/dominance 6, 11, 12, 25, 29, 38, 53, 58, 63n9, 67, 85, 94, 100, 101, 104, 133, 134, 137, 145, 146, 147, 148, 151, 153, 154, 155, 158, 162, 166, 167n1, 173
drama 17n6, 23, 35, 40n10, 43, 47, 50, 51, 53, 56, 57, 62, 82, 152, 156, 171, 190n10; *see also* theatre
dualism/duality 12, 70, 77, 155, 181, 189n4
Dutch 8, 10, 14, 45, 66, 100, 102, 103, 105, 107, 109, 111, *113*, 114, 115, 116, 117, 120, 122, 123, 124
Dutch East Indies 100
dynasty 34, 42, 45, 152

East Asia 2, 15, 17n10, 110, 158, 160
Eliot, T.S. 32, 183
English 1–4, 9, 10, 14, 16, 17n2, 17n3, 17n5, 17n6, 17n8, 27, 36, 43, 44, 47–50, 57–60, 69, 70, 75, 100, 110, 111, 114, 115, 119–123, 132, 137, 142, 159, 174–185, 189n4; *see also* anglophone

epistemology/epistemological 2, 12, 14, 16, 67, 70, 172
essentialised/essentialist/essentialism 16, 25, 55, 56, 61, 153, 172, 178, 186, 187
ethnic identity 146, 161; *see also* racial identity
ethnicity 1, 6, 15, 43, 54, 55, 56, 57, 59, 61, 62, 102, 103, 104, 122, 123; *see also* race
equivalence 16, 18n11, 173, 188
Eurasian 14, 33, 47, 101, 103, 104, 105, 123, 124, 137, 143, 144, 158
Eurocentric 2, 3, 5, 10, 12, 68, 107, 111, 118, 119

Fairclough, Norman 133
Faiq, Said 132, 133, 135
feminine 7, 77, 86, 88, 90, 96, 140, 147, 180, 181, 188
femininity 13, 16, 43, 59, 83, 84, 88, 91, 139, 174
feminisation/feminised 48, 55, 177, 178
feminism/feminist 4, 78, 147, 177, 185, 187, 188
fiction 8, 11, 14, 22, 23, 24, 26, 35, 39n1, 40n9, 42, 44, 46, 74, 75, 78, 82, 97, 102, 110, 111, 121, 122, 132–149, 164
fictional/fictionalised 24, 46, 74, 78, 104, 105, 117, 134, 137, 157, 160, 167n2, 176, 178
fidelity 18n11, 77, 123, 174, 190n8
film 4, 8, 9, 12, 13, 15, 31, 32, 35, 74, 78, 82, 83, 91–98, 108, 110, 151–167, 188, 190n10; *see also* cinema
Filipino 16, 171, 172, 173, 174, 175, 179, 180, 181, 182, 183, 184, 185, 186, 187, 188, 189n3
francophone 101
Freeman, Elizabeth 25
French 54, 66, 84, 87, 92, 98n1, 104, 111, 158, 188
French feminism 188
folklore 68, 69, 72
Foucault, Michel 173

gay *see* homosexuality
German 104, 107, 111, 153, 176
gender: identity 12, 13, 14, 42, 59, 60, 82, 96, 97, 132, 187; relations 8, 52, 76, 90
genre 7, 10, 14, 35, 36, 38, 43, 44, 75, 82, 83, 84, 97, 145, 146, 148, 151
Gentzler, Edwin 4
Ghulam-Sarwar Yousof 79n6

globalisation/globalised 1, 4, 13, 22, 43, 49, 59, 60, 61, 100, 132, 133, 136, 148, 171, 188
glocalisation/glocalised 14, 60
Goh, Daniel P. S. 162

Halberstam, Judith 24, 25
Han, Byung-chul 78
Hang, Li Po 11, 12, 42–63
harimau jadian see were-tiger
hegemony 1, 15, 16, 43, 100, 110, 123, 136, 148, 155, 159
Hermansen, Martha 145
Heryanto, Ariel 17n7
Heterogeneity/heterogeneous 4, 6, 39, 57, 103, 123, 163
heteronormative/heteronormativity/ies 6, 24–26, 32, 35–39, 174, 175, 181, 183, 189n3
heterosexual/hetero/heterosexuality/ies 6, 8, 26, 30, 52, 173, 175, 179–181
Hindu/Hinduism 66, 73, 79n1
hispanophone 101
history/historical 3, 5, 6, 7, 8, 10, 11, 12, 22, 23, 24, 26, 28, 29–32, 34–39, 40n9, 42–63, 67, 68, 82, 83, 86, 87, 94, 97, 98n1, 100, 101, 109, 110, 132–134, 136, 144, 151–160, 165, 166, 182, 185, 187
Holden, Philip 23, 39n1, 162
Hollywood 3, 15, 110, 134, 151, 152, 153, 154, 156, 160, 163, 166
homogenising 1, 48, 57, 135, 174
homophobia 18n13
homosexual/homo/homosexuality 7, 16, 18n13, 26, 39n6, 171, 173–187, 189n4
Hung, Eva 5
hybridity 1, 3, 4, 38, 40n10, 53, 54, 56, 57, 61, 173

identity 1, 3, 5, 6, 7, 8, 10, 11, 12, 13, 15, 23, 24, 27, 30, 38, 42, 43, 44, 45, 46, 48, 49, 50, 51, 52, 53–57, 59, 61, 62, 63n9, 82, 92, 94, 97, 134, 135–136, 138, 143, 144, 145, 146, 147, 148, 152, 161, 167, 172, 174, 175, 176, 177, 178, 179, 180, 181, 183, 184, 186, 187, 189n4
ideology/ideological 1, 3, 5–7, 9, 11, 13, 15, 16, 24, 26, 43, 44, 46, 50, 51, 53, 54, 59–61, 62n5, 83, 87, 89, 91, 94, 102, 105, 123, 124, 132, 135, 136, 139, 145, 147, 148, 157, 162, 186

imaginary/imaginaries 6, 9, 10, 11, 14, 16, 38, 43, 73, 134, 153, 158, 187
independence 1, 3, 13, 23, 26, 52, 56, 62, 82, 124, 132, 136, 138, 148
India 2, 44, 63n10, 79n3, 160
Indigenous/indigeneity 8, 10, 11, 12, 13, 18n16, 47, 48, 53, 66–79, 101–105, 107, 109, 136, 160, 162, 175, 186, 187
individualism/individualistic 143, 152
Indonesia 2, 3, 5, 7, 8, 9, 12, 14, 18n13, 31, 32, 45, 68, 69, 71, 75, 78, 79n1, 100–124, 135, 148, 159, 160, 162
intercultural 6, 14, 17n10, 66, 164, 174
interlingual translation 15, 158
interpretation 3, 7, 9, 32, 53, 56, 176, 182
interracial 29, 52, 62, 102, 110, 118, 136
intersemiotic translation 83
intertextual/intertextuality 5, 7, 9
intervention/interventionist 10, 12, 14, 16, 70, 78, 172
intralingual translation 12, 83, 85, 91
intramale 16, 174
Islam 5, 14, 15, 26, 45, 46, 47, 48, 49, 52, 63n8, 66, 68, 69, 79n1, 104, 108, 132–149; *see also* Muslim
Ismail S. Talib 17n8

Japan 2, 34, 36, 110, 160
Japanese occupation 23, 32, 33
Jaswal, Balli Kaur 23, 39n4; *Inheritance* 24, 25, 39n4, 73
Jatakas 84, 98n2
Jedamski, Doris 101, 102, 117
Joaquin, Nick 181

Khing, Hoc Dy 82, 84
Khmer 8, 10, 12, 13, 82–98
Khmer literature 8, 12, 13, 82–98
Khoo, Kay Kim 34, 38, 42, 46, 51
knowledge/knowledges 2, 6, 7, 22, 23, 24, 31, 34, 40n11, 62, 67, 70, 79n1, 100, 101, 116, 117, 119, 122, 123, 133, 136, 137, 140, 173, 181
Kommer, Herman 101, 104, 105, *106*, 107, 108, 109, 111, 117, 120, 123, 124; *see also* Tjerita Njonja Kong Hong Nio 104, 105, *106*, 108, 109, 111; *Tiga Tjarita* 104; *Tjerita Siti Aisah* 104; *Tjerita Nji Paina* 104
Koos, Arens 102, 103, 104, 105, 107
Kurniawan, Eka 69, 75, 76, 77; *Lelaki Harimau* 69, 70, 75; *Man Tiger* 69, 75, 76–78, 79n5

Kwa, Lydia 3, 11, 22–40; *This Place Called Absence* 11, 22–40; *Pulse* 39n4
Kwan, Kevin 3, 15, 151, 161, 163, 166, 167n1, 167n3; *Crazy Rich Asians* 15, 151–167; *China Rich Girlfriend* 167n1; *Rich People Problems* 167n1

Lana, Jun 188, 190n10; *Die Beautiful* 188, 190n10
Laos 2
Lee, Ann 43, 62n3, 63n11; *Hang Li Poh—Melakan Princess* 43, 50, 56–61
Lee, Kuan Yew 62n4, 162
Lefevere, André 155
Legend 11, 12, 42, 44, 46, 48, 50, 52, 53, 56, 57, 58, 61, 62, 158
lesbian *see* homosexuality
LGBTQ 6, 7, 11, 18n13, 25, 26
LGBT *see* LGBTQ
liberal/liberalism 13, 26, 32, 47, 60, 120
Lindsay, Jennifer 4, 44, 55, 57, 59
Linguistic 4, 5, 6, 7, 9, 14, 15, 17, 18n11, 18n18, 22, 56, 57, 58, 59, 60, 62, 68, 70, 83, 97, 100, 102, 121, 122, 123, 132, 136, 159, 171, 174, 175, 179, 181, 185
literary form 1, 8, 84, 148
literary representation 68, 97, 134
literary studies 2
Loh, Vyvyane 23, 39n3, 163; *Breaking the Tongue* 39n3
Lowe, Lisa 157
lusophone 101
Lyk, Rary 98n5; *Women's Fate* 98n5

Magsaysay, Ramon 176, 189n6
Mahathir Mohamad 49
Maier, Henk 101, 102, 109, 122
Malacca *see* Melaka
Malay 1, 10–12, 14, 17n6, 29, 35, 36, 42, 43–62, 63n8, 66–79, 100–105, 107, 108, 109–111, *112*, 114, 115–123, 132, 133, 135, 136, 137, 138, 140, 143, 144, 145, 148, 154, 159, 162
Malay Annals see Sejarah Melayu
Malay Archipelago 12, 66–79
Malaya/Malayan 23, 32–34, 36, 39n2, 51, 62n2, 71, 77
Malaysia 2, 3, 5, 7, 8, 9, 11, 12, 17n6, 17n8, 22–40, 42, 43, 44, 45, 46, 47, 49, 50, 52, 53, 56, 57, 59, 61, 62, 63n8, 68, 69, 71, 135, 136, 141, 159, 160, 163, 167n2

Malaysian Chinese 11, 12, 42, 43, 45, 46, 48, 49, 51, 53, 55, 57, 58, 62
Mandarin 44, 50, 57, 58, 66, 102, 120, 159, 162
Manicka, Rani 23, 39n3; *The Rice Mother* 39n3; *The Japanese Lover* 39n3
Mantel, Hilary 22
marginal/marginality/marginalised/marginalisation 5, 7, 17n7, 17n8, 26, 28, 29, 48, 52, 59, 100, 156, 166, 187
masculine 6, 13, 48, 52, 140, 175, 176, 179, 180, 186
masculinity 8, 46, 76, 77, 175
McHugh, Susan 70
Melaka 42, 44, 45, 46, 48, 50, 51, 52, 54, 56, 57, 58, 60, 63n12
Melayu Islam Beraja 132, 135
mestizo 101, 102
metaphorical translation 9
metatextual 11, 26, 30, 33, 38
Mignolo, Walter 67
minority/minorities 26, 32, 47, 53, 55, 63n9, 145, 153, 154, 156, 163, 166, 167, 183, 186
misogyny 177
modern/modernist/modernity 3, 12, 13, 24, 25, 29, 44, 49, 50, 56, 60, 61, 62, 67, 68, 69, 70, 73–79, 83, 85, 86, 88, 91, 92, 93, 96, 97, 98, 101, 102, 134, 136, 164, 172, 174, 179, 181, 184, 186, 187
monarchy 47, 48, 66, 132, 135, 138, 143, 147
monodrama 43, 50, 56
monocultural 46, 47, 51, 57, 60, 61, 171, 175
monolingual 46, 51, 53, 55, 61, 97, 98n1, 171
Montano, Severino 171, 174–182, 187, 189n5; *The Lion and the Faun* 171, 174, 175; "Sabina" 189n8; "The Love of Leonor Rivera" 189n8
M.T.F. 118, 119, 121, 122; *My Chinese Marriage* 102, 118, 119, 120, 121, 122; *Akoe poenja Pernikahan dengan Saorang Tionghoa* 119, 122
multi-ethnic 46, 51, 61, 123
multicultural 9, 23, 33, 40n10, 51, 60, 61, 62n1
multilingual 3, 4, 9, 36, 42, 43, 46, 51, 56–61, 66, 159
Munday, Jeremy 66

Muslim 8, 26, 43, 47, 48, 53, 56, 71, 73, 102, 108, 109, 133–149; *see also* Islam
Myanmar 2, 7, 159, 160
Myth/mythology 11, 12, 42, 68, 69, 70, 71–74, 77, 78, 79, 91, 108, 178, 181, 183, 184

Nagata, Judith 56
Nakamura, Fuyubi 5
narration 44, 52, 57, 63n8, 96
narrative 5, 12, 13–16, 23, 24–27, 29, 30, 31–33, 34, 35, 37, 38, 39, 46, 52, 60–62, 69, 70–73, 75, 77, 78, 92, 95, 96, 111, 115, 123, 134, 135, 139, 142, 144–148, 151, 156–161, 163–167, 173, 174, 177, 178, 181, 186
nation 1, 3, 6, 7, 10–13, 16, 24–26, 29, 35, 39, 42, 43, 46, 47, 49, 50, 51, 55, 56, 59, 61, 62, 71, 78, 92, 122, 132, 135, 137, 142, 159
national culture 11, 13, 23, 47, 49, 53, 57
national identity 1, 13, 42, 94, 136, 143, 145, 148
nationalism/nationalist/nationalistic 3, 13, 18n17, 46, 48, 50, 53, 56, 61, 94, 102, 122, 137, 146, 147, 172
nation-state 1, 3, 6, 7, 11, 12, 13, 16, 26, 50, 56, 71
the Netherlands Indies *see* Dutch East Indies
neo-colonial 47
Nguyen, Viet Thanh 160, 161, 166
Niranjana, Tejaswini 4, 100, 155
Noor Azam Haji-Othman 135, 136
Norsiah Haji Abd Gapar 138–141; *Pengabdian* 132, 135, 137, 138, 140, 143, 144, 145, 146
Norodom, Sihanouk 82, 91, 98n4; *Apsara* 82, 91, 98n4
Nou, Hach 82, 86, 87, 88, 98n3; *The Faded Flower* 82, 86–88, 90

Ooi, Keat Gin 66
Ong, Aihwa 158
Orientalism/Orientalist 6, 69, 40n10, 110, 133, 146, 157, 164, 165
Oswin, Natalie 25

paternalism/paternalistic 6
patriarchy/patriarchal 76, 78
Peranakan 14, 45, 57, 102, 159
performance 4, 5, 7, 9, 11, 12, 42–63, 71, 74, 77, 92

performance translation 12, 44, 57
performative/performativity 44, 55, 174, 187
Philippines 2, 3, 7, 8, 9, 16, 17n5, 67, 100, 171–190
Polyglossia/polyglossic 9, 16, 57
Porter, Katherine Anne 118, 119, 121; *My Chinese Marriage* 102, 118, 119–122
postcolonial(ism) 1, 2, 3, 4, 6–8, 10, 12, 13, 14, 16, 17n5, 23, 26, 42–44, 50, 57, 62, 68, 69, 70, 73, 75, 82, 83, 85, 91–97, 134, 142, 143, 144, 151, 152, 154, 155, 156, 157–164, 166, 172, 173, 174, 175, 181, 182, 183, 185, 186, 187, 188
postcolonial literature 2, 4, 82, 95
postcolonial studies 2, 10, 160, 173
postcolonial translation 14, 69
postmodern/postmodernism/postmodernity 24, 25, 50, 56, 60, 164
power 1, 4, 6, 7, 10, 15, 24, 29, 30, 31, 34, 44, 45–48, 52, 55, 58, 60, 62, 68, 69, 70, 72, 76, 93, 95, 100, 109, 110, 116, 117, 122, 123, 124, 133, 142, 147, 152, 155, 158, 166, 167, 173, 181
P. Ramlee 69, 74, 75, 77; *Sitora Harimau Jadian* 69, 70, 74, 77, 78
precolonial 7, 8, 10, 11, 12, 46, 48, 52, 71
prose 28, 43, 69, 75, 78, 82, 83, 84, 85, 87, 88, 91, 93, 97, 98n1, 104, 111
psychoanalysis/psychoanalytic 176, 188
psychology/psychological 9, 10, 14, 17n8, 32, 38, 175
Pym, Anthony 185

queer: space 24, 30, 39; studies 24, 25, 39n5, 172; time 11, 24, 25, 36, 39

race 1, 4, 5–12, 14, 15, 23, 24, 29, 42–44, 47, 48, 50–59, 61, 62, 62n4, 102, 104, 109, 110, 115, 117, 118, 122, 123, 135–137, 145, 146, 148, 157, 158, 161–163, 165, 188n1; *see also* ethnicity
racial 7, 14, 15, 26, 29, 47, 53–56, 61, 62n4, 102, 109–111, 115–118, 121–124, 134–136, 143–144, 146–148, 151, 153–158, 160–166
racial identity 53, 136, 146, 161; *see also* ethnic identity
racialised, racialisation 10, 11, 14, 43, 46, 55, 56, 57, 103, 108, 110, 115–117, 122, 123, 145, 147

racism 14, 110, 114, 115, 116, 122, 123, 153, 157
Rahmah Bujang 43, 50, 51, 52, 53, 54, 59, 61, 62n2; *Puteri Li Po* 43, 50, 51–56, 62n2
Reid, Anthony 48
religious/religiosity 6, 13, 14, 18n13, 26, 37, 43, 46, 50, 84, 98n2, 102, 108, 109, 114, 118, 133–135, 137, 138, 140, 142, 146, 147, 174, 181, 184
religion 6, 51, 66, 82, 102, 108, 109, 134, 136, 141, 142, 145–147
representation *see* literary representation
resistance 1, 14, 29, 33, 54, 57, 96, 146, 173, 185, 186
revision/revisionist 7, 9, 11, 12, 42, 44, 50, 61
Ricci, Ronit 5, 68, 133, 134, 149
Rim, Kin 82, 86, 88, 98n3; *Sophat* 82, 86, 88–91, 98n3; *The Story of Samapheavy* 98n3
Ritter, Wilhelm Leonard 103–105, 107–109, 117; *De Dubbele Moord* 102, 103, 104, 105, 114, 118, 119; *Pieter Erberveld* 103; *Sara Specx* 103; *De Arme Rosetta* 103; *Si Tjonat de Landrover* 103; *Toeloecabesie* 103
Rohmer, Sax 110, 111, 114–117, 127n31, 127n32; *The Mystery of Dr. Fu-Manchu* 102, 110, 111, *112, 113*, 114, 117–120; *Het Geheim van Dr. Fu-Manchu* 111
Ruzy Suliza Hashim 42, 45, 48

Said, Edward 155, 164
Salmon, Claudine 17n9, 45, 101, 102, 111, 118
Sejarah Melayu 43, 44, 46, 47, 52, 55, 57, 71
semantic 14, 114, 120, 123, 180, 187, 188
semiotic 5
Sengupta, Mahasweta 100, 155, 166
sexuality 1, 4–11, 14, 16, 23–27, 30, 36, 119, 172, 181, 185–188, 188n1, 189n3
Siegel, James T. 108, 122
Simon, Sherry 4
Singapore 2, 3, 7–9, 11, 15, 17n5, 17n8, 22–33, 39, 39n1, 39n2, 39n3, 39n4, 39n6, 40n8, 62n4, 71, 75, 135, 151–166, 167n1, 167n3
Sinha, Vineetha 67
Sino-Malay 45
Sinophone 1, 5, 17n3, 159

Smyth, David 17n4, 17n9
social hierarchy/social hierarchies 139, 145, 148
source text 18n11, 104, 105, 107, 109, 111, 114–117, 119, 120, 122, 123
South Asia 2, 17n10, 115, 148, 160
Southeast Asia 1–8, 10, 15, 16, 17n2, 17n10, 38, 48, 59, 63n10, 66–68, 78, 79n3, 100, 133, 134, 149, 151, 153–162, 164–167, 167n4
Southeast Asian literatures 1, 2, 3, 6, 8, 10, 16, 17n2, 17n9, 160, 188n1
Spanish 67, 100, 111, 175, 180
Spivak, Gayatri Chakravorty 4, 167
stereotype 8, 54–57, 59–61, 82, 84–86, 90–97, 109, 110, 118, 133, 143, 146, 147, 154, 177
straight *see* heterosexual
subaltern 10, 28
subordinate/subordinated/subordination 7, 11, 17n7, 46, 48, 52, 57, 62, 87, 91, 100
subversion/subversions 56
subversive 56, 57, 60, 147, 174
supernatural 48, 75, 79n3
Sutedja-Liem, Maya 102, 105
Syariah 14, 18n12, 134, 135
symbol 5, 6, 8, 10, 12, 13, 16, 30, 31, 34–36, 39, 44–49, 52, 61, 77, 85, 86, 117, 138, 143, 144, 153, 156, 157, 162, 180
syncretic/syncretism 51, 56, 63n10, 171, 174, 186

Tagalog 10, 66, 100, 171, 179, 181, 182, 189n4
Tan, E.K. 5
Tan, Michael L. 178, 181
Tan, Sooi Beng 51, 53, 63n10
Tan, Tjin Kang 111, *112*, 114, 115, 116, 117; *Rasianja Dr. Fu Manchu* 111
Tan, Twan Eng 3, 11, 23, 24, 26, 32–39, 39n3, 40n9, 40n10, 40n11; *The Gift of Rain* 11, 23, 24, 26, 32–39, 39n3, 40n9; *The Garden of Evening Mists* 39n3, 40n9
target text 18n11, 104, 111, 114, 115, 116, 119, 174
temporal/ temporality/temporalities 5–7, 13, 24, 25, 29, 32, 35–37, 39, 56, 71
Thailand/Thai 7, 66, 79n6, 18n18
theatre 17n6, 44, 47, 50, 53, 57, 62n3, 102, 162, 165, 175–178

Thompson, Kristin 163
Tinio, Rolando S. 171, 174, 181–185, 187, 190n9; "A Parable" 171, 181–185
Toer, Pramoedya Ananta 103, 105
Torop, Peeter 83
transfer 18n11, 83, 85, 87, 97
transform 13, 33, 48, 59, 71, 72, 74, 77, 78, 79n1, 96, 104, 124, 173, 185, 187
transformation/transformations 9, 12, 35, 51, 53, 55–57, 68–70, 73, 74, 102, 160, 174, 188
transformative 4, 7, 77
transgender 174, 175, 186–188, 190n10
translation 1, 3–5, 7–12, 14–16, 17n9, 17n10, 18n11, 22–24, 26, 30, 38, 39, 44, 45, 51, 53, 55, 56–58, 61, 66–70, 75, 77–79, 82, 83, 85, 91–93, 96, 100, 102, 103–105, 107–111, *112, 113*, 114–124, 128n37, 128n39, 133, 134, 142, 148, 151, 152, 154–161, 164–167, 167n1, 171–175, 183, 185, 186, 188, 189n3
translation studies 4, 5, 9, 12, 14, 17n9, 17n10, 18n11, 66, 68, 70, 78
translational 4, 9, 10, 14, 16, 50, 54, 68, 111, 142, 143, 148, 155, 160, 161, 166, 171, 172, 174, 179, 180, 184–188
translational politics 3, 7, 50, 104, 108, 109, 118, 124, 155
transcultural 14, 173, 185
transnational 1, 3, 4, 6, 7, 11, 14, 22, 23, 39, 50, 51, 60, 61, 142, 148, 158, 167
Trivedi, Harish 4, 100
Tymoczko, Maria 4, 100

the UK 3, 23, 103, 137, 140, 141, 144, 145, 189n1
the US 2, 3, 23, 103, 118, 119, 145, 146, 147, 151, 156, 157, 160, 166, 176, 182, 184
United States *see* the US
United Kingdom *see* the UK

van der Putten, Jan 5
Vietnam 94, 160
Villa, Jose Garcia 181
violence 7, 15, 32, 157, 159, 160, 161

Wakabayashi, Judy 5
Wang Zhaojun 45
Warren, James Francis 28
Waugh, Patricia 23
were-tiger 12, 66–79

Wessing, Robert 71, 73, 74
West/Western 8, 13, 14, 16, 17n7, 18n17, 25, 26, 40n10, 67, 68, 71, 78, 100–103, 105, 110, 111, 114, 117, 118, 119, 122, 123, 124, 133, 134, 144, 145, 146, 151, 164, 172, 178, 180, 181, 185–187, 189n4
Western-centric *see* Eurocentric
Wheeler, Alexandra-Mary 70
white/whiteness 15, 54, 67, 76, 110, 111, 116, 118, 119, 141, 143–147, 151, 153, 155–157, 166
Wilson, G. Willow 145, 146

Woodward, Wendy 70
Worden, Nigel 43, 44, 46, 48, 49
world literature 2, 4, 75, 144, 160
World War: First 110; Second 23, 33, 175, 189n6

Xiongnu 45

Yamada, Teri Shaffer 17n4, 17n9
Yamashita, Shinji 100

Zainal Abidin bin Ahmad 71, 72
Zhang, Yimou 164, 165

Printed in the United States
By Bookmasters